Swift and Science

Swift and Science

The Satire, Politics, and Theology of Natural Knowledge, 1690–1730

Gregory Lynall
Lecturer in English, University of Liverpool, UK

First published 2012 by
PALGRAVE MACMILLAN

Palgrave Macmillan in the UK is an imprint of Macmillan Publishers Limited, registered in England, company number 785998, of Houndmills, Basingstoke, Hampshire RG21 6XS.

Palgrave Macmillan in the US is a division of St Martin's Press LLC, 175 Fifth Avenue, New York, NY 10010.

Palgrave Macmillan is the global academic imprint of the above companies and has companies and representatives throughout the world.

Palgrave® and Macmillan® are registered trademarks in the United States, the United Kingdom, Europe and other countries.

ISBN 978–0–230–34364–1

This book is printed on paper suitable for recycling and made from fully managed and sustained forest sources. Logging, pulping and manufacturing processes are expected to conform to the environmental regulations of the country of origin.

A catalogue record for this book is available from the British Library.

A catalog record for this book is available from the Library of Congress.

10   9   8   7   6   5   4   3   2   1
21 20 19 18 17 16 15 14 13 12

Printed and bound in Great Britain by
CPI Antony Rowe, Chippenham and Eastbourne

Contents

List of Illustrations

Acknowledgements

For over a decade, Marcus Walsh, as tutor, now friend and colleague, has been unstinting in his encouragement of my studies, and I owe much to him. I was privileged to work as a postdoctoral assistant for Professor Walsh on the Cambridge edition of *A Tale of a Tub and Other Works* (2010) whilst conducting research towards this monograph, and I am delighted that collaborations between us have continued beyond that volume. My other colleagues at the University of Liverpool have also provided a wealth of assistance. I am especially obliged to Paul Baines, Jill Rudd and Michael Davies of the School of English for generously sharing their time and experience with me.

The book developed from papers read before the British Society for Eighteenth-Century Studies, the British Society for Literature and Science, and the University of Liverpool Eighteenth-Century Worlds seminar, and I enjoyed discussing issues at these fora. I was honoured to attend the Sixth Münster Symposium on Jonathan Swift, and there benefited from the wisdom and encouragement of many scholars, including Andrew Carpenter, Chris Fox, Brean Hammond and James Ward. Early draft sections of this book have been read by Nick Davis, Judith Hawley, Anne McDermott, Hermann Real, Jonathan Roberts and Valerie Rumbold, and I am grateful for their insights and corrections. Professor Real and Dr Rumbold kindly made available to me writings prior to their publication. The anonymous readers' comments were also hugely beneficial.

My research has been carried out in Liverpool University Library, Birmingham University Library, the British Library, Birmingham Central Library, the Bodleian Library, the Wellcome Collection, and the library of the Ehrenpreis Center for Swift Studies, Westfälische-Wilhelms-Universität, Münster. I am much obliged to the staffs of these repositories. EEBO and ECCO have also been invaluable resources. My work was partially funded by a Research Councils UK early career fellowship. I offer my gratitude to the RCUK, and also to Phil Davis of the University of Liverpool for his help in securing this funding.

Some materials in Chapters 1 and 4 have been published in different forms previously: in *Swift Studies*, 26 (2011), 7–21, and *British Journal for*

Eighteenth-Century Studies, 28 (2005), 19–32. I acknowledge the generosity of the respective editors, Hermann Real and Matthew Grenby, in allowing me to draw upon these articles.

My family and friends have been tireless in their support, but above all, my wife Anna, to whom this book is dedicated, has kept faith in me over all this time.

List of Abbreviations

CJS	*The Correspondence of Jonathan Swift, D. D.*, ed. David Woolley, 4 vols (Frankfurt am Main: Lang, 1999–2007)
Ehrenpreis	Irvin Ehrenpreis, *Swift: The Man, His Works, and the Age*, 3 vols (London: Methuen, 1962–83)
LCC	*The Leibniz-Clarke Correspondence*, ed. H. G. Alexander (Manchester: Manchester University Press, 1956)
LRJS	Dirk F. Passmann and Heinz J. Vienken, *The Library and Reading of Jonathan Swift: A Bio-Bibliographical Handbook, Part 1: Swift's Library in Four Volumes* (Frankfurt am Main: Lang, 2003)
Memoirs	*The Memoirs of the Extraordinary Life, Works, and Discoveries of Martinus Scriblerus*, ed. Charles Kerby-Miller (New Haven, CT: Yale University Press, 1950; repr. Oxford: Oxford University Press, 1988)
NP	*The Newton Project* <http://www.newtonproject.sussex.ac.uk>
OED	*Oxford English Dictionary*, 2nd edn (Oxford: Oxford University Press, 1989)
Oxford DNB	*Oxford Dictionary of National Biography*, eds Colin Matthew and Brian Harrison (Oxford: Oxford University Press, 2004)
Poems	*The Poems of Jonathan Swift*, ed. Harold Williams, 2nd edn, 3 vols (Oxford: Clarendon Press, 1958)
PW	*The Prose Works of Jonathan Swift*, eds Herbert Davis and others, 14 vols (Oxford: Blackwell, 1939–68)
RAML	William Wotton, *Reflections upon Ancient and Modern Learning* (London, 1694; repr. Hildesheim: Olms, 1968)
Tale	*A Tale of a Tub and Other Works*, ed. Marcus Walsh (Cambridge: Cambridge University Press, 2010) [*The Cambridge Edition of the Works of Jonathan Swift*, I]

TE   *The Twickenham Edition of the Works of Alexander Pope*, eds John
Butt and others, 11 vols (London: Methuen, 1939–69)

WRB *The Works of Robert Boyle*, eds Michael Hunter and Edward
B. Davis, 14 vols (London: Pickering & Chatto, 1999–2000)

Introduction: Altitudes of Authority

> Authority, which did a Body boast,
> Though 'twas but Air condens'd, and stalk'd about,
> Like some old Giants more Gigantic Ghost;
> To terrifie the Learned Rout
> With the plain Magick of true Reasons Light,
> He chac'd out of our sight.[1]

So Abraham Cowley, in his ode 'To the Royal Society', romantically figures Francis Bacon's reformation of natural philosophy as the overthrow of the tyranny of scholastic learning. During the seventeenth century, the authority of the ancients had been challenged by new experimental and empirical methodologies far removed from the 'Magick' in Cowley's paradoxical metaphor. Despite the ode's claims, in the late seventeenth and early eighteenth centuries the new natural philosophy had not yet established supremacy: many rival narratives of nature competed for cultural acceptance. This book examines the ways in which Jonathan Swift, writing at this time of great transition, engaged with developments in knowledge of the external observable world, and with the culture of scientific discovery and practice, including the textual transmission of ideas. More particularly, the study focuses upon the theological, political and socio-cultural resonances of scientific knowledge in the early eighteenth century, and considers what they tell us about Swift's literary strategies and the growth of his often satiric imagination.

Although the politics and theology of the new sciences in the early eighteenth century could be explored in relation to a number of literary writers, Swift offers arguably the most complex, and often misunderstood, relationship to natural knowledge (the aim of those enquiries we now term the 'sciences'). While this topic has been addressed in

1

a number of short studies, it is evident that there are significant questions which remain to be answered. It is often thought that Swift was vehemently opposed to the methods and purposes of science,[2] but this study interrogates that assumption, bringing new perspectives to his most famous works, and making a case for the intellectual importance of some of his more neglected poems and prose satires. The book explores to what extent Swift's attitudes to scientific developments were determined by personal, political and social, as well as theological and philosophical factors, and investigates if there were particular issues about which Swift and his contemporary natural philosophers shared the same concerns. This is not to say that science did not in many instances constitute a significant target of Swift's satiric wrath, but where this is the case it is often accompanied by a sense of revelry in the new imaginative resources science provided.

Swift's response to the statesman, natural philosopher and archetypal 'Modern' Francis Bacon (1561–1626) serves to indicate the complex nature of his relationship to the new experimental philosophy. For Cowley, Bacon's progressive scheme brought 'true Reasons Light' by encouraging inductive and empirical ways to knowledge, in the place of Aristotelian deduction and the acceptance of inherited authority (figured in the ode as a satanic ruse).[3] The Royal Society adopted Bacon as their founding father, seeing their institution as the fulfilment of 'Salomon's House' in his utopian *New Atlantis* (1627).[4] Bensalem is undoubtedly one of the models for the flying island of Laputa, and the *Tale*-narrator's prose is often reminiscent of Bacon's aphoristic style.[5] However, as Bacon's 'survival' in *The Battel of the Books* (*Tale*, p. 244) perhaps confirms, the numerous echoes of his writings are not necessarily of a parodic nature. In *A Tale of a Tub* the allusions lend rhetorical weight to the narrator's many absurd pronouncements, while it has been argued that in *Gulliver's Travels* they function to show how Bacon's followers did not live up to their ideals.[6]

Moreover, the *Battel's* fable of the Spider and the Bee, traditionally understood as an anti-Modern, pro-Ancient allegory, has in recent years been interpreted as a 'restatement of Bacon's manifesto of empiricism as against Aristotelian and scholastic rationalism',[7] and Chapter 2 complicates the reading of this allegory further, suggesting that Swift pits the Modern, Cartesian 'Spider' Thomas Burnet (whose writings, for Swift, resemble Ancient scholasticism) against the Modern, Newtonian 'Bee' John Keill (whose works give due respect to the biblical and classical traditions). Likewise, two of Swift's early odes each suggest that Swift saw Bacon's plea for conceptual and methodological reform, in order to strip away the foundations of scholastic learning, as an important epistemological and moral step. Perhaps inspired by Cowley's spectral simile, the 'Ode to the Honble Sir William Temple' figures such received knowledge as a 'troubled Ghost' which 'still haunts' the schools, while the 'Ode to the Athenian Society' laments that 'Philosophy, as it before us lyes' is full of '*Doubts*, Impertinence, and Niceties'.[8] Swift's biographer John Boyle, Earl of Orrery, goes so far as to suggest that in the 'Voyage to Laputa' Swift pursues the 'same plan' as Bacon's (to expose the 'vain pursuits of ostentatious pedants'), but in a comic manner. Furthermore, Orrery privileges Swift's satire over Bacon's serious analysis because it places the 'imaginary schemes of all pretenders, in a more ludicrous, and therefore in a more proper light'.[9] The unique abilities of the satiric mode as a kind of philosophical critique will become apparent at various points in this book.

Bacon's vision, in *The Great Instauration* (1620), of a natural history based on the collection, description, comparison and classification of specimens, involving 'hard labour, investigation and world-wide survey', seems to be endorsed by the Bee's echoing statement that '*an universal Range, with long Search, much Study, true Judgment, and Distinction of Things, brings home Honey and Wax*'.[10] However, while many 'virtuosi' (John Woodward being the most famous and satirically vilified) saw such pursuits as offering important evidence for their natural and providential histories, their studies were often ridiculed (by Swift and many others) as pedantic, unseemly, ignoble and trivial.[11] For instance, the naïve narrator of the *Tale*'s 'Digression in the Modern Kind', parodying William Wotton's *Reflections upon Ancient and Modern Learning* (1694), celebrates how 'every Branch of Knowledge has received such wonderful Acquirements' within highly specialized fields of investigation, such as '*Flies* and *Spittle*'.[12] Bacon's call also contributed to a fascination with the exotic and monstrous, which Gulliver indulges when donating three Brobdingnagian wasp stings to the Royal Society's repository at Gresham College (*PW*, XI, 110).

As the eclecticism of these activities and subjects suggests, 'science' as we know it did not exist in Swift's time. In the early eighteenth century, the word 'science' (*scientia*) referred to any knowledge acquired by study and ratiocination, and was often applied more particularly to the knowledge of demonstrable truths which can be reduced to general laws. This 'science' was distinct from knowledge based on perception or intuition (*cognito*), or derived from received authority (*eruditio*). However, by the nineteenth century, particularly when a professional elite had been established, it came to mean empirical knowledge of the external observable world.[13] Nonetheless, in the eighteenth century 'science' was often used to refer to 'philosophy', including natural philosophy, as in Pope's reference to 'proud Science' in *An Essay on Man*.[14] Despite the historicity of the word, 'science' is still attractive as a term to describe the context of this study: 'natural philosophy' would not quite capture the array of emerging disciplines with which Swift engaged. Indeed, the eighteenth century is no longer seen as a time of divide between C. P. Snow's 'two cultures' of art and science, but is viewed as 'pre-disciplinary' in its organization of knowledge.[15] As Ludmilla Jordanova argues, the present-day demarcations between discrete categories of knowledge were not in place because few of the scientific institutions existed to maintain them. The polymathic career of Swift's good friend John Arbuthnot (1667–1735), the physician, mathematician, antiquarian and satirist, is surely testament to this. On the other hand, John Christie and Sally Shuttleworth contend that the ideological boundary present between the disciplines by the nineteenth century can to some extent be traced back to the creation of the Royal Society in the mid-seventeenth century.[16]

This study appreciates that Swift was responding not to a single discipline of 'science', but to a range of social and cultural practices and epistemological perspectives, and makes apparent that Swift's works reflect, or even contribute to, the development of boundaries between arts and sciences, and between methods of scientific enquiry. The demarcation and relative importance of different ways of knowing was fundamental to the intellectual contest in which Swift was directly involved at the start of his career, although his loyalties within this affair are not as easily assumed by critics as they used to be.[17] Sir William Temple (1628–99), the retired diplomat for whom Swift worked as a secretary in the 1690s, reinvigorated the Ancients and Moderns debate within England by arguing in his *Essay upon the Ancient and Modern Learning* (1690) that the knowledge and the genius of the Ancients had not been surpassed by modern discoveries or compositions. For instance, while Temple acknowledges that the 'Copernican system' and 'Harvey's circulation of the blood' are probably 'new' to the Moderns, he could only bring himself to state these discoveries 'have been of little use to the world, though perhaps of much honour to the authors'.[18] This skirmish escalated when the Royal Society chose to enter the 'battle of the books' by requesting one of its fellows, William Wotton (1666–1727), to answer Temple, in his *Reflections* (1694). Wotton's survey of knowledge sought to celebrate the achievements of modern learning, particularly the new sciences, in an enlightened vision of progress.

However, it was questioned by some, notably John Locke, whether the new natural philosophy was 'capable of being made a Science' because its empirical method improved knowledge '*only by Experience and History*' and therefore could not attain absolute certainty.[19] We can associate some of Swift's suspicion of natural philosophy, or at least of the claims of its comprehensive knowledge and formulation of general laws, with a similar epistemological attitude, informed by a Christian 'fideist skepticism' he broadly shared with Erasmus, Rabelais, Robert Burton and Montaigne.[20] This position is traceable to Pauline arguments against philosophical speculation: that the only certainty man can find, especially in relation to the most important articles of faith, is contained in Scripture.[21] The sermon *On the Trinity* perhaps illustrates best his philosophical outlook:

> It is against the Laws of Nature, that a Human Body should be able to walk upon the Water, [...] or that a dead Carcase should be raised from the Grave after three Days, when it began to be corrupted; which those who understand Anatomy will pronounce to be impossible by the common Rules of Nature and Reason. Yet these Miracles, and many others, are positively affirmed in the Gospel; and these we must believe. (*PW*, IX, 165–66)

Similarly, in *Further Thoughts on Religion*, Swift counters theories of spontaneous generation by arguing that 'The Scripture-system of man's creation, is what Christians are bound to believe, and seems most agreeable of all others to probability and reason' (*PW*, IX, 264). According to Swift, even if God revealed his mysteries 'we should not be able to understand them, unless he would at the same time think fit to bestow on us some new Powers or Faculties of the Mind' (*PW*, IX, 165). Swift does not take this idea of uncertainty to its fullest conclusion, but instead suggests that man can use his understanding within his own sphere: 'I am in all opinions to believe according to my own impartial reason; which I am bound to inform and improve, as far as my capacity and opportunities will permit' (*Thoughts on Religion*, in *PW*, IX, 261). For Temple, it is the realization of this limitation that fundamentally differentiates Ancients from Moderns. Ancient learning 'led them to a sense and acknowledgement of their own ignorance, the imbecility of human understanding, the incomprehension even of things about us, as well as those above us', while Modern knowledge, exemplified by the new experimental philosophy, 'leads us to presumption, [...] and makes us think we do, or shall know, not only all natural, but even what we call supernatural things'.[22] This is a sentiment echoed in the humbleness of the ghost of Aristotle on the island of Glubbdubdrib (*PW*, XI, 198), although Swift's endorsement of this polarized view is not wholly guaranteed.[23]

Swift's distrust of any human claim to ultimate truth is apparent in the 'Introduction' to the *Tale*, which is principally concerned with those who 'hath an Ambition to be heard in a Crowd', and therefore exalt themselves to a 'certain Degree of Altitude' (p. 34). This section of the *Tale* asks: who has the theological, political or cultural authority to speak publicly to disseminate their ideas; from where does this power originate; and what grants some discourses more authority than others? The comedy of the 'Introduction' implies that it is related to nothing more than how and where people stand: the 'altitude' from where they speak, rather than the substance of their words. In *The History of the Royal-Society* (1667), which Swift is said to have joked was the 'best book in the English tongue', Thomas Sprat similarly observes:

> How many rewards [...] have been still snatch'd away by the easie vanity of *fine Speaking?* [...] of all the Studies of men, nothing may be sooner obtain'd, than this vicious abundance of *Phrase*, this trick of *Metaphors*, this volubility of *Tongue*, which makes so great a noise in the World.[24]

For Swift, the new sciences are themselves related to this wider debate about who has the right to utterance in the public domain. The new forms of knowledge sought validation through social acceptance, which relied upon rhetorical and institutional power for successful communication. As Swift's choice of metaphor suggests, natural knowledge could also be used as a satiric device to express in new ways his concerns about public authority and, more specifically, how 'truth' (whether religious, political or philosophical) was established through socio-cultural processes.

While Section I of the *Tale* focuses upon interrogating the oral means of obtaining authority, elsewhere in Swift's works it is the textual transmission of ideas which is paramount within his parodic and satiric schemes. Indeed, on several occasions scientific developments are figuratively and sometimes literally implicated in the problems of print culture, suggesting that writing has become more a material than an intellectual performance. In the *Tale*, Swift finds an appropriate metaphor for the composition of Grub Street writing in the alchemical concept of '*Reincrudation*', describing hack authors as infusing their own crude productions with plagiarized material; and the goal of Section V's alchemical recipe is the creation of '*an infinite Number of Abstracts* [...] *reducible upon Paper*' to be ravenously 'digested' by Modern readers (pp. 43, 82).[25] Swift modifies this conceit for the new scientific 'Academy of Lagado', in which 'Projectors in speculative Learning' have designed a mechanical 'Frame' of 'several Bits of Wood' annotated with the Laputian language which they hope will randomly produce a 'compleat Body of all Arts and Sciences' (*PW*, XI, 182, 184). As this satiric contrivance suggests, Swift and his 'Scriblerian' friends (Pope, Gay and Arbuthnot) were well aware that the new forms of knowledge had themselves infiltrated contemporary culture primarily via the medium of print. They also suspected that the natural philosophers saw textual proliferation more as a means of self-promotion than as part of the Baconian project for universal improvement. In the *Memoirs*, for instance, Martinus Scriblerus is yet again characterized as the archetypal virtuoso because 'Whatever he judg'd beneficial to Mankind, he constantly communicated [...] by some method or other in which Ostentation had no part'. These innumerable publications include 'Accounts to the Royal Society', as one would expect (p. 169).

Roger D. Lund argues persuasively that early eighteenth-century culture expected 'widely disseminated, rapidly updated, accessible and useful forms of information', and it was the new sciences which were at the forefront of the production of knowledge.[26] The natural philosopher's insistence on getting into print immediately, so as to become the '*freshest Modern*' (*Tale*, p. 85), is satirized at the end of *The Mechanical Operation of the Spirit*. This mock-treatise, which encapsulates what Swift sees as a cultural tendency to reduce all to the physical, is framed as a letter apparently from a man of '*Gresham*' (i.e. probably a member of the Royal Society) who concludes his account of the '*Phœnomenon of Spiritual Mechanism*' in 'great Haste' because 'the Post is just going' (*Tale*, pp. 170, 175, 187). The narrative suggests that if this gentleman had given himself time to think, he might have learnt from Diogenes Laertius' story that he himself cites, of the 'Philosopher, who, while his Thoughts and Eyes were fixed upon the *Constellations*, found himself seduced by his *lower Parts* into a *Ditch*' (p. 187). Swift's structural irony here is, of course, that the putative author's account has itself descended into one concerned with baser subject matter, including an ejaculatory description of the 'Height and *Orgasmus*' of religious fervour (p. 186).

For Swift and the Scriblerians, not only was the contemporary desire to immediately disseminate new ideas via print detrimental to the quality of the thoughts conveyed, but also produced stylistic failings, and these were most apparent in scientific writings. In his *History*, Sprat explained that the Royal Society thought new scientific theories and discoveries should be communicated through a discourse of 'primitive purity' (p. 113). This commitment to a 'plain style' of writing was satirized in Martinus's aim to convey his proposals without 'Ostentation', and also by the language schemes of the 'Academy of Lagado'. *A Meditation upon a Broom-Stick*, as well as Swift's other early works (most obviously the *Tale* and *Mechanical Operation*), offered parodic models to the Scriblerians for their collective attacks on the new forms of writing. As Brean Hammond contends, their joint satires, such as *An Essay concerning the Origine of Sciences* (1732), often parodied the 'sub-literary kinds' (including the learned essay or critical treatise) generated by the new 'professional' scholars who seemed to mechanically apply the emerging scientific methodologies to all forms of learning.[27] As Chapter 1 in particular will highlight, for Swift the transgressions of literary standards committed by natural philosophers (and their popularizers) often included contravening their own linguistic prescriptions. While Sprat thought that 'Whatever discoveries shall appear to us afresh, out of the hidden things of *Nature*, the same words, and the same waies of Expression will remain' (*History*, p. 324), in practice the natural philosophers had recourse to construct elaborate analogies or coin new (and often compound) technical terms in order to explain the physical phenomena they observed in their experiments.

The Royal Society sought to distinguish itself as the purveyor of 'Real Knowledge' of nature through its methods and practices, including its prose style and, more insistently, the 'right *Art* of *Experimenting*' (Sprat, *History*, p. 79). Sociological studies over the past forty years or so have challenged the absolute authority of science. It is now often viewed as one among many competing modes of discourse of equal legitimacy, and this is reflected in recent studies of 'literature and science', which place an emphasis upon the historically specific contexts which both 'the science' and 'the literature' share (if such distinctions are valid), and upon identifying the tropes and metaphors on which they both draw. Yet George Levine argues that 'Literature has been unable to avoid science because science asserts an epistemological authority so powerful that it can determine even how we allow ourselves to imagine the world, or to resist that authority'.[28] The prominence of science within early eighteenth-century British culture meant that it could not exist independently of the outside world, and its cultural resonance inevitably compelled Swift to explore the wider consequences of experimental enquiries into nature.

As historians of science such as Steven Shapin, Simon Schaffer and Larry Stewart have shown, the coexistence of rival accounts of nature meant that by asserting the legitimacy of their representations natural philosophers would consequently disqualify other knowledge systems and practices. Such conflicts would ultimately take place in the cultural field, making use of political, moral and aesthetic resources. But science itself would play a significant role in defining the authority and legitimacy of public institutions such as the House of Hanover (as Chapter 5 will explore).[29] While not denying that Swift sometimes inveighed against specific scientific theories, practices and discourses for purely 'philosophical' reasons, a central claim of this study is that animosities for and between individuals and institutions over single matters could boil over to encompass all affairs. Science therefore became an important battleground for Swift's assault upon his social enemies. For instance, William Wotton and Richard Bentley are named targets of the *Tale* and *Battel*, often function as representatives of all 'Modern' kinds of learning and writing, and are sometimes ridiculed in relation to natural philosophy, but it is difficult to determine if Swift vilifies them primarily because of their scientific interests, or whether this is just another front on which they can be tackled in revenge for their assault on Temple.

Furthermore, Chapters 2 and 3 make the claim that any interpretation of the *Tale* and *Battel* must be wary of seeing these works as the attacks of an 'Ancient' upon 'Modern' learning. The categories of 'Ancient' and 'Modern', and the placing of Swift and his fellow Scriblerians within them, are more fluid than they might first appear. In the *Memoirs*, for example, Cornelius's eccentricities seem to be judged against the satiric norm of his brother Albertus: 'a discreet man, sober in his opinions, clear of Pedantry, and knowing enough both in books, and in the world, to preserve a due regard for whatever was useful or excellent, whether ancient or modern' (p. 113). In contrast, Cornelius 'had a most superstitious veneration for the Ancients; and if they contradicted each other, his Reason was so pliant and ductile, that he was always of the opinion of the last he read' (p. 125). It is uncertain as to whether Swift contributed to or was even aware of this passage, given Pope's editorial control of the *Memoirs* over many years,[30] but it still serves as evidence that some caution is advisable when positioning a writer of occasional satires within distinct intellectual groupings.

Sir Isaac Newton's domination of 'science' in the period, both philosophically and institutionally, meant that for Swift and many of his contemporaries the signifier of 'Newton' functioned as a metonym for

(British) natural philosophy as a whole.[31] This is apparent notably in the 'Voyage to Laputa' where, as I argue in Chapter 4, several of the flying island's inhabitants resemble the Royal Society's President, as Swift's satire works at its most occasional. Even if reading without this specificity in mind, one is struck by how similar the philosophers of Laputa all are; serving as a reflection of the ubiquity of the Newtonian philosophy, which through iatromechanists like Archibald Pitcairne and George Cheyne had even infiltrated medical discourses. Moreover, the Laputians' universal interest in science perhaps reflects a sociological shift in the variety of people engaged in natural philosophy by the 1720s.[32] Publications such as *The Spectator* promoted interest in natural philosophy as a source of refinement: 'It heightens the Pleasures of the Eye, and raises such a rational Admiration in the Soul'. Science became a focus of public consumption, another form of spectacle for the fashionable classes to wonder at. To be fair to *The Spectator* itself though, one of its articles anticipates the 'Voyage to Laputa' in its joke about the prevalence of absent-minded and socially deficient men 'wholly fixed on some particular Science' who ignore the beautiful women before their eyes.[33]

In Laputa this cultural ubiquity is literalized in a 'Race of Mortals [...] singular in their Shapes, Habits, and Countenances', and with a corresponding mental uniformity they all require a bash of a bladder to the mouth or ear to remove them from their 'intense Speculations' (*PW*, XI, 159). The homogeneous identity of this mass is suitably depicted in Johann Sebastian Müller's copper-plate image of the royal court, which was included in John Hawkesworth's 1754 edition (see Figure 1). Indeed, in this illustration the King is only differentiated from his subjects by the throne upon which he sits, and the two flappers which are required to attend to him. In contrast, whilst Gulliver was 'a Sort of a Projector' himself in his 'younger Days' (*PW*, XI, 178), he is immediately recognizable amongst this crowd, standing to the left of the illustration, with a face suggesting both wonder and bemusement at these curious specimens.

Although Swift was keenly aware of the socio-cultural power of assemblies and societies, especially those institutions concerned with Modern forms of learning, and in his works often grouped men and women of similar folly together, he also held the satiric possibilities of the individual in focus. Swift noted in *The Examiner* that 'In describing the Virtues and Vice of Mankind, it is convenient, upon every Article, to have some eminent Person in our Eye'. This would seem to be a reasonable approximation of his compositional method in many, if not all, of his

Figure 1 Johann Sebastian Müller, copper-plate of the royal court of Laputa, in *The Works of Jonathan Swift, D. D. Dean of St. Patrick's, Dublin, Accurately revised in Twelve Volumes, adorned with copper-plates, with some account of the author's life, and notes historical and explanatory*, ed. John Hawkesworth, 12 vols (London, 1754–55), II, following p. 278. By permission of the Cadbury Research Library: Special Collections, University of Birmingham.

satires, and is commensurate with his friend Pope's focus on personal targets, as explained in *An Epistle to Dr Arbuthnot* and the correspondence which inspired the poem's dedication.[34] The specificity of Swift's satires involving science inevitably raises questions about readership. Many of Swift's caricatures or lampoons of individual natural philosophers or theologians, or allusions to particular philosophical disputes, suggest that they would have only been appreciated by a small clique of like-minded and well-read thinkers, such as the Christ Church 'Wits', who assisted Temple in the *Phalaris* quarrel with Wotton and Bentley.

Such target-specificity is not ubiquitous in Swift's satires, but it lends itself particularly well to their engagements with natural philosophy. Steven Shapin argues compellingly that judgments regarding the veracity of knowledge-claims involve assessments of their sources, and so to build a body of knowledge its agents must be perceived as trustworthy. Shapin claims that late seventeenth-century natural philosophers, such as Robert Boyle, presented themselves as gentlemen to invoke the associations of gentility with truthfulness and honour.[35] Likewise, Swift was deeply aware that attempts to disparage an institution or mode of thought were far more successful if one attacked an individual (with exploitable human flaws) who represented such a target synecdochically, rather than engaging in more detailed – and probably less funny – critiques of the scientific validity of a theory. Therefore, nearly all of the chapters are focused upon Swift's responses to individual theorists, practitioners or popularizers, reflecting not only his satiric strategies, but also the recent critical emphasis upon the humanization and historicization of science. Swift was also able to use (for his own, opposing, ends) the same discourse of gentility employed by the natural philosophers themselves, undermining their symbolic identities. An important example of this rhetorical strategy is at work within *Polite Conversation*, in which Newton is portrayed as a lowly 'Instrument-Maker' and 'Workman in the Mint', as Chapter 4 highlights.

Metonymy is a common Swiftian device. Phillip Harth, for instance, has explored the synthesis of Puritanism and Occultism in Section VIII of the *Tale*, while John R. R. Christie has written of Swift's 'creative miscegenation' of targets in the 'Voyage to Laputa'. Elsewhere, I have noted how Swift self-consciously figures this satiric strategy as a form of alchemy.[36] These schemes of association and conflation can occasionally undermine the very purpose of the satire, deflecting ridicule away from the intended butt. Moreover, Swift's treatment of enquiries into nature reveals a fascination with and an indulgence in the discourses science offers, but these are often simultaneously undercut by a sense of distrust. Swift's satires involving the sciences are therefore elusive pieces which attempt to evade full interpretation.

Thomas Sheridan (the younger) conjectured that if Swift had applied himself to the speculative sciences at Trinity College, Dublin, he 'might have proved the foremost Logician, Metaphysician, or Mathematician of his time; [...] and instead of writing a Laputa, he might have himself been qualified for a professorship in the academy of that airy region'.[37] How realistically one can take this remark is debatable, but the intricacy and detail of Swift's allusions to the culture of natural philosophy and related forms of learning suggest that some of this potential was fulfilled, but in parodic and satiric form. The groundbreaking studies by Marjorie Nicolson and Nora Mohler demonstrated that many of the Lagadan experiments in the 'Voyage to Laputa' are burlesques and conflations of actual ones which were reported in the Royal Society's *Philosophical Transactions*, and Frederick N. Smith has argued that the *form* of the journal's papers (which assert their credibility through presenting themselves as neutralized observations of phenomena) also had an effect on his imagination.[38] But Swift's reading in the new forms of learning was far wider than just a few volumes of the *Transactions*, and included Wotton's *Reflections*, Joseph Glanvill's *Scepsis Scientifica* (1665), Burnet's *Theory of the Earth* (third edition, 1697), and Newton's *Principia* (second edition, 1713), amongst others. It is also possible that Swift became aware of some scientific ideas through more 'literary' (and moreover, satiric) sources such as Samuel Butler's *Hudibras* (1663), Thomas Shadwell's *The Virtuoso* (1676), and William King's *The Transactioneer* (1700), which are obvious antecedents to some of Swift's satires on science.

While most of Swift's encounters with the new sciences are textual, it seems safe to assume that he also learnt of developments in natural knowledge in conversation with his several good friends who were active natural philosophers and mathematicians, including his tutor at Trinity College, St George Ashe (1658–1718), his fellow Scriblerian Arbuthnot, friend Thomas Sheridan (1687–1738), and personal physician Richard Helsham (1683–1738). Patrick Delany even recalls that when Swift fell into the acquaintance of 'men of learning' (probably including Sheridan and Helsham) during his time in Dublin between 1714 and 1720, to ensure he could understand their conversation 'he applied himself even to mathematics, [...] and made some progress'.[39] It is also known that in 1710 Swift attempted to visit the Royal Society's Repository (then at Gresham College), but 'the keeper was not at home'. Swift may well have made a more successful visit on another day, witnessing at first hand its loadstone *terrella* ('little earth') of four and a half inches in diameter, paralleling Laputa's diameter of 'about four miles and a half'.[40] Swift was evidently an opportunist who seized information about science from wherever he could, and his close friendships with men of science suggest we should temper our more extreme readings of his satires on natural philosophy.

Swift's relationship with science is, evidently, a capacious topic, and I make no claims of comprehensiveness, offering instead a selective study of intersections of the satiric, political, theological and natural philosophical in his writings. Certainly, there are several issues which are notable omissions from this study. Swift's engagements with alchemy, astrology and technology have been excluded in the main, for reasons of not only space but also coherence. It should be acknowledged, though, that the contested demarcations of alchemy, astrology and technology from 'science' are to some extent merely a convenient method of delimiting my focus. In the cases of alchemy and astrology, it is the difficulty involved in the untwisting of these practices from their 'enlightened' counterparts chemistry and astronomy which Swift and the Scriblerians exploit in some of their satires upon learning, especially the *Memoirs*. The Scriblerians seemed intensely aware that natural philosophers asserted the legitimacy of their narratives of nature by disqualifying other knowledge systems and practices. Sprat's *History*, for instance, denied that Royal Society members had any connection with increasingly outmoded ideas, such as alchemy, which would otherwise undermine the Baconian notions of utility and empiricism that the new institution sought to follow (p. 113). This could work in the opposite way, however, in that more esoteric forms of knowledge might seek cultural acceptance through connecting their theories and practices with learning of the mainstream. Swift had certainly noticed this: his Bickerstaff persona, for instance, attempts to assert his place within the '*Republick of Letters*' by claiming that the continental scholars Leibniz and Jean Le Clerc had cited his predictions (*PW*, II, 159–61). The differentiation between bogus and credible forms of knowledge in popular perception seemed to be so slim that this gap could be bridged easily by a satirist such as Swift, and formed an important part of his caricatures and lampoons of Newton, as we will see in Chapter 4.[41]

As Marjorie Nicolson has shown, the unprecedented technological developments of the seventeenth and eighteenth centuries were instrumental in Swift's most imaginative work.[42] In the microscope Swift found one inspiration for his satiric strategies of diminution and expansion; in magnetism he discovered a suitable explanation for keeping the Laputians' heads literally up in the clouds, to complement their solipsistic negations of the outside world. Nevertheless, this study will be limited in its consideration of human inventions. Similarly, issues associated with medicine and physiology will be addressed only when they are significantly related to debates in natural philosophy, such as those involving mechanical models of the body. I have also, in the main, limited consideration of Swift's place in connection to the Irish scientific context. Swift probably learnt many things concerning the new experimental philosophy from his friends Ashe and Helsham, amongst others, but the extensive study this subject perhaps warrants is outside the scope of this book, which instead focuses primarily on the major intellectual battles predominantly sited within and between Moor Park, London, Oxford and Cambridge.

Each chapter normally sketches one episode or theme within Swift's writing. The chapters are organized chronologically, following Swift's literary career. The first chapter concentrates upon *A Meditation upon a Broom-Stick*, the *Tale* and other early works in relation to the ideas of Robert Boyle, whilst hinting at the resonance of particular tropes within *Gulliver's Travels* and other later writings. The second and third chapters discuss the *Battel* primarily, and are concerned with the theological appropriation of Cartesian and Newtonian ideas respectively, and some of the responses to such borrowings. The fourth and fifth chapters are broadly interested in the political significance of Newton 'the man', his associates, and his philosophy in general during the 1710s and 1720s, which were reflected particularly in *Gulliver's Travels*, 'Directions for a Birthday Song', and *Polite Conversation*. Much of the book is therefore devoted to Swift's responses to Newton and Newtonianism, reflecting the immense cultural impact of this thinker and his work during the period.

While this study remains vigilant that tracing the specificity of Swift's local satires offers only one reading of complex works, it simultaneously resists Swift's own claims for the universal. Swift's attitudes to science and its practitioners and popularizers alter over time and between texts, and reflect his changing cultural allegiances; we may also discern that some of the more extreme stances taken and energies unleashed are rhetorical ploys rather than ideological statements. There are unquestionably similarities in theme one can find between, say, the *Tale* and 'Directions for a Birthday Song', but they each respond to their own intellectual and personal contexts. Of course, the general appeal of much of Swift's literary output demonstrates the fruitfulness of ahistorical (or only broadly periodized) readings. However, the universalizing tendency of readers is something Swift exploits in his satires, often subjecting his opponents to ridicule through placing them within a timeless viewpoint or grouping. Needless to say, this is but one of several sophisticated satiric methods Swift employs in relation to the culture of natural knowledge. Therefore, while I will make a case for *why* Swift attacked science (on those occasions he does), the more general task of this book is to explore *how* he incorporates scientific knowledge within his writing, using it as a source of creative potency, but also exploiting the comic possibilities of scientific experiment, debate and contemplation.

1

Meditations and Mechanisms: Swift and Robert Boyle's *Occasional Reflections upon Several Subjects*

> The sword of wit, like the scythe of time, cuts down friend and foe, and attacks every object that lies accidentally in its way. But, sharp and irresistible as the edge of it may be, Mr. BOYLE will always remain invulnerable.[1]

Robert Boyle (1627–91) would have been an appropriate and archetypal target for an attack on the new natural philosophy, despite some critics finding its satiric effectiveness doubtful. His many achievements included demonstrating the role of atmospheric pressure, the function of air in respiration, and that sound could not be transmitted in a vacuum. Boyle was therefore one of Wotton's key players in the overthrow of ancient knowledge, with the 'Comparison between the *Ancient* and *Modern Physicks*' in the *Reflections upon Ancient and Modern Learning* (1694) primarily designed to 'determine who Philosophized best, *Aristotle* and *Democritus*, or Mr. *Boyle* and Mr. *Newton*'.[2] As one of the *Tale's* main objectives was to pour scorn on Wotton and his *Reflections*, ridiculing Boyle would have served this purpose well. However, such a tactic would have to be carried out with subtlety. In his attacks on Wotton and Bentley, Swift received vital support from the 'wits' of Christ Church, including Robert Boyle's great nephew Charles, the future Earl of Orrery. To satirize the relative of a key ally in a blatant lampoon would have provoked more tension in an intellectual scuffle already tense and reduced to personal attack. From a practical point of view also, to name *Robert* Boyle as a champion of the Moderns within *The Battel of the Books* would have confused the action, in which *Charles* Boyle is heavily involved as a defender of the Ancients. Hence those few critics who have considered Boyle's work in relation to the *Tale* and its associated works have argued for rhetorical, tonal and stylistic similarities rather than for the existence of specific allusions. By the time he was writing *Gulliver's Travels*, however, Swift considered some of Boyle's studies to be perfect for burlesque transformation in the 'Academy of Lagado'.[3]

Talking Flowers

That Swift would have found Boyle a worthy satiric butt cannot be questioned. The most striking piece of evidence is one of Swift's marginal annotations in John Lyon's copy of Gilbert Burnet's *History of His Own Time* (1724–34). Burnet emphasized Boyle's devotion to his studies by remarking how the virtuoso 'neglected his person, despised the world, and lived abstracted from all pleasures, designs, and interests'.[4] At this time, solitude could be viewed as a state conducive to creativity, and to the improvement of one's own soul (through the *vita contemplativa*, or contemplative life). Alternatively, it could also be seen as a threat to the rationality of the human mind, which was normally regulated through social interaction.[5] As the depiction of the Spider in the *Battel* suggests (*Tale*, pp. 149–52), Swift would not have applauded Boyle's solitary contemplation of nature and misanthropic rejection of society, because it would lead to the production of knowledge useful only (or perhaps, even harmful) to Boyle himself. Indeed, in the margin next to Burnet's remark Swift scribbled that 'Boyle was a very silly writer'; an emphatic judgement, especially given that this was written in a borrowed copy. This annotation was perhaps an appropriate blunt dismissal of Boyle's attitude to the world (as reported by Burnet), but the emphasis on this natural philosopher as a 'writer' suggests that Swift had more in mind here, and it is generally thought that Swift was referring to Boyle's *Occasional Reflections upon Several Subjects* (1665).

    In his *Occasional Reflections*, Boyle writes in a seventeenth-century tradition pursued by many authors, but exemplified best by the *Occasional Meditations* (1630) of Joseph Hall, in which quaint conceits and events seemingly trivial become the inspiration for higher contemplations.[6] Composed around 1647–48, Boyle's *Reflections* espoused a natural theology which constituted an early attempt at the 'physico-theological' arguments he formulated later in his career. Boyle set out a scheme for the moral contemplation of objects and experiences, based on the assumption that an ordinary man could search for divine mysteries by looking into the Book of Nature, grounded in a voluntarist theology which sees God as directly involved in all of the universe's activity.[7] There is consequently something resembling the developing scientific mind-set in Boyle's interest in the detailed observation of natural phenomena. Moreover, the emphasis upon the spontaneity of each meditation is reminiscent of the immediacy of experience presented in Boyle's natural philosophical writings: a rhetorical device he used in order to establish his experimental accounts as authoritative testimony.[8]

While Boyle's meditations are primarily theological, his major innovation in the genre was to produce secular ones, finding they have 'also a Political, an Oeconomical, or even a Physical use' in the production of knowledge (*WRB*, V, 30).[9] He was also the first to theorize the genre's method and form, including the establishment of its terms of reference, calling his meditative practice '*Meleteticks*', which supplies 'Religious and hansome Reflections, upon the most Obvious Works of Nature, and the most Familiar Occurrences of humane Life', working the soul to 'Heavenly Mindedness' (*WRB*, V, 19, 52). The topics subject to contemplation include not only those we might expect from a natural philosopher, such as '*Looking through a Prismatical or Triangular Glass*' and '*Upon Clouds rising out of the Sea, and falling down in Rain*', but also the more mundane: '*Upon my Spaniel's fetching me my Glove*' and '*Upon the Sight of a fair Milk-maid singing to her Cow*' (*WRB*, V, 91, 124, 90, 98). Boyle sees great value in 'these little Fragments, or Parcels of Time, which [...] would be dissipated, and lost, [if not] managed by a skilful Contemplator, and [...] improv'd by the Celestial fire of Devotion' (*WRB*, V, 24).

Using terms from classical rhetoric and dramatic criticism, Boyle divided the comparative argument of each meditation into two sections: the former being the '*Protasis*, wherein we display and consider the minute particularities of the Theme', with the latter constituting the '*Apodosis*', containing 'an Application [...] may be some important Moral Instruction, or perhaps some Theological Mystery', usually accompanied by appropriate scriptural quotation (*WRB*, V, 12, 15). As Boyle's description suggests, the '*Apodosis*' always involves the construction of analogies or the use of metaphors. This heavily stylized method in particular may have incited Swift's criticism, since Boyle himself admits that there may be places in which he has 'a little Strain'd the Similitude' (*WRB*, V, 11). The images which Boyle often conjures up for analogical purposes would invite ridicule from a satirist such as Swift, who generally thought that language should reflect ordinary, reasonable conversation, and promote common sense.[10] For instance, Boyle's justification of his distinctive 'way of Thinking' (*WRB*, V, 21) paradoxically demonstrates its limitations:

since, ev'n the illiterate Husbandman can, with the most abject Dung it self, give a flourishing growth to [...] fragrant Flowers; why may not a wise Man, by the meanest Creatures, and slighted'st Object, give a considerable Improvement to the noblest Faculties of the Soul, and the most lovely Qualities of the Mind? (*WRB, V,* 39)

The excremental metaphor seems to be invoked in all seriousness, which cannot but help produce an element of bathos, especially when it is in combination with the pompous self-declaration of being a 'wise Man'. There are other unintentionally comic instances such as this, and so it is perhaps no wonder that Swift considered Boyle to be 'a very silly writer'. However, the *Occasional Reflections* were immensely popular, inspiring many others to compose privately, and sometimes publish, meditations of a similar style.[11] Moreover, Boyle's '*Meleteticks*' offered a seminal moment in prose style and epistemology which contributed to the development of the early novel, in the emphasis on the accumulation of detail and the subjectivity of response, although this claim should be moderated with not only an acknowledgement of the wider and earlier tradition of the occasional meditation, but also recognition that Boyle's prose had itself been influenced by French heroic romance.[12]

Thomas Sprat famously declared that the Royal Society's linguistic schemes involved the rejection of 'all the amplifications, digressions, and swellings of style' and instead sought a 'return back' to a language of 'primitive purity' in which 'men deliver'd so many *things*, almost in an equal number of *words*'.[13] While Swift's own *Proposal for Correcting, Improving and Ascertaining the English Tongue* (1712) supported linguistic correctness, in the Lagadan Academy's 'School of Languages' he couldn't resist burlesquing the Royal Society's suggestions to improve communication. The first project sought to 'shorten Discourse by [...] leaving out Verbs and Participles; because in Reality all things imaginable are but Nouns'. The emphasis on the imagination is the key here: it is the diminution of creativity through narrow modes of discourse that Swift is concerned about, as we will see in *A Meditation upon a Broom-Stick*. The second linguistic scheme is for 'abolishing all Words whatsoever', and 'since Words are only Names for *Things*, it would be more convenient for all Men to carry about them, such *Things* [...] they are to discourse on' (*PW,* XI, 185). The concretization of the abstract, reducing things into only their material components, is again an effective satiric strategy, not only revealing the impracticality of the Lagadans' (and early Royal Society's) concept of condensing all language into a fixed system of signs (from a golden age of discourse which never existed), but also functioning as a caricature of the natural philosopher's sole concern with the physical, measurable world.

Like Sprat, Joseph Glanvill preferred a '*way* of *writing* […] which is more gratified with *manly sense*, flowing in a *natural* and *unaffected Eloquence*, then in the *musick* and curiosity of *fine Metaphors*', and this is illustrated in his own attempts to tone down the use of imagery between editions of his works.[14] In practice, however, the Society's natural philosophers could not emulate mathematical precision in their writing and so inevitably relied upon metaphorical or allegorical language to some extent.[15] Sprat himself was accused of hypocrisy by the satirist Samuel Butler, one of the Society's earliest and staunchest critics: 'The historian of Gresham College endeavours to cry down oratory and declamation while he uses nothing else'. Nevertheless, the language ideals of the Society's rhetoricians, particularly John Wilkins, which were ostensibly hostile to metaphors as vehicles of knowledge, seem far removed from accommodating the method of '*Meleteticks*' pursued in the *Occasional Reflections*.[16] While Boyle's meditations were composed some time before the Royal Society and its discursive concerns were established, Swift may well have found it striking to discover Boyle to be the advocate of an excessively figurative type of discourse.

There were certainly others who shared Swift's opinion of Boyle. In Thomas Shadwell's play *The Virtuoso* (1676), Sir Nicholas Gimcrack speaks of Sir Formal as 'the finest speculative Gentleman in the whole world and in his cogitations the most serene animal alive', continuing:

Not a creature so little but affords him great curiosities. He is the most admirable person in the *meletetiques*, viz., in reflections and meditations, in the whole world. Not a creature so inanimate to which he does not give a tongue, he makes the whole world vocal; he makes flowers, nay, weeds, speak eloquently and by a noble kind of prosopopeia instruct mankind.[17]

The acute particularity of *The Virtuoso*'s satire is well known. Shadwell alludes to numerous scientific debates, discoveries and publications, centred upon the Royal Society, and especially upon Boyle.[18] Through Sir Formal's description of Gimcrack, Shadwell highlights a number of concerns. The repetition of 'whole world' not only ridicules Boyle's immense public reputation, but also highlights the new scientists' claims of universality with regard to their theories. The irony of the oxymoron 'serene animal' reduces the value of Boyle's 'cogitations', whilst also mocking the traditional Aristotelian definition of man as a 'rational animal'.[19] As Barbara M. Benedict notes, this has social implications, with Sir Nicholas the 'Gentleman' descending to a lower order of species.[20]

Shadwell's critique then increases in specificity, emphasizing the triviality of Boyle's objects of meditation, and of scientific enquiry (that a 'creature so little [...] affords him great curiosities'), and poking fun at the pomposity of his special coinage, *'meletetiques'*. Finally, Shadwell derides the method of Boyle's *Occasional Reflections* (of finding moral lessons in nature) through the absurdity of giving dignified, sophisticated utterance to flora.

Shadwell's caricature seems to be alluding to a particular (but hitherto unknown) passage, where Boyle makes claims for the diverting and ethical pleasure of meditation. Boyle prescribes his kind of reflection to his reader as a form of 'self-help', making all of one's time useful to one's soul:

> he that can (as it were) make the World vocal, by furnishing every Creature, and almost every occurrence, with a Tongue to entertain him with, and can make the little Accidents of his Life, and the very Flowers of his Garden, read him Lectures of Ethicks or Divinity; such a one, I say, shall scarce need to fly to the Tavern, or a worse place, [...] to help him to get rid of his time. (*WRB*, V, 22)

The *Occasional Reflections* descends into bathos again, with the half-ridiculous argument that a libertine would find 'talking to flowers' a viable alternative to his usual wanton pursuits (where human tongues might entertain him in other ways). Sir Formal's description shows that, despite Boyle's claims, this instruction comes from Gimcrack/ Boyle himself, the agent of a personification which 'makes Flowers, nay Weeds, speak'. Shadwell condemns Boyle's project as a shallow rhetorical exercise which grants insight only into one's self-love rather than the providence of the divine author.

Shadwell's contemporary Butler also satirized Boyle's reflections, but would concentrate on one aspect in particular: the trifling and undignified nature of subject matter. 'An Occasional Reflection on Dr. Charleton's Feeling a Dog's Pulse at Gresham College by R. B. Esq.' combines parody of Boyle's *'Meleteticks'* with more general ridicule of the Royal Society's experiments. Rather than satirizing the natural theological use of Boyle's observations, Butler instead parodies the Society's utilitarian claims:

> though a dog's leg in the language of the vulgar signifies a thing worth nothing, yet even that may teach us that there's nothing so contemptible but may, if rightly applied to, contribute something to the public good of mankind and commonwealth of learning.

Through sexual innuendo, the narrator emphasizes his amazement that Walter Charleton, a physician 'whose province lies in the cabinet of fair ladies, [...] should nevertheless condescend to animadvert the languishing diastole of an expiring mongrel'. From this contrast, the narrator then constructs his self-reflecting apodosis, that 'we may receive matter of instruction from objects of the meanest and most contemptible quality as well as from things of higher and more sublime condition'.[21] Arguably, the success of Butler's parody is limited by its ambitious dual satiric purpose, and lacks the sharp conciseness of Shadwell's caricature.

Topsy-turvy Trees

By means of elaborate and acute parody, Swift would join Shadwell and Butler in subjecting the moralizing Boyle to ridicule. *A Meditation upon a Broom-Stick* was probably composed in 1702,[22] when Swift worked as chaplain to Charles Berkeley (1649–1710), Lord Justice of Ireland. During this period, Swift was often requested to read the *Occasional Reflections* to either Lady Elizabeth, Countess Berkeley, or her daughter, Lady Betty Berkeley, later Germain (there are two, differing, accounts). On one occasion, Swift apparently recited his own spoof instead, which fooled his recipient into believing that he was reading from one of Boyle's genuine meditations.[23] The published version, unable to achieve the same form of hoax, explained the focus of the parody through the subtitle, 'According to the Style and Manner of the Honourable *Robert Boyle*'s Meditations' (*PW*, I, 239). Swift's 'personation' (as he might have called it) captures Boyle's conversational but pious tone, emulates the method of '*Meleteticks*', and is abundant with verbal and thematic parallels from a number of the reflections.[24] As a parody it was very successful, but Swift's early critics generally saw the *Broom-Stick* as a controversial and unwarranted attack on a man universally known as a genius.[25] This is not to say that the *Broom-Stick* did not have some admirers, including Swift's friend Anthony Henley, who was inspired to write a darkly humorous 'Reflection upon Death'.[26]

The piece begins with 'a single stick [...] lying in [a] neglected Corner', then quickly moves from this domestic space, as the narrator apparently 'once knew [this stick] in a flourishing State in a Forest'. The Meditator then admits:

> When I beheld this, I sighed, and said within my self SURELY MORTAL MAN IS A BROOMSTICK; Nature sent him into the World strong and

lusty, [...] wearing his own Hair on his Head [...]; till the Axe of Intemperance has lopped off his Green Boughs, and left him a withered Trunk: He then flies to Art, and puts on a *Perriwig*; valuing himself upon an unnatural Bundle of Hairs, all covered with Powder. (*PW*, I, 239–40)

Swift imitates the several ejaculatory and personal declarations in the *Occasional Reflections*, exemplified by Boyle's response whilst recovering from illness: 'Good God! said I, in my self, what a multitude of unpleasant Medicines have I been order'd to take' (*WRB*, V, 82). The *Broom-Stick* also directly transposes Boyle's contemplation of man's mortality, degeneration through self-indulgence, and the ageing of hair:

how many evitable Mischiefs our own Appetites, or Vices, expose us to, by acts of Intemperance, [...] and practices of Sin, whereby we provoke the Creator to punish us; when [...] I consider all this, and consequently how many Mischiefs he must escape that arrives at Gray-hairs; I confess, the commonness of the Sight cannot keep me from thinking it worth some wonder, to see an Old man, especially if he be any thing Healthy. [...] For so many, and so various are the unfore-seen accidents to which we poor Mortals are expos'd. (*WRB*, V, 64)[27]

Swift incorporates a brilliant homophonic pun into his verbal parody, figuring 'acts of Intemperance' in a concretive metaphor as an 'Axe of Intemperance' hacking away at this tree-broomstick-man.

Next the Meditator, in deducing from this illustration of man's vanity that we are 'Partial Judges [...] of our own Excellencies, and other Mens Defaults!' (*PW*, I, 240), inverts Boyle's praise for the objectivity of occasional reflections:

our own Consciences being the Makers of the Application, we cannot suspect the Reprehensions to come from Persons, that either mistake us, or are partial against us; and that Truth which a man's Conscience applies to him, [...] extracting from Objects that which every Considerer would not have pick'd out thence; it may very often happen, that the same Reflection will discover to a man his Excellencies, as well as make him take notice of his faults. (*WRB*, V, 29)[28]

This is, of course, an attack which is only fully brought to light through specific knowledge of the pre-text. However, Swift's *Broom-Stick* then proceeds to undermine, in a more general fashion, the method and purpose of the meditation genre. After comparing man to a broom-stick, the narrator speculates:

> a *Broom-stick*, perhaps you will say, is an Emblem of a Tree standing on its Head; and pray what is Man but a topsy-turvy Creature? His Animal Faculties perpetually mounted on his Rational; his Head where his Heels should be, groveling on the Earth. [...] [He] rakes into every Slut's Corner of Nature, [...] and raiseth a mighty Dust where there was none before; sharing deeply all the while in the very same Pollutions he pretends to sweep away. (*PW*, I, 240)

Like Boyle, the Meditator is self-reflexive in the vocabulary he uses within the analogical process ('Emblem'),[29] although it is the narratee who is apparently taking this visual image and using it to express the moral. Exaggerating Boyle's tendency to 'Strain [...] the Similitude', the correspondence between man and a broom-stick is not sufficient itself. There is too large a gap between the protasis and its apodosis, and so the intermediary analogy of 'a Tree standing on its Head' is pursued. Furthermore, the interrogative phrase 'what is Man but a topsy-turvy Creature' locates in rhetorical structure the reductionist logic behind the formation of any similitude.[30] The naïve narrator is the victim of a structural irony in which his analogies are extended to the point of absurdity, drawing attention to themselves as merely rhetorical exercises applied to spontaneously chosen and arbitrary subjects. The analogies also violate literary decorum through base images seemingly inappropriate for a 'meditation', and crucially, the narrator uses these correspondences to construct what at first appears to be a rational argument, but which paradoxically demonstrates that man is not a rational creature.

Leslie Moore suggests that Swift chose the broom-stick analogy because Boyle refers to the *Occasional Reflections* as 'loose sticks' bundled up into 'Faggots', and included a meditation on an 'Instructive Tree', alluding to the vine and branches of John 15.1–6. Moore consequently places Boyle's 'Instructive Tree' and Swift's *Broom-Stick* within this scriptural context to discuss the satiric reduction of theological metaphors, inevitably reading the spoof in one way as an allegory of the Fall of Man, beginning in a 'flourishing state' and concluding in being 'kicked out of Doors'.[31] While this analysis is persuasive, the central conceit of Swift's parody should be placed additionally in relation to two familiar classical images which suggest that in the *Broom-Stick* Swift seeks to comment upon natural philosophical and physico-theological schemes associated with Boyle, as well as his devotional meditations. Indeed, it is questionable as to whether these types of discursive activity can be separated, and Swift may well have considered them to be part of the same project, especially given the claims for the theological utility of natural knowledge made by apologists such as Wotton.[32]

The correspondences the Meditator draws out from the initial analogy invert the classical but enduring topos of man looking aloft to the heavens. Swift could have encountered this commonplace motif in a number of authors he is known to have read, including Ovid: 'man was made to hold his head / Erect in majesty and see the sky'. The Ancients, at least as far back as Plato, believed that it was man's upright posture which distinguished him from the animals: 'man alone is rightly called man (*anthrôpos*), because he looks up at (*anathrei*) what he has seen (*opôpe*)'.[33] This bodily stance suggested he also possessed the mental capacity to contemplate higher things, both physical and spiritual, and confirmed the existence of man's rational faculty.[34] For Aristotle, plants and animals shared the vegetative and sensitive parts of the soul with man, but 'the function of man is an activity of soul in accordance with, or not without, rational principle'.[35] While it was still generally accepted in the seventeenth century that man's erect posture indicated his natural predisposition for heavenly meditation, the idea was beginning to encounter opposition, especially because developments in natural history and global exploration demonstrated that upright stature was not singularly possessed by mankind, but also by creatures like the penguin and the mantis.[36]

Swift's conceit in the *Broom-Stick* therefore functions in part to ridicule the very basis of the classical topos: that man's mental capacity is dependent upon his physical gait. However, there is also a long intellectual history of the arboreal inversion of man, the Meditator's intermediary analogy, and this image is implicit in Boyle's 'Instructive Tree':

> as the loaded Branch makes use of the moisture it attracts from the dirty ground, to recede as much as it can from the Earth, and spends its sap in shooting up towards Heaven, and bearing Fruit for Men: so the devout Christian improves the Blessings he receives of this inferiour World, to elevate his mind above it. (*WRB*, V, 50)

For Plato, man's spiritual nature, possessing 'that kind of soul which is housed in the top of our body and raises us', meant that he was like a plant with its roots in the heavens. Aristotle made a similar comparison, but gave a naturalistic reason: 'in plants the roots are the equivalents of mouth and head, while the seed has the opposite significance, for it is produced above at the extremities of the twigs'.[37] The Platonic and Aristotelian images of man as *arbor inversa* can be encountered in numerous hermetic, patristic, medieval and Renaissance authors, including Francis Bacon.[38] The credibility of this analogy might have been sustained into the early modern period by anatomical illustrations of man's uncannily branch-like arterial system (see Figure 2).

The obvious comic potential of this motif had almost inevitably been exploited before Swift, by Butler in 'A Speech Made at the Rota': 'philosophers say that a man is a tree inverted, and that his head is the root by which he takes in his nourishment, and his arms and legs the branches. If that be true, it must follow that his rump is the head'.[39] Prior to writing the *Broom-Stick*, Swift had himself already alluded to, but ironically reinverted Plato's idea (and Boyle's metaphor), in the penultimate paragraph of *The Mechanical Operation of the Spirit*:

> however Spiritual Intrigues begin, they generally conclude like all others; they may branch upwards towards Heaven; but the Root is in the Earth. Too intense a Contemplation is not the Business of Flesh and Blood; it must by the necessary Course of Things, in a little Time, let go its Hold, and fall into *Matter*. (*Tale*, p. 187)

Here the topos, joined with Christ's warning to Peter in Matthew 26.41, not only acts as an appropriate aphorism concerning man's sexual appetite, but also serves as a strike against the mentality of the occasional meditator.

In both the *Broom-Stick* and *Mechanical Operation*, Swift is clearly enjoying the opportunity of inhabiting but distorting the meditative genre, indulging in an analogy extended to breaking point: an exercise in adynaton, or expressing *impossibilia*, which makes light of traditional conceptions of man.[40] However, there is perhaps real satiric intent aimed at Boyle behind the stylistic parody and mock-taxonomic re-classification in the *Broom-Stick*, and this can be directly related to the classical topoi Swift draws upon. Boyle's primary intention for the *Occasional Reflections* is to cultivate man's inquisitive and contemplative faculties. This aim is revealed in a passage which Swift seemed to have in mind when composing his spoof:

> if Experience did not convince the contrary, I could never suspect that [...] rational Creatures, especially professing Christianity, should

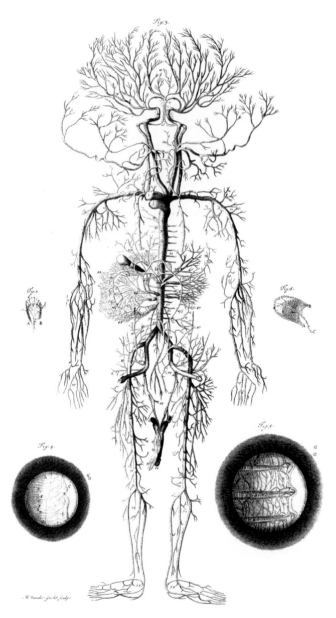

Figure 2   Michael Vandergucht, engraving of 'The Trunks and large Ramifications of all the Arteries of a Humane *Fœtus*, Injected with Wax, and Display'd after Dissection', in William Cowper, *The Anatomy of Humane Bodies* (Oxford, 1698), Appendix: The Third Table. By permission of the Wellcome Library, London.

either keep idle, or confine to Employments worse than Idleness, so noble and improvable *a Faculty,* that enables an Ingenious Man to pry into the innermost Recesses of mysterious Nature, and discover there so much of the Wisdom, Power, and Goodness, of the Author, as are most fit to give the Discoverer a high and devout Veneration for those Excellencies. A *Faculty,* whereby an Inquisitive Soul may expatiate it self through the whole Immensity of the Universe, [...] by whose help the restless mind having div'd to the lowermost parts of the Earth, can thence in a trice take such a Flight, that having travers'd all the corporeal Heavens, [...] she roves about in the ultra-mundane spaces, and considers how farr they reach. (*WRB,* V, 34–35)

Boyle's hyperbole imagines the soul in flight, in a Lucretian fantasy of cosmological surveyance continued in physico-theological poetry such as John Reynolds's *Death's Vision* (1709).[41] This extravagant image of man's potential to move his mind through cosmic spaces of knowledge is countered in Swift's *Broom-Stick* with base images of a sexual and bestial nature ('mounted', 'groveling', 'Slut's corner'), which depict the 'Rational' faculties of man in continual subservience to their oppressive 'Animal' masters. Moreover, man is granted the oxymoronic epithet of 'reasoning Vegetable' (*PW,* I, 239), satirically deflating man's proud status as a 'rational Creature'. The narrator's absurd arguments and low images demonstrate man's tendency to grovel on the earth, to deal with dirty things, mocking the belief that man's erect posture indicated his natural predisposition for heavenly meditation.

The *Broom-Stick* therefore functions as a precursor to Gulliver's fourth voyage, which challenges the definition of man as 'a Creature pretending to *Reason*' (*PW,* XI, 267). Of course, in a letter to Pope Swift declares: 'I have got Materials Towards a Treatis proving the falsity of that Definition animal rationale, and to show it should only be *rationis capax*'. Swift's joke, amongst other things, serves to highlight how absurd it would be to define a species according to its potentialities: Bolingbroke, seeming to treat this definition in all seriousness, finds that it 'will not bear examination'.[42] Swift held a sceptical attitude towards the absolute authority of man's rational capacity, as he expresses in his sermon *On the Trinity*: '*Reason* itself is true and just, but the *Reason* of every particular Man is weak and wavering, perpetually swayed and turned by his Interests, his Passions, and his Vices' (*PW,* IX, 166).[43] It is fairly certain we should see Swift not as a misanthrope who believed in the doctrine of original sin, but as a follower of Anglican rationalists such as John Tillotson, who thought the Fall had weakened but not destroyed man's higher faculties.[44] Both Swift and Boyle consider man to be capable of reason, but not always following its directions. However, Swift is perhaps suspicious of how Boyle puts his own 'higher faculty' into practice, especially in relation to his natural philosophical pursuits, and so the *Broom-Stick* ironically satirizes man's reason through the means of rational argument.

It is easy to see why this section of the *Broom-Stick* has been interpreted as an allegory of the satirist's eternal problem, of his potential to rake up 'Dust' and 'shar[e] deeply' in his target's faults, to be guilty of proliferating the opinions he seeks to attack, or to be proud of his own position of superiority while he condemns the pride of others.[45] However, the images function not only as a critique of the methods and objectives of satire, but also as an account of the use and power of natural philosophy, derived from a discourse which Swift would have encountered explicitly in Joseph Glanvill's *Scepsis Scientifica* (1665), and more implicitly in Boyle's *Occasional Reflections*. Dedicated to the Royal Society, *Scepsis Scientifica* (a revision of *The Vanity of Dogmatizing*, published 1661) attacks scholastic learning and promotes the new experimental philosophy. It is certain that Swift knew the work, dismissing it in a letter to John Winder as a 'fustian piece of abominable curious Virtuoso Stuff'.[46] One of Glanvill's central concerns is to explore how man must deal with the epistemological consequences of the Fall:

> whereas our ennobled understandings could once take the wings of the morning, to visit the World above us, [...] they now lye grovelling in this lower region, muffled up in mists, and darkness: the curse of the Serpent is fallen upon *degenerated* Man, *To go on his belly and lick the dust.* (pp. 5–6)

The prelapsarian Adam's naming of the animals (Genesis 2.19–20) was assumed to signify that he had possessed knowledge of all nature, but the first sin had led to the corruption, or at least the privation, of both man's moral *and* rational faculties, causing 'the *shortness* of our *intellectual sight*, the *deceptibility* and impositions of our *senses*, the tumultuary *disorders* of our *passions*' (p. 6). The narrative of the Fall played an important role in the development of natural knowledge in the seventeenth century. Many natural philosophers, including Glanvill, saw experimentalism and empiricism as a way of counteracting the current deficiencies of man's intellectual faculties.[47] Glanvill emphasizes the 'higher degree, to which *Philosophy* sublimes us. For, as it teacheth a generous contempt of what the grovelling desires of *creeping* Mortals

Idolize and dote on; so it raiseth us to love and admire an Object, that is as much above terrestrial, as *Infinite* can make it' (pp. 179–80). Natural philosophy, in Glanvill's opinion, allows Adam's descendants new access not only to truth but also to morality, as 'next after the *divine Word*, it's one of the best friends to *Piety*' (p. 182).

Moreover, for Glanvill 'those generous *Vertuosi* [...] dwell in a higher Region then other Mortals' and, significantly, he combines the metaphors of height and depth with the idea of man as *arbor inversa* in order to describe the depravity of the present condition of the vulgar: 'the greatest part of miserable Humanity is lost in *Earth*; and, if Man be an *inversed Plant*; these are *inversed Men*, who forgetting their *Sursum*, which Nature writ in their Foreheads, take their Roots in this sordid Element' (pp. 176, 178). In response to the optimism of Boyle and Glanvill's epistemological attitudes, in the *Broom-Stick* Swift uses the topos of man as an inverted tree to satirize not only Boyle's '*Meleteticks*', but also natural philosophy and the physico-theological project (finding God in laws of nature written by mankind). Swift borrows Glanvill's images of fallen man intellectually 'lost in *Earth*', and employs Boyle's own method of similitude against him, with the comparison of man to a broom-stick functioning as a highly useful conceit.

While both Swift and Boyle consider man to be capable of reason, but not always following its directions, Swift is perhaps suspicious of how Boyle puts his own 'rational faculty' into practice. The *Broom-Stick*, employing what could be called 'a compensating disproportion',[48] argues that for all their aspirations to absolute knowledge, all men, including natural philosophers, are condemned through their fallen natures to be 'groveling on the Earth', not looking upwards. In Swift's opinion, despite Boyle's pompous posturing, his meditations are always trapped in the 'lowermost parts of the Earth' (*WRB*, V, 35), as his trivial choices of subjects for contemplation demonstrate. As a striking riposte to the physico-theological designs of Boyle and Glanvill, the *Broom-Stick* shows that instead of finding God in the 'innermost Recesses of mysterious Nature' (*WRB*, V, 34), through the restoration of Adamic knowledge, the natural philosopher merely 'rakes into every Slut's Corner of Nature' through his enquiries, becoming not only physically but also morally contaminated by his 'dirty' objects of study (*PW*, I, 240). The sexual metaphor implicit in Boyle's account is made explicit in Swift's parody, perhaps in order to emphasize the exploitation of the natural which he sees at work in the Christian virtuoso's many schemes. Moreover, the intellectual deficiencies of man brought to light in the *Broom-Stick* parallel what Douglas Lane Patey has called the 'inverted physico-theology' of *Gulliver's Travels*, where both the Brobdingnagian scholars and the Houyhnhnm master list Gulliver's physical limitations, ridiculing the pride invested in human concepts of benevolent design.[49]

The image of man as an inverted tree in the *Broom-Stick* can be read as a caricature of Boyle, and of the natural philosopher more generally, as Swift utilizes classical and biblical tropes that are imbued with significant resonance within natural philosophical writing of the period. Appropriately, inversion is the principal satiric method. The contemptible images conjured up by Swift function as topsy-turvies of the pretentious piety of Boyle and Glanvill, who see their enquiries into nature as a route to spiritual illumination. Swift figures these studies as merely sweeping in the dirt, or more brutally, as muck-raking, rather than as a means of restoring Adamic knowledge or 'expatiat[ing] [...] through the whole Immensity of the Universe'. This inversion is accompanied by a strategy of satiric literalization. Swift's Meditator concretizes Boyle's figurative language in order to show that, for all of the claims made for the utility of occasional meditation as a discursive practice, rhetorical trimmings do not produce valid forms of knowledge (*WRB*, V, 149). In this sense, the *Broom-Stick* can be read as a self-conscious allegory of its own act of *reductio ad absurdum*, wearing Boyle's orotund prose from a heavily metaphorized 'flourishing state' down 'to the Stumps' (*PW*, I, 239).

Tritical Texts and Contemptible Insects

In their concern with the debasement of writing and the interests of the virtuoso, and the achievement of structural ironies through the use of naïve putative narrators, there are clear connections between the *Broom-Stick* and *A Tritical Essay upon the Faculties of the Mind*. As its title implies, the *Tritical Essay* (dated 6 August 1707) is a patchwork of trite quotations, aphorisms, and proverbial phrases, many of which involve ideas broadly associated with natural philosophy (man as microcosm, Epicurean atomism, tidal movements, Euclidian geometry, the existence of vacuums in nature, the mind of man as a *tabula rasa*), as well as allusions to mythology and antiquity. Ehrenpreis supposes that the anonymous 'Lover of Antiquities' to whom this mock-treatise is addressed is Swift's good friend Sir Andrew Fountaine (1676–1753), to whom he once wrote, perhaps with some irony: 'you are a Bookish Gentleman and admired far and near for your Towardlyness in deep learning' (6 March 1712/13, in *CJS*, I, 470). A graduate of Christ Church, Oxford, from 1707 Fountaine was Gentleman-Usher of the Black Rod, assisting the newly appointed Lord Lieutenant of Ireland, Thomas Herbert, eighth Earl of

Pembroke (1656/7–1733), who shared his interest in antiquarianism and art collecting, and friendship with Swift. Pembroke owned what was generally acknowledged to be the finest collection of classical objects in the British Isles, had served as President of the Royal Society in 1689–90, and was a friend and patron of John Locke, becoming the dedicatee of *An Essay Concerning Human Understanding* (1691). In Ireland, he cultivated a similar network with men of learning, including St George Ashe, and in November 1707 he was elected President of the Dublin Philosophical Society (although he left for London, with Fountaine and Swift, soon after).[50] Swift met with Pembroke, Fountaine, Ashe and others at Dublin Castle in 1707, forming a coterie that could see the funny side of their interests (immortalized in 'A Dialogue in the Castillian Language'). It is likely, therefore, that in addition to Fountaine, Swift also had Pembroke (and his circle as a whole) in mind as an audience for the essay, especially given some of its pseudo-Lockean content.

Identifying the possible readers of the *Tritical Essay* aids us in determining its satiric objectives. The work puts forward the standard repertoire of complaints against the virtuoso: that with great pomp he pursues useless, abstract knowledge involving ignoble and banal objects of enquiry that should be beneath the interests of the gentleman.[51] But it is more concerned about, or at least playing around with, the effects of such pursuits upon the written word. The mock-treatise is presented as the virtuoso-narrator's curious collection of *textual* specimens, assembled within the repository of the book as he might adorn a cabinet with physical objects of art and nature. Rather than a display of literary rarities which inspires wonder in its viewers, the writing is derivative and stylistically indecorous; self-consciously digressive, and punctuated with 'but' and 'however' as it moves between convoluted analogies. The essay's diverse contents seem to be thrown together indiscriminately rather than following a particular taxonomy, serving as a satiric metonym and metaphor for the fragmentary nature of Modern knowledge, with the virtuoso-narrator concerned only with amassing plagiarized 'facts' and nuggets of supposed wisdom, and not with the epistemological or rhetorical usefulness of such objects themselves.[52] As part of the structural irony, the narrator complains that critics are 'but the Drones of the learned World, who devour the Honey, and will not work themselves', and asserts that their empty heads settle 'the long Dispute [...] about a *Vacuum*' (*PW*, I, 249), whilst readers never lose sight of the hackneyed writing in front of them.

Like the *Broom-Stick, A Tritical Essay upon the Faculties of the Mind* appears to burlesque the *Occasional Reflections* in its meditations and admonitions, although Boyle's work should not be seen as an exclusive target of this multifarious piece. Even the title of this skit may allude to Boyle, who saw '*Meleteticks*' as conducive to the 'exercise and improvement of divers of the faculties of the mind' (*WRB*, V, 32). In the Preface, the narrator states: 'I have been of late offended with many Writers of Essays and moral Discourses, for running into stale Topicks and threadbare Quotations, and not handling their Subject fully and closely' and so proposes his work as a 'Pattern for young Writers to imitate' (*PW*, I, 246). As J. Paul Hunter has shown, the genre of the occasional meditation enjoyed enormous popularity in the late seventeenth century, and much (but not all) of this was down to the success of Boyle's reflections.[53] It is likely that the sorts of 'moral discourses' Swift has in mind include those by Boyle. However, as the irony of the Preface suggests, far from 'not handling their subject fully and closely', Boyle's meditations could be seen as 'too Elaborate, or too Pompous, for the Themes whereunto they are accommodated' (*WRB*, V, 13), as Boyle himself admits. Consequently, *A Tritical Essay* at times parodies both Boyle's style and philosophical method.

Boyle's physico-theological reasoning seeks to find the Creator by 'pry[ing] into the innermost Recesses of mysterious Nature' (*WRB*, V, 34). Swift's 'Tritical Essayist', however, removes all mention of an originating divine Author:

> Nature does nothing in vain; if we were able to dive into her secret Recesses, we should find that the smallest Blade of Grass, or most contemptible Weed, has its particular Use; but she is chiefly admirable in her minutest Compositions, the least and most contemptible Insect most discovers the Art of Nature. (*PW*, I, 247–48)

There is an 'argument from design' of sorts here, with 'Nature' figured as an artist, but divine providence is replaced with a pantheistic theology. This performs discursively what Swift perhaps sees as having been carried out in sentiment by those who concentrate exclusively on the 'secret Recesses' of 'Dame Nature' (a common phrase which is implied but not stated by the narrator in his feminizing metaphor).[54] Swift emphasizes the triviality and indecorousness of the subject matter of such meditations, drawing upon the common image of the virtuoso (found in Shadwell, Butler, Mary Astell, William King, and others), obsessed with the 'minutest Compositions', such as 'the least and most contemptible Insect'.[55] However, this constitutes no *reductio ad absurdum*, but imitates Boyle's method without exaggeration. For instance, Boyle the physico-theologian finds the glow-worm 'a small and contemptible Insect, yet the Light which shines in his Tail [...] is a noble and heavenly Quality' (*WRB*, V, 15). In Boylean fashion, Wotton similarly considers insects and arachnids to be 'small Productions of the Divine Mechanicks' (*RAML*, p. 269). Boyle's *Occasional Reflections*, therefore, should be considered to be a significant object of satire of the *Tritical Essay*, in its exploration of the moral utility of new forms of knowledge and, perhaps especially, in its rhetoricity. The effect of the innumerable philosophical clichés compiled in Swift's travesty of the learned essay is to argue that the new forms of knowledge are created purely through the manipulation of language, divorced from an empirical basis in physical reality.

Corpuscular Clothes

Considering Swift was in all likelihood still at work on the *Tale* in some way during the period he was reading Boyle's *Occasional Reflections* to the Berkeley ladies, it is surprising that connections between the two works remain unexplored.[56] Surely Boyle's meditations constituted an archetype of the sort of writing Swift lays waste to in the *Tale*'s satire on the productions of '*Gresham* and of *Will*'s' (p. 40)? Moreover, in its general exposure of a physicalizing and mechanizing tendency Swift saw infiltrating Modern culture and thought, the *Tale* derives much satiric power from the kinds of dense metaphor, convoluted analogy and crude literalization Boyle deploys. Significantly, it seems more than a coincidence that there are echoes in phrasing and in the use of analogical reasoning between the *Broom-Stick* and Section II of the *Tale*, which burlesques philosophical and commercial materialism by reducing all to surface appearance, describing how the worshippers of the Taylor-Deity 'held the Universe to be a large *Suit of Cloaths*, which *invests* every Thing' (p. 49). The *Broom-Stick* asks 'what is Man but a topsy-turvy Creature?' (*PW*, I, 240), whilst the *Tale*-narrator wonders 'what is Man himself but a *Micro-Coat*[?]', as well as 'What is that which some call *Land*, but a fine Coat faced with Green? or the Sea, but a Wastcoat of Water-Tabby?' (p. 49). These interrogative phrases locate in rhetorical structure the reductionist logic inherent in Boyle's method of finding similitudes.

On the level of simple conceit, in the *Broom-Stick* the 'Axe of Intemperance' lops off the 'Green Boughs' of the child, leaving the man a 'withered trunk' who 'puts on a *Perriwig*' in the form of broom-hairs (*PW*, I, 239–40). The clothes analogy in Section II of the *Tale* almost inevitably leads to a description of the fashion of the '*vegetable* Beaux': 'Observe how sparkish a Perewig adorns the Head of a *Beech*' (p. 49). Of more significance, the *Broom-Stick* and Section II both ridicule Boyle's avowal of the superior faculties of men as 'rational Creatures'. In the *Occasional Reflections*, Boyle uses the term metonymically to refer to mankind (*WRB*, V, 34), while the *Tale*-narrator's 'due Course of Reasoning' leads to his insistence that 'those Beings which the World calls improperly *Suits of Cloaths*, are in Reality the most refined Species of Animals, or to proceed higher, [...] they are Rational Creatures, or Men' (p. 50).[57] The *Broom-Stick* reminds us that such definitions reflect the presumptuous pride of man, who forgets what sway his animal instincts possess over his reason.

Before getting carried away with these parallels, it should be acknowledged that there seems to be an aggregation and accumulation of various systems of knowledge within the sartorial cosmology, parodying the analogies of part to part which many philosophers, not only Boyle, employ. For instance, Thomas Vaughan (in the words of his intellectual adversary, Henry More) saw the 'whole World' as 'an *Animal*' whose '*flesh* is the *earth*, whose *bloud* is the *water*', whilst Phillip Harth has identified echoes of Hobbes' *Leviathan*. There are also several possible parallels for the clothes analogy itself, including Thomas Stanley's description of Democritus' cosmology, in which the world is 'compassed about with a coat' and 'interwoven with Stars'.[58] Despite these other potential pretexts, the narrator's methods and intellectual assumptions in this part of the *Tale* cannot help but remind us of Boyle's '*Meleteticks*', and the style and verbal register used here resemble Swift's other parodies of these meditations. Furthermore, the reduction of all matter in the universe to a single substance is reminiscent of Boyle's corpuscular philosophy.

In contrast to the Epicureans, in Boyle's opinion all matter was universally the same, and created and controlled by the divine author, who divided it into 'an innumerable multitude of very variously figur'd Corpuscles' and put them into motion in the 'Grand Fabrick or System of the World'.[59] The physical properties of any given body were determined by the size, shape and motion of its component corpuscles. For Boyle, this mechanical universe did not follow laws of impact and inertia, where particles collided and transferred their motion, as Cartesians and Epicureans might envisage.[60] Instead, Boyle considered the world mechanism to be constructed like a clock: a 'curious Engine' framed so that the 'various Motions of the Wheels, and other parts concur to exhibit the *Phænomena* design'd by the Artificer' (*WRB*, III, 248). That this 'Engine' is the passive instrument of its 'Opificer' was not a negative thing for Boyle, as it would have been for Descartes, but instead showed 'a Machine so Immense, so Beautiful, so well contriv'd'.[61]

The Taylor-worshippers' system is not analogized as an 'Engine', but as another form of manufactured artifice: a 'large *Suit of Cloaths*'. The Taylor-deity, who created by 'Manufactory Operation' (p. 49), and Boyle's God are therefore similar in their roles as divine artisans or 'Opificer[s]' of a universe comprising component parts of different sizes in regularity and harmony, and made from the same substance (clothes/ corpuscles). Section II shows that all systems of thought that attempt to explain the precise workings of God's universe (and especially those that believe omnicompetent knowledge only comes from taking things to pieces) reduce the complexity of things by turning surface metaphors into matters of fact. These artificial manufactures, of vulgar social origin (perhaps to represent a lower sphere of understanding), can only result in materialism, for the spiritual universe will be forever unknown to earthly man. Moreover, the vision of man as a *'Micro-Coat'* ignores the scriptural tenet that man is in the image of his Creator. The expansion of this literalizing, 'physico-logical' scheme to encompass abstract nouns makes the materialism at the heart of the extended analogy more evident, with all things reduced to the physical. The similitudes contrived by the *Tale*-narrator resemble the analogical apodoses of Boyle in his *Occasional Reflections*, but also serve to parody mechanical philosophies in order to draw attention to their inherent materialism.

The system of the Taylor-worshippers functions as a burlesque of numerous concepts and discourses, and tensions between these narratives of nature inevitably manifest themselves in Swift's parodic cosmology. Not only did Boyle follow the biblical account in considering man to have been created in God's image, and so objected to the Paracelsians' micro- and macrocosm analogy, he also rejected the idea of 'Nature' acting as a second cause, seeing it more as a system of rules.[62] In Boyle's opinion, that the universe was an immense system of manufactured components interacting, but also requiring incorporeal assistance, underpinned his physico-theology:

> it *more* sets off the Wisdom of God in the Fabrick of the Universe, that he can make so vast a Machine, [...] *than* if he imployed from time to time an Intelligent Overseer, such as *Nature* is fancied to be, to regulate, assist, and controul.[63]

His comments seemed to be directed at the Cambridge Platonist Ralph Cudworth, whose concept of *'Plastick Nature'* sought to account for the 'vital motions' of living things.[64] For Cudworth, God's indirect involvement could explain the imperfections in nature, while for Boyle this removal diminished the glory of the omniscient and omnipotent Creator.[65] Moreover, in Boyle's opinion, placing emphasis upon this secondary agent also had the potential to encourage the deist conflation of God with Nature.

In Section II of the *Tale*, the narrator invites the reader to 'Proceed to the particular Works of the Creation, [and] find how curious *Journey-man* Nature hath been, to trim up the *vegetable* Beaux' (p. 49). Like in the *Tritical Essay*, Nature is personified, but this time not as a woman whose 'secret Recesses' are penetrated by the gaze of the 'reflecting' virtuoso (a gender reversal perhaps intended to enhance the appropriateness of the 'Man as "*Micro-Coat*"' conceit). The Taylor-God has constructed a harmonious 'Fabrick', but its maintenance is provided by the intermediary, artisanal hireling '*Journey-man* Nature', not by its original 'Opificer', as it would be in Boyle's voluntarist conception.[66] Nevertheless, Swift's conflation of philosophies in Section II seems to include the '*Meleteticks*' and 'mechanism' of Boyle, not only in the numerous inter-textual connections between the *Tale*, *Broom-Stick* and *Tritical Essay*, but also in the sheer scale and intricacy of the analogy pursued by the Taylor-worshippers and, by extension, the narrator. However, this is not to argue that Swift's intellectual parodies are consistent with their 'real' counterparts, for the conflation, diminution, reduction, and exaggeration upon which satire relies will inexorably distort its targets.

In *A Meditation upon a Broom-Stick* and its contemporaneous works, Swift presents Boyle's '*Meleteticks*' as a form of mechanization of thinking. While Boyle's natural philosophical writings promote a mechanical philosophy of all matter in nature, Swift suggests that his moralizing reflections encourage the systematization of textual composition and of the human imagination itself. Swift seems to imply that, ironically, the standardization of reflection which Boyle prescribes in order to encourage man's special '*Faculty*, whereby an Inquisitive Soul may expatiate it self' through the universe (*WRB*, V, 34) can only serve to diminish or remove completely the sort of moral insight the Christian virtuoso seeks through such contemplations. Swift shows that similitudes do not always produce useful forms of knowledge, and especially not of the philosophical and/or theological magnitude Boyle claims. Instead, Swift insinuates that Boyle's reductive 'meditations', which catalogue experience after experience, reflect what he sees as the dull systematizing and arrogance of the Royal Society's version of the Baconian mindset, which believes that the collection of data, no matter how trivial, is of value because of its very accumulation, and results in the cultural acceptance and appreciation of such contributions to knowledge as a 'Dissertation upon *Tea*' (*Tale*, p. 84). Of more concern to Swift, however, seems to be the focus placed in Boyle's meditations on the natural world and its interaction with the individual human subject as a site of theological significance. Despite Boyle's preservation of Scripture as a means to God, albeit in combination with evidence from natural phenomena, his emphasis upon nature and human reason, apparently above revelation, in Swift's eyes seemed to have the potential to lead to deism and enthusiasm.

Curious Engines

As the Taylor-worshippers' system suggests, mechanical philosophers including Boyle applied their laws to all phenomena in the universe, and so even to man himself. Following William Harvey's groundbreaking discovery of the circulation of the blood (which demonstrated that the heart functions as a pump), the seventeenth century witnessed the development and increasing acceptance of a mechanistic physiology. Descartes' *Discours de la méthode* (1637) and *Traité de l'homme* (1648) explained the operations of the body in terms of matter and motion, utilizing mechanical metaphors and analogies, finding 'life' only in the human soul.[67] Pioneering anatomists such as Marcello Malpighi (whose works Swift would have encountered through reading Wotton's *Reflections*) also saw the human body as an assemblage of components with mechanical or chemico-mechanical functions.[68] These complex pieces were subject to and acted in accordance with physical and/or chemical laws, performing as valves, levers, pulleys, tubes, and so forth. Iatromechanism and iatrohydraulics offered ways of conceptualizing the regulation of the body's system which were far more compelling than physiological accounts based on humoural flows which, after centuries of dominance, were finally superseded. By the 1680s, mechanistic models had become generally accepted, and particularly through the work of Thomas Willis were perceived to have medical application, especially in relation to the nerves and brain.[69]

Between the 1650s and 1680s, Boyle became more and more convinced that not only was the system of the world analogous to an 'Elaborate Engine', but also that the body could be explained in mechanistic terms, it being 'a curious engine, admirably framed and contrived'. It is suspected that his embrace of these concepts occurred through reading Descartes, given the similarity of their mechanical allusions, especially in relation to physiology.[70] The entrenchment of these ideas within Boyle's thinking reflected and also shaped the wider approval of the mechanical philosophy, as one would expect from the most influential British natural philosopher of the period. Although the *Occasional Reflections* is thought to have been written in 1647–48, Boyle's mechanistic view of human physiology is already evident in this early composition, and one 'meditation' seems to be of particular significance to Swift's writing. Concentrating upon non-nervous anatomy, the remainder of the chapter explores the echo of Boyle's mechanistic writing on the body within Swift's works, showing how the human frame as a site of knowledge is exploited as an object of satire. Swift's attitude to the body has been explored in much detail elsewhere,[71] but I wish to emphasize how the conception of the human form as analogous to mechanism suggested to Swift a unique way of discussing human fragility and error, and offered what appeared to be the epitome of the mind-set which developed through the new experimental philosophy.

Of the six sections in the *Occasional Reflections*, the whole of the second is devoted to Boyle's meditations upon 'the Accidents of an Ague', constituting a change to a more autobiographical genre resembling St Augustine's *Confessions* and Donne's *Devotions upon Emergent Occasions* (1634). Boyle's first contemplations when contracting the disease parallel various parts of the *Tale*, and it is almost certain that Swift read this passage, given that it includes the phrase 'acts of Intemperance' explicitly parodied in the *Broom-Stick*. His attempts at philosophical self-anatomy in the *Occasional Reflections*, of using the meditations as not only a method of finding God in Nature, but also a form of enquiry into the nature of identity and the self (and especially its moral formation), are manifested as a literal autopsy:

> to what a strange number and variety of Distempers these frail Carcasses of ours are Obnoxious; for, if I had call'd to mind what my Curiosity for Dissections has shown me, and remembred how many Bones, and Muscles, and Veins, and Arteries, and Grisles, and Ligaments, and Nerves, and Membranes, and Juices, a humane Body is made up of, I could not have been surprised, that so curious an Engine, that consists of so many pieces, whose Harmony is requisite to Health, [...] should be subject to Pain, or Sickness, [like] an Instrument with above a thousand Strings (if there were any such) should frequently be out of Tune, especially since the bare change of Air may as well discompose the Body of a Man, as untune some of the Strings of such an Instrument; so that ev'n the inimitable Structure of humane Bodies is

scarce more admirable, than that such curious and elaborate Engines can be so contriv'd, as not to be oftner out of order than they are; the preservation of so nice and exact a Frame being the next wonder to its Work-man-ship. And indeed, when I consider further, how many outward accidents are able to destroy the Life, or, at the least, the Health, [...] and how easily the Beams of a warm Sun, or the Breath of a cold Wind, [...] or an infectious Vapour, [...] are able to produce Sickness, and perhaps Death. (*WRB*, V, 63–64)

Boyle has experienced what appears to be a life-threatening illness, but in trying to make sense of his fragile form the dehumanizing focus on the human anatomy as an 'Engine' removes him from the reality of mortality. He admits his great 'Curiosity for Dissections' and lists with relish the many pieces the 'humane Body is made up of', expressing not only the complexity of the human frame, but also his own mastery over anatomy through this knowledge. The corporeal human form becomes for Boyle an object of intellectual fascination, and one analogous to artificial mechanism: 'so curious an Engine'.

In Boyle's reflection, even bodies imbued with life are figured as 'frail Carcasses'. Boyle's analogy of man as a machine is most similar to Descartes' in this respect, who claimed that the image of a corpse illustrated most readily man's mechanistic anatomy:

the difference between the body of a living man and that of a dead man is just like the difference between [...] a watch or other automaton (that is, a self-moving machine) when it is wound up [...] and, on the other hand, the same watch or machine when it is broken.[72]

The difficulties philosophers encountered in accounting for the interaction of the incorporeal soul with the body, satirized by Swift in the *Tale* and *Mechanical Operation*, did much to reduce man to mere mechanism.[73] However, the analogies employed by Boyle and Descartes highlight that the advances in anatomy, which reveal the 'elaborate Engines' at work inside the body, also put at risk the conception of man as a partly spiritual being, leaving him as just matter in a highly structured form. Through Boyle's reductionism, 'Sickness' becomes merely the 'untuning' of 'an Instrument'. Boyle's pathology sees the human frame as a device of mechanical regularity, but subject to malfunction through external, environmental conditions. With the normal tension and elasticity of its components disrupted, the instrumental harmony of the body is lost, and the mental and bodily motions powered by the 'engine' are rendered 'out of order'. The paradox of the human body's preservation despite its fragility, which Boyle identifies as 'the next wonder to its Work-man-ship', is revealed through the body's similarity to the productions of art: its harmonious structure is 'scarce more admirable' than 'such curious and elaborate Engines can be so contriv'd'. Here Swift would find an example of the presumptuousness of the virtuoso in declaring an affinity between the works of the Creator and the works of man. In its strange mixture of the polite with the gruesome, Boyle's meditation hints at the cruel objectification of the human body which, for Swift, the anatomical eye intrinsically pursues.

The beginning of Section V of the *Tale*, the mock-panegyric 'Digression in the Modern Kind', reminds Martin Price of the voice of a 'Christian virtuoso' like Boyle, and the similarities here can be taken much further.[74] Reminiscent of Marvell's satiric anatomy of Samuel Parker in *The Rehearsal Transpos'd*,[75] the narrator figures his enquiries as a kind of dissection, but the metaphorical is soon confused with the literal, and in its cold detachment magnifies Boyle's clinical observation of the human form:

> I have [...] dissected the Carcass of *Humane Nature*, [...] till at last it *smelt* so strong, I could preserve it no longer. [...] I have been at a great Expence to fit up all the Bones with exact Contexture, and in due Symmetry; so that I am ready to shew a very compleat Anatomy thereof to all curious *Gentlemen and others*. (p. 81)[76]

The narrator admits that his project is 'fit up': an artificial contrivance which is reductionist in method, despite his declaration of comprehensive knowledge. Of course, the irony of this claim is that only the 'Carcass' has been examined, rather than the whole body (and importantly, the mind) in a state of animation. This inherent flaw renders any 'anatomy' of '*Humane Nature*' deficient, and so it will not provide 'curious *Gentlemen*' with the deepest answers; while the possible pun on '*Humane*' reveals the indecorum and perhaps immorality of his intellectual interests.

More apposite to Boyle's contemplations on his 'Ague', however, are the musings of the narrator in the *Tale*'s 'Digression on Madness'. Not only does Section IX take Boyle's conceit that 'the bare change of Air may as well discompose the Body of a Man' to its *reductio ad absurdum*, it also contains the same strange mixture of logical thoughts with speculations unrestrained by moral imperatives. Swift's adaptation of medical theories of the 'vapours' to explain frenzied psychological states in this

'Digression' has been much explored. However, Michael DePorte suggests that in the emphasis on the 'mechanical operation' of vapours Swift diverges from his primary source, Henry More's *Enthusiasmus Triumphatus* (1656).[77] Swift's mock-symptomology blends together humoural and mechanical pathologies of hysteria. For instance, despite the initial aerial tropes, the narrator figures his system of vapours in overtly mechanical terms to account for the sexual appetite of Henri IV of France (1553–1610): 'What secret Wheel, what hidden Spring, could put into Motion so wonderful an Engine? It was afterwards discovered, that the Movement of this whole Machine had been directed by an absent *Female*, whose Eyes had raised a Protuberancy' (p. 106). For Boyle, the entire human frame is 'so curious an Engine', while the *Tale*-narrator ironically finds 'so wonderful an Engine' in the mechanisms of sexual stimulation, which has the power to move the 'whole Machine' and not just its component 'parts'. There is, no doubt, much to be made of the irony that it is a king who becomes 'subject' to the 'secret Wheel' and 'hidden Spring'. The absence of conscious will – with the king's lust attributed to his physiology, as a purely involuntary response to an external stimulus – leaves the world of the 'Digression on Madness' as one of moral chaos, and thus satirizes proleptically the libertine mechanism of Julien Offray de La Mettrie's *L'Homme Machine* (1748), in which the erection of the penis is attributed to a 'singular spring'.[78] The idea of one sexually stimulated 'Movement' in control of the 'whole Machine' also serves as a satiric inversion of Glanvill's celebration of 'this admirable *Engine* of our Bodies, whose functions are carryed on by such a multitude of *parts*, and *motions*, which [...] by an *harmonious Sympathy* promote the perfection and good of the whole' (*Scepsis Scientifica*, p. 32). Swift's satire is probably not implying that man's consciousness has no control over his own actions, but that mechanism cannot explain, and man does not possess the sort of understanding needed to perceive, such subtle harmonies at work in his own body.

Explaining why 'great Introducers of new Schemes in Philosophy' acquire so many 'Disciples' (*Tale*, pp. 107–108), 'A Digression on Madness' also figures the human mind as a passive piece of musical apparatus perhaps, as Harth suggests, again parodying Glanvill.[79] The *Tale*-narrator focuses upon the variation in pitch of a 'peculiar *String* in the Harmony of Human Understanding' (p.108) to account for the social relativity of madness, Glanvill figures the 'power of one man's imagination upon another's' as the reverberation of strings on a lute (*Scepsis Scientifica*, pp. 146–47), while for Boyle, the entire human body is a delicate 'Instrument with above a thousand Strings' (*WRB*, V, 63). Boyle's analogies have a crude phenomenological basis in physical reality (the 'Muscles, and Veins, and Arteries' and so on do resemble 'strings' to some extent), while the *Tale*-narrator speculates upon the workings of the mind in a way which assumes the validity of mechanistic accounts of consciousness and, by corollary, materialist conceptions of the soul. This stance produces a structural irony, in that the narrator's physicalized system places himself in the ranks of the reductive 'Innovators in the Empire of Reason' (p. 108).

Despite the *Tale*-narrator's pseudo-physiological explanations of human motivations and appetites, he later offers an empiricist critique of 'that pretended Philosophy which enters into the Depth of Things': 'the Sight and the Touch [...] never examine farther than the Colour, the Shape, the Size, and [...] then comes Reason officiously, with Tools for cutting, [...] and piercing, offering to demonstrate, that [Bodies] are not of the same consistence quite thro' (p. 111). The narrator's comments betray a feeling of lament that the senses 'never examine farther' than the external qualities, but the method of achieving knowledge of an object's inner attributes is far from celebrated. Swift plays with two meanings of 'officiously': 'Reason' presents itself as courteously supplying the means to wisdom, 'offering to demonstrate' to a polite audience of willing spectators. However, the velocity of 'then comes' suggests that in reality 'Reason' is obtrusively putting forward its results even if the onlookers can no longer bear to watch. The onomatopoeia of 'cutting' and 'piercing' accentuates the intellectual violence that 'Reason', using its crude 'Tools', will perform upon its subject, suggesting that any conclusions will offer little worth.

The narrator then literalizes the anatomical metaphor, and the pragmatic voice is replaced by confessions of intellectual enquiries which suggest a morally dubious appetite for knowledge:

in most Corporeal Beings, [...] the *Outside* hath been infinitely preferable to the *In*: Whereof I have been farther convinced from some late Experiments. Last Week I saw a Woman *flay'd*, and you will hardly believe, how much it altered her Person for the worse. Yesterday I ordered the Carcass of a *Beau* to be stript in my Presence; when we were all amazed to find so many unsuspected Faults under one Suit of Cloaths: Then I laid open his *Brain*, his *Heart*, and his *Spleen*; But, I plainly perceived at every Operation, that the farther we proceeded, we found the Defects encrease upon us in Number and Bulk: from all which, I justly formed this Conclusion to my self; That whatever Philosopher or Projector can find out an Art to sodder and patch up the Flaws and Imperfections of Nature, will deserve much better of Mankind, and teach us a more useful Science, than that so much in present Esteem, of widening and exposing them. (p. 112)

The narrator offers this personal testimony as 'useful' knowledge, and is ignorant of the uncertain ethics of the 'late Experiments'. Swift associates the scientific impulse, despite its insistence upon the value of individual experience, with an unfeeling, objectifying outlook which could even classify torture as a valid method of enquiry; although, as Claude Rawson identifies, there is a sense of cruel fantasy on the author's part here, suggesting 'if not literal endorsement of the hideous punishment, a distinct animus against the victim', and a correlation between anatomical and satiric exposure.[80] This insensitive attitude, belying the personal nature of the response, is detached from the reality of physical cruelty, emphasized through ironic understatement ('you will hardly believe'). The narrator's curiosity is characterized as a sexual lust in which the 'Carcass' is 'stript' and its 'innermost Recesses' (as Boyle would say) are penetrated. As the autopsy progresses, and 'the Defects encrease upon us', this desire is eventually satiated.[81]

Both Boyle and the *Tale* narrator acknowledge the 'Imperfections' of the human body and magnify them through a form of imaginative violation analogous to contemporary anatomy. However, while Boyle celebrates the 'curious and elaborate Engines' man contrives which almost rival the human frame, the *Tale* narrator states a desire for human progress which is as yet unsatisfied. At the end of the *Tale* passage, the reasonable argument appears to return, offering an 'apodosis' with an apparently useful moral dictum. The narrator believes he is putting forward a sensible case, but the polite manner in which he has dealt with the horrific details of assaults upon the human form paradoxically reveals his brutality. The irony is heightened through the coarse vocabulary ('sodder', 'patch up') he uses to describe such 'Art'. In moments of the *Tale* such as this, one can fleetingly glimpse the opinions of the 'Swift' hiding amongst the patchwork of discourses. But such identifications can only be reductionist in method, in that much of the power of this passage comes from the clash of seemingly paradoxical moral values within the narratorial persona. Moreover, such contradictory impulses are also at work in the meditations of Boyle, offering the reader the thoughtful reflections of the moral philosopher and Anglican apologist, whilst revealing the desires of the curious virtuoso.

Fundamentally, the 'Digression on Madness' seeks to show how mechanistic conceptions of man are associated with an erosion of morality.

However, for Swift the image of man-as-machine also functioned as a useful conceit (and sometimes for its comic value alone). For example, in a scene which evokes many questions about the human as an object of science,[82] the diminutive Gulliver is mistaken for an automaton:

> The King [...] had been educated in the Study of Philosophy, and particularly Mathematicks; yet when he observed my Shape exactly, and saw me walk erect, before I began to speak, conceived I might be a piece of Clock-work (which is in that Country arrived to a very great Perfection) contrived by some ingenious Artist. But when he heard my Voice, and found what I delivered to be regular and rational, he could not conceal his Astonishment. (*PW*, XI, 103)

It is easier for the King of Brobdingnag to believe that Gulliver is an artificial construct than to consider (as a physico-theologian might) that Nature (or the divine creator) contrived such a man to exist: as the 'three great Scholars' point out, Gulliver's structure does not seem to possess the capacity to preserve his life, 'either by Swiftness, or climbing of Trees, or digging Holes in the Earth' (*PW*, XI, 103). The King can conceive of the possibility that the vertical gait and movements of the human frame can be replicated, but it is Gulliver's 'regular and rational' utterances which, somewhat ironically, convince him that clockwork motion could not be responsible for the creature before him. In his study of philosophy and mathematics, therefore, the King may well have encountered a Brobdingnagian Descartes, whose European counterpart claims that language (other than simple mimicry) could not be produced mechanically:

> we can certainly conceive of a machine so constructed that it utters words, [...] But it is not conceivable that such a machine should produce different arrangements of words so as to give an appropriately meaningful answer to whatever is said in its presence.[83]

This factor does little to aid Gulliver's classification by the King's three 'virtuosi', however, who conclude he is 'only *Relplum Scalcath*, which is interpreted literally *Lusus Naturæ*', an indefinable 'thing of nature' (*PW*, XI, 104). Gulliver's encounter with the Brobdingnagian philosophers serves to satirize the taxonomic impulse, and the arbitrary and empty nature of signification, and ultimately highlights the limitations of human and Brobdingnagian knowledge. While Gulliver's speech proves his consciousness to the King, the 'three great Scholars' show that language may be 'regular and rational', but still empty.

In the *Memoirs*, Swift and his Scriblerian friends imagine the construction of a 'real' (and not just suspected), functioning automaton. The 'Society of *Free-Thinkers*' inform Martinus that they have employed

> a great Virtuoso at Nuremburg, to make a sort of Hydraulic Engine, in which a chemical liquor resembling Blood, is driven through elastic chanels resembling arteries and veins, by the force of an Embolus like the heart, and wrought by a pneumatic Machine of the nature of the lungs, with ropes and pullies, like the nerves, tendons and muscles: And we are persuaded that this our artificial Man will not only walk, and speak, and perform most of the outward actions of the animal life, but (being wound up once a week) will perhaps reason as well as most of your Country Parsons. (Chap. XII, p. 141)

In his *Occasional Reflections*, Boyle finds the body analogous to 'so curious an Engine', while in *A Free Enquiry into the Vulgarly Receiv'd Notion of Nature*, he develops his conception further, seeing the human frame as 'an Hydraulical, or rather Hydraulo-pneumatical Engine, that consists not only of Solid and Stable Parts, but of Fluids [...] in Organical Motion' (*WRB*, X, 540). The Scriblerians take this idea to its *reductio ad absurdum*, with the Nuremburg virtuoso's 'artificial Man' manufactured from those man-made components which resemble the natural human anatomy. While the punch-line is a simple poke at the intelligence and commitment of the lower clergy, the Scriblerians' conceit of an automaton made from 'a sort of Hydraulic Engine' is the culmination of their sustained attack on mechanistic accounts of the soul, treading a path previously explored by Swift in the *Mechanical Operation*.[84]

In 'My Lady's Lamentation and Complaint against the Dean' (dated 'July 28, 1728') mechanism functions as a metaphor in a more light-hearted vein. Probably one of the earliest poems written whilst staying with Sir Arthur and Lady Anne Acheson at Market Hill (near Armagh), it is notable for its impersonation of the Lady's voice, involving shifts in perspective which allow Swift to scrutinize himself.[85] The speaker's many grumbles include:

> When my elbows he sees
> Held up by my knees,
> My arms, like two props,
> Supporting my chops,
> And just as I handle 'em
> Moving all like a pendulum;

> He trips up my props,
> And down my chin drops,
> From my head to my heels,
> Like a clock without wheels;
> I sink in the spleen,
> An useless machine. (ll. 25–36, in *Poems*, III, 852)

The finely balanced motion of the 'pendulum' of Lady Acheson, belied by the hypermetric disorder of the line in which the simile appears, is disturbed by the japery of the Dean (who would often tease his hostess), serving as a half-serious symbol of the domestic disruption Swift's visits bring to her home. One set of components is rendered inoperative and the whole system grinds to a halt, 'Like a clock without wheels'. However, this would be only a momentary malfunction if the embarrassment did not bring Acheson (characterized as a typical 'nervous' female of the eighteenth century) to 'sink in the spleen', lose control of her rational faculties and so, in Cartesian terms, become 'An useless machine'. Arno Löffler views this study of 'splenetic sensibility' as a burlesque of Robert Burton's depiction of the melancholic mind,[86] but what Swift adds to this Burtonian analysis is an emphasis upon more contemporary discussions of hysteria, which could only make sense of abnormal physiologies through the application of mechanistic analogies. The focus on the fragility of Lady Anne's body, and the reduction of its functions to matter and motion, also features in a newly discovered poem from this same period, 'An excellent new Panegyric on Skinnibonia' (1728). The prevalence of metaphors of mechanism, and emphasis upon materiality, in the Market Hill poems reflects the Lady's interest in Lucretius, which Swift had encouraged; another instance that suggests the Dean's occasional ambivalence (rather than outrage) towards materialist ideas.[87]

Although Swift is simultaneously suspicious of, but imaginatively attracted to, mechanistic conceptions of human anatomy held by philosophers like Boyle, it is clear that in the 'Digression on Madness' he captures but wildly distorts the mind-set and epistemology he finds exemplified in Boyle's apparently 'moralizing' reflections. In the discursive confusion of the refined with the repugnant, and the logical with the wildly irrational, Swift shows that the emphasis which the method of '*Meleteticks*' places upon the value of the self in generating knowledge can result, for all its good intent, in the production of learning of dubious usefulness or morality. Boyle's meditations are in method initially rooted in the empirical observation of the world, but then 'officiously, with Tools for cutting'

(*Tale*, p. 111) they attempt to offer moral truths. Paradoxically, however, these 'important Moral Instruction[s]' or 'Theological Myster[ies]' (*WRB*, V, 15) are obtained through the construction of analogies which only function through surface comparisons, and therefore can in no way offer the true nature of things. *A Meditation upon a Broom-Stick, A Tritical Essay upon the Faculties of the Mind* and several key parts of the *Tale* show that Swift found the inductivist application of trivial observations of the 'most contemptible Weed' to the formation of universal conclusions to be philosophically unsound and theologically dangerous. For Swift, this method was not only 'very silly' in that it promoted a 'mechanized' and laborious way of writing (and ultimately, thinking) that involved the accumulation of trite similitudes, it was also morally worrying. Swift saw Boyle's 'meditations', despite their basis in a voluntarist conception of God's place in the universe, as reflecting a new tendency towards the deistic and mechanistic emphasis upon second causes and the negation of divine providence. In spite of claiming to make 'short Flights Heavenwards' (*WRB*, V, 25), Boyle's reflections spent far too long delving in the 'secret Recesses' of Nature.

2

Sinking the *'Spider'*s Cittadel': *The Battel of the Books* and Thomas Burnet's 'Philosophical Romance' of the Earth

In *The Battel of the Books* Swift chose to enshrine the most recent quarrel between the Ancients and the Moderns in a mock-heroic: a 'terrible Fight' between the books in the King's Library (*Tale*, p. 146). The *Battel* was written whilst Swift was working as Temple's secretary at Moor Park, and its intellectual context is firmly grounded in the debates of the 1690s, with a substantial number of its specific satiric targets directly related to what became a very personal feud. To demonstrate the superiority of Ancient writing, Temple had unfortunately picked the *Epistles* of Phalaris, the tyrant of Acragas, which the scholar, royal librarian and physico-theologian Richard Bentley (1662–1742) proved to be a forgery from a much later date, in a dissertation appended to the second edition of his friend Wotton's *Reflections* (July 1697). Charles Boyle (1674–1731) of Christ Church, Oxford had prepared an edition of Phalaris to support Temple's intellectual position and defend his personal reputation, and Bentley's dissertation provoked several replies from the 'Wits' at Boyle's college, the most significant being the collaborative *Dr. Bentley's Dissertations [...] Examin'd* (February 1698), published under Boyle's name. Composition of the *Battel* probably started after Swift read Bentley's *Dissertation* and must have continued at least until after the publication of the Christ Church *Examin'd*, a work of 'great Learning and Wit' according to the 'Bookseller' (p. 141). Indeed, evidence suggests that key segments of the *Battel* could not have been composed before 1699.

The *Battel*'s skirmishes pit the works of Galen against those of Paracelsus, Aristotle against Bacon and Descartes, Pindar against Cowley, and the combat ends with Charles Boyle vanquishing both Bentley and Wotton in one strike, their books bound together. However, Swift's attitude to Temple is now considered to be more complex and

ambivalent than previously thought,[1] and many of the individual con-
tests are left unresolved or their results obscured by pretended hiatuses
in the manuscript, meaning that the *Battel*'s support for the Ancients
is not without some degree of hesitation. Furthermore, the form of the
mock-heroic does little to honour either party.

Whilst keeping the main arena within its sights, this chapter is concerned principally with a digression within the *Battel*, but one which
dominates interpretation of the work as a whole: the fable of the
Spider and the Bee.[2] The narrator tells us that in the 'highest Corner
of a large Window' in the King's Library 'there dwelt a certain *Spider*'
whose web is called variously a 'Palace', 'Castle', and 'Mansion'. This
fortress is disturbed when a 'wandring *Bee* [...] happened to alight upon
one of the outward Walls of the *Spider*'s Cittadel; which yielding to
the unequal Weight, sunk down to the very Foundation' (p. 149). An
argument between the Spider and Bee ensues, in which the Spider criticizes the Bee's livelihood for being '*an universal Plunder upon Nature*',
while celebrating that his '*large Castle (to shew my Improvements in the
Mathematicks) is all built with my own Hands, and the Materials extracted
altogether out of my own Person*' (p. 150). The Bee answers '*I visit, indeed,
all the Flowers and Blossoms* [...] *but whatever I collect from thence, enriches
my self, without the least Injury to their Beauty, their Smell, or their Taste*',
while the Spider merely possesses '*an over-weening Pride, which feed-
ing and engendering upon it self, turns all into Excrement and Venom*'
(p. 151).

Several critics have noted that in using the spider to represent
Modern system-builders, Swift draws upon a common emblem in the
seventeenth century.[3] Although not the originator, Francis Bacon was
influential in disseminating this figuration, arguing in one of *Novum
Organum*'s aphorisms that 'The empirics, in the manner of the ant, only
store up and use things; the rationalists, in the manner of spiders, spin
webs from their own entrails; but the bee takes the middle path: it col-
lects its material from the flowers of field and garden, but its special gift
is to convert and digest it'. In *The Advancement of Learning*, Bacon associates the spider with scholastics, who 'spin out vnto vs those laborious
webbes of Learning', whilst bees were often identified with the common
interest, organized society, and industry.[4] It is generally assumed that
Swift uses the Moderns' own insect metaphors against them, with the
Spider no longer representing the Ancient scholiast but the Modern
system-builder, and the Bee as the Ancient, not the Baconian natural
philosopher.[5] What is rarely acknowledged, however, is that it is a
character within the *Battel*, the book of Æsop, who moralizes the fable,

asking his Ancient friends and Modern enemies whether '*any thing*
[was] *so* Modern *as the* Spider [who] *Spins and Spits wholly from himself,
and scorns to own any Obligation or Assistance*', and contending that '*the*
Antients [...] *are content with the* Bee, *to pretend to Nothing of our own*
[and] *fill our Hives with Honey and Wax*' rather than 'Dirt *and* Poison'
(pp. 151–52).[6] Æsop's moral produces a 'Tumult' among the books, and
they decide to resolve their animosities through the battle which forms
the remainder of the narrative (p. 152). That it is the book of Æsop
who appropriates the images for his own figurations problematizes the
suggestion that the Spider and the Bee unequivocally represent the
Moderns and the Ancients respectively, and has implications for readings of Swift's relation to the new natural philosophy.

Spinning Sacred Theories

The quarrel between the Ancients and Moderns was not confined to
assessments of the relative value of authors, or to debates about the
nature of literary scholarship, but revealed wide philosophical and
theological differences. Temple stated that his *Essay upon the Ancient
and Modern Learning* (1690) had been provoked by a piece 'in French
upon the Plurality of Worlds' and another 'upon the Antediluvian
World'.[7] These two works of considerable notoriety, Bernard le Bovier
de Fontenelle's *Entretiens sur la Pluralité des Mondes* (1688) and Thomas
Burnet's *Sacred Theory of the Earth* (1684; first published in Latin as
Telluris Theoria Sacra [1681]), had both celebrated the contributions
of the Moderns to learning. The Ancient Temple could not help but
be inflamed by their audacious comments. Burnet, for instance, made
the comparison that 'Ancient Learning is like Ancient Medals, more
esteemed for their rarity, than their real use'.[8]

Burnet's system used theories from Cartesian natural philosophy in
aid of a literal interpretation of the biblical account of the creation, fall,
flood and conflagration. Burnet (c. 1635–1715), who was a fellow of the
Royal Society, and had been Master of the Charterhouse and Chaplain
to William III, proposed that the Earth's surface had been smooth at
its creation, but that because of the Fall it became fractured, allowing
the waters lying in the abyss to rise up and flood the Earth in the great
Deluge. This left the world in the uneven, ruined state which modern
man saw around him, with mountains, valleys and seas as scars upon
God's creation. Burnet's cosmogony would set in motion the production of many other pseudo-geological theories over the next century.
Their authors were inspired by the breadth of Burnet's undertaking, but

were very often concerned that the *Theory* had not taken into account the rapidly accumulating geological and palaeontological data. For instance, John Woodward, the frequent butt of the Scriblerians' satires (such as the *Memoirs* and *Three Hours after Marriage*), wrote *An Essay toward a Natural History of the Earth* (1695), which attempted to show that fossils were the remnants of antediluvian creatures. Meanwhile, physico-theologians such as Bentley and William Derham insisted upon the utility of mountain ranges in their arguments from design, rather than seeing them as a reminder of man's sin.[9]

Burnet's account of the conflagration was an excessively literal interpretation of II Peter 3.10, which foresees the dissolution of the Earth by fire. Burnet believed that evidence from outside scripture, in the form of the discoveries and theories of the new natural philosophy, could be employed as a way of countering claims that the biblical text must be read allegorically. The events outlined in the Petrine conflagration 'will all be literally true', because to make it an allegory is 'not only to contradict S. *Peter,* but all Antiquity, Sacred or Prophane. [...] the present Heavens and Earth shall be destroyed in a literal Sence, and by material Fire'.[10] What makes Burnet's eschatology distinctive is that secondary (i.e. natural) causes are suggested as the agents of the millennial transformation. The immense heat needed to accomplish this would originate in geological and astronomical phenomena; in volcanoes, minerals like coal, and meteors. Using the book of Daniel, Paul's Epistles to the Thessalonians, and the Revelation of John, the Protestant propagandist Burnet believed that the conflagration would begin with the annihilation of the Antichrist at Rome, and for him this was substantiated by the volatile geology of the Italian region. This 'Sea of fire' would then progress to cover 'the whole Globe of the Earth'.[11]

Significantly, these natural causes would envelop and destroy the souls of the sinful, including the prince of devils, following Revelation 20.9–10:

> if we suppose *Beelzebub,* and his Apostate crew, in the midst of this fiery furnace: [...] It will be hard to find any part of the Universe, or any state of things, that answers to so many of the properties and characters of *Hell,* as this. (Book III, Chap. 12, pp. 73–74)

Burnet acknowledges that his apocalyptic vision of the universal inferno 'would seem to most Men a Romantick Scene. Yet we are sure there must be such a Scene' (p. 72). The grand style of Burnet's prose and particularly the epic nature of his imagination were celebrated by many authors in the following century, including Richard Steele:

> When this Admirable Author has reviewed all that has passed, or is to come, which relates to the Habitable World, and run through the whole Fate of it, how could a Guardian Angel, that had attended it through all its Courses or Changes, speak more emphatically [...] than does our Author, when he makes, as it were, a Funeral Oration over this Globe [...]?[12]

Theologically and philosophically, however, Burnet's theory was on much more fragile ground. On the one hand, Burnet's biblical herme-neutics followed a literal reading of scripture, but used natural phi-losophy to prove its validity. On the other, however, Burnet was also attempting to follow the Augustinian theory of accommodation, arguing that Moses did not 'Philosophize or Astronomize', but instead presented 'a narration suited to the capacity of the people, and not to the strict and physical nature of things' ('A Review of the Theory of the Earth', in *Theory*, p. 183).

It was this belief that got Burnet into trouble. For instance, Burnet corresponded with Newton during the composition of the *Theory*, and their letters indicate that although Newton was receptive to the accommodation hypothesis, he was unsure as to whether Burnet was employing it correctly.[13] Once published, Burnet's *Theory* encountered responses far more condemnatory than Newton's, because its very approach provoked questions about the limits of human reason in rela-tion to the authority of revelation. Burnet's *Archaeologiae Philosophicae* (1692) sought to defend his interpretation, but along the way argued that the Fall of Man must also be read with the accommodation hypothesis in mind, and was used by deists such as Charles Blount and Charles Gildon to argue against the scriptural account of man's origins altogether. These appropriations led to Burnet losing his chaplaincy in the early 1690s.[14] By the time of the *Battel*, therefore, Burnet's *Theory* had become a source of great controversy.

Ernest Tuveson established that the fable of the Spider and the Bee is at least partly concerned with the contemporary debate regarding the interpretation of scripture using discoveries and theories of natural phil-osophy, including Burnet's *Theory*, but also Woodward's *Natural History* and William Whiston's cometographical *A New Theory of the Earth* (1696). However, detailed analysis of this digression reveals the intense specificity of Swift's satiric allegory in targeting Burnet's work, and source study shows that the attack drew upon criticism of Burnet's ideas within the community of natural philosophy. Certain echoes of vocabulary within the episode suggest that Swift had read the *Theory* (and we know he owned the third edition), and chose to associate Burnet's system of the Earth with the Spider's cobweb. In Swift's allegory, the Spider's fragile web is not only figured as a castle suspended in the air, making use of the architectural trope of knowledge common in the seventeenth century,[15] but also represents what Swift sees as the intricate but flimsy, transient nature of Burnet's conjectures. Simultaneously, through the use of parodic echo the web is mock-heroically transformed into Burnet's vision of the Earth itself. Fittingly, Swift's figuration of the Spider as system-builder is perhaps partly derived from Burnet's account in *Archaeologiae Philosophicae* of the 'Brachmin' legend of 'a certain immense Spider' who created and governs the universe, imaged as a gigantic web.[16]

Burnet's *Theory* is parodied both stylistically and substantively in the *Battel*. Tuveson notes that 'Chasms', 'Ruins' and 'Dilapidations' were 'favorite terms in Burnet's theory', but the allusions go much deeper than this, as Swift seeks to highlight the most worrying aspects of Burnet's scriptural readings.[17] The Spider felt the 'terrible Convulsion' caused by the Bee unsettling the web and feared that '*Nature* was approaching to her final Dissolution' (p. 149); in the *Theory* 'The Earth shakes and trembles, in apprehension of the [...] convulsions that are coming upon her; And the Sun often hides his head, [...] as if all Nature was to suffer in this Agony'. For Burnet, such portents signify the beginning of the 'second dissolution by Fire': the first being at the time of the universal Deluge.[18] The Spider beholds 'the Chasms, and Ruins' of his 'Fortress'; in Burnet's opinion, the surfaces of the contemporary Earth are the 'Ruines' of 'that first World' and the seas and oceans were formed by the rains of the Deluge filling the 'Chasms' made by the Sun's heat. The Spider then fears that the great 'Convulsion' signals that '*Beelzebub* with all his Legions, was come to revenge the Death of many thousands of his Subjects'. Beelzebub is, of course, the lord of the flies, but what makes the conceit of Burnet-as-Spider especially appropriate is Burnet's eschatological vision of the souls of sinners destroyed by physical phenomena, in a 'Deluge of [volcanic] fire'.[19]

Swift's parody appears to ridicule Burnet's account of divine retribution using secondary causes, finding it erroneous for mechanical principles as devised by mortal man to be used to describe the conditions in which God's power is exercised. That Burnet's apparent privileging of natural causation above divine providence is the focus of the satire is confirmed later in the paragraph, when the Spider 'wisely gather[s] Causes from Events' to determine that the Bee has brought about the destruction of his castle (p. 149). Like the Spider, Burnet confesses to taking pleasure in tracing out the 'Causes of Effects, and the depend-ance [sic] of one thing upon another in the visible Creation' (Book I, Chap. 1, p. 1). Swift is no doubt also engaging in more general satire on Modern natural philosophers here, targeting their pride in seeming to determine ultimate causes, but Burnet is a suitable archetype because he sees it as the 'proper business' of a Philosopher to 'describe in compre-hensive Theories the *Phaenomena* of the World, and the Causes of them' (sig. A4ᵛ). Burnet's explanation of the last judgment over-reaches his own boundary, as it assigns material agents to divine acts. The attitude implicit in Swift's attack therefore resembles the concerns of the Lower House of Convocation, in their polemic *A Representation of the Present State of Religion* (1711), a copy of which Swift owned. This proclama-tion, sometimes attributed to the Christchurch man and friend of Swift, Francis Atterbury (1663–1732), identified that the 'Attempts made to shew, how [...] the Creation of the World, [was] to be accounted for by the known Laws of Motion; and the Destruction of it, by the Deluge' have a tendency to 'confine the Thoughts of Men to second Causes, and to intimate, how little the Wisdom of God was concern'd'.[20] This is not to say that Swift himself did not find something imaginatively use-ful in the figuration of God's powers as physical phenomena. 'On the Day of Judgement', normally ascribed to Swift, seems to draw upon the interest in eschatological theories, and there he revels in the spectacle of the great conflagration: 'Jove, arm'd with Terrors, burst the Skies, / And Thunder roars, and Light'ning flies!' (ll. 5–6, in *Poems*, II, 578).[21] However, the framing of the entire fable as a 'material Accident' (p. 149) invites the suspicion that Burnet's approach is materialist in all but name, with an 'Accident' allowing no place for authorship or providence of events.[22]

Although Burnet is defending the literal truth of the biblical account, as opposed to reading it allegorically, Swift is perhaps concerned about Burnet's favouring of reason over revelation, through using the external evidence provided by natural philosophy. The subordination of the bib-lical text is made explicit from the outset of the *Theory*: ''Tis a dangerous thing to engage the authority of Scripture in disputes about the Natural World, in opposition to Reason; lest Time [...] should discover that to be evidently false which we had made Scripture to assert' (Preface, sig. A4ᵛ). Burnet insists upon using individual reason, which can fall into similar error, as his doomed appropriation of Cartesian theory verifies.

The 'Wandring *Bee*' Alights

The many parodic verbal echoes, and hence the precision of the satiric targeting outlined so far, reveal that Swift almost certainly possessed knowledge of Burnet's *Theory* when writing the *Battel*. This is not much of a revelation given that Swift's employer Temple had read Burnet and responded to it in his *Essay upon the Ancient and Modern Learning*. What is more surprising is that Swift's attack, expressing his unease at Burnet's method of biblical hermeneutics, may have been encouraged and inspired by criticism of his grand system within the community of natural philosophy, most notably in John Keill's *An Examination of Dr Burnet's Theory of the Earth* (1698). Keill's book does not appear in Swift's library catalogue, and there is no reference to it in his correspondence, but it is possible that Temple received a copy of the work, judging by its relevance to the Ancients and Moderns debate. Evidence from within the *Battel* suggests that Swift was aware of some of the particulars of Keill's argument against Burnet, granting some insight into Swift's satiric technique and purpose within the fable, and showing that Swift shared the same attitude towards the pseudo-geological theorists as some Newtonians.

Keill (1671–1721) had studied at Edinburgh University under David Gregory (1659–1708), one of the first to accept the accomplishments of Newton's *Principia*. Gregory moved to Balliol College in 1691 when he was appointed Savilian Professor of Astronomy. Keill soon followed Gregory to Oxford, and his courses as Sedleian deputy (from 1699) were the first to express 'Love of the *Newtonian Philosophy*', as John Theophilus Desaguliers, one of his most famous students, put it (this devotion would be most emphatically manifest in Keill's accusation that Leibniz's system of differential calculus had plagiarized Newton's theory of 'fluxions').[23] Gregory, and presumably Keill, associated with members of Christ Church, including the Dean, Henry Aldrich (1648–1710), who was also the university's vice-chancellor. At some time around 1700, Gregory transferred from Balliol to Christ Church, with Keill following his mentor there in 1703.[24] Swift received his MA from Hart Hall in July 1692, and in November that year would comment that at Oxford: 'I had all the civilities I could wish for, and so many [showed me] favours, that I [...] have been more obliged in a few weeks to strangers, than ever I was in seven years to Dublin College'.[25] It is not known who these affable Oxford men were, but the controversy over the authenticity of the Phalaris letters later in the decade certainly brought Swift into contact with the 'Christ Church Wits' who defended Charles Boyle's edition against Bentley.

When the *Tale* first appeared, Atterbury informed Bishop Trelawny that 'It comes from Christ Church': whether this was because he considered Swift to be a member of the college, or the result of mistaken attribution, is not clear, but highlights that this work of 'wit, humour, good sense, and learning' and fervent opposition to Catholicism and Dissent (but alleged profanity) would find a suitable home at this institution.[26] The connection between Swift and members of the college would remain strong: after meeting with Atterbury in March 1711/12, Swift wrote to Stella that 'they have this long time admitted me a Christchurch man' (*PW*, XVI, 514). Swift's correspondence reveals that he also knew both Gregory and Keill personally, perhaps through the Christ Church connection, but it is unclear as to when he first met them.[27]

It has been argued that the Phalaris affair escalated from one based in issues of textual philology to reflect divisions between High and Low Church, Tory and Whig, Ancient and Modern, gentleman-amateur and professional scholar, Oxford and Cambridge. This thesis can account for some of the differences: in issues of episcopacy, doctrine and monarchical succession, Christ Church members were firmly High Church and, in several cases, suspected of Jacobite Tory tendencies; whilst Wotton and Bentley (and Newton, at least publicly) were Low Church Whigs. However, Anita Guerrini's study of the 'Tory Newtonians' has shown that these dichotomies belie the more complex picture of loyalties.[28] The principal Christ Church 'Wits' – Aldrich, Boyle, Atterbury, George Smalridge (1663–1719), and William King (1663–1712) – can all be identified as 'Ancients' within this dispute, but the college welcomed Keill and Gregory, and included another acquaintance of Swift's, the physician John Freind (1675–1728), who attempted to reconcile his position as both Ancient and Newtonian by arguing that many of Hippocrates' opinions had been corroborated by Newtonian theories of the body.[29] It is also difficult to identify Charles Boyle as exclusively an 'Ancient': he became a fellow of the Royal Society in 1706, and was later the patron of George Graham, whose astronomical display instrument the 'orrery' was named after the Earl.

For all of the usual associations of the new sciences with a discourse of progress, as instigated by writers like Wotton, some Newtonians, and Newton himself, saw Modern natural philosophy as restoring Ancient wisdom (the *prisca sapientia*). In their opinion, the writers of remote antiquity had hidden their discoveries from the vulgar through elaborate allegories. Newton's draft scholia to Book III of the *Principia* reveal that he constructed detailed Ancient genealogies for his doctrines, and it is known that Newton allowed Gregory to incorporate materials from the scholia into *Astronomia physicae et geometricae elementa* (1702).[30] Keill followed his two mentors in his *Astronomical Lectures*, where he also presents contemporary natural philosophers as rediscovering lost Ancient astronomy: Pythagoras had learnt the 'true System of the Universe' from the Egyptians, and was the first in Greece to teach the heliocentric system and the axial motion of the Earth.[31] Keill may have viewed himself, therefore, as an 'Ancient' in a narrative of restoration, rather than progress, through Modern natural philosophy.

Like his Christ Church friends, Keill was presumed to be a Tory by his contemporaries. Writing to Robert Hunter on the occasion of Gregory's death in late 1708, and Keill's wish to succeed his friend as Savilian Professor, Swift lamented that 'Party reaches even to Lines and Circles, and [Keill] will hardly carry it, being reputed a Tory, wch yet he utterly denyes'. Keill failed to gain the chair in this instance (although he was eventually elected in 1712), but benefited from governmental roles offered by Robert Harley.[32] Swift, of course, also profited from this source of patronage when working as a Tory propagandist between 1710 and 1714, but his political identity, particularly at the time of the *Tale*, has been subject to much critical disagreement. In around 1702, Swift admitted to John, Baron Somers (1651–1716), Whig Lord Chancellor and President of the Royal Society (1698–1703): 'I found myself much inclined to be what they call a Whig in politics; [...] But, as to religion, I confessed myself to be an High-churchman'. His ecclesiastical allegiance is fairly certain, especially when acknowledging the vehemence of the *Tale*'s attacks on Dissent and occasional conformity, but his political self-description is more problematic, in that High Church and *Tory* issues often intersected at this time.[33] Moreover, the dedication from the *Tale*'s putative bookseller to Somers is often considered to be ironic, and Ian Higgins has identified much else in the *Tale*'s satire that is consonant with Tory party-political attitudes.[34]

Whether or not their political persuasions intersected at this time or later, Swift would have found much in Keill's theological position which corresponded with his own. For Keill, augmenting the Bible with reference to natural philosophy is not necessary:

> our holy Faith stands so well confirmed by real miracles, that [...] we are not to detract from [their] value [...] by pretending to deduce them from *Natural* and *Mechanical* causes, when they are no ways explicable by them. It is therefore both the easiest and safest way, to refer the wonderful destruction of the old world to the Omnipotent hand of God, who can do whatsoever he pleases. (*Examination*, p. 33)

Like many Newtonians, Keill was reluctant to deny the agency of the miraculous in the formation and transformation of the Earth as described in Scripture, fearing that otherwise he would be assisting the atheist cause, and so he subordinated a scientific account to a literal interpretation.[35] This is not to say, however, that Keill does not provide a thorough critique of Burnet's natural philosophy. Keill's specific arguments against Burnet concern: the unexplained origin of the water which caused the Deluge; the settling of the Earth from Chaos according to the weight of liquids and solids; the perpetual Spring of Eden explained by the changing position of the Earth's axis; the raising of the vapours from underneath the Earth's crust, which the Sun's heat would not be strong enough to achieve; that mountains are not just evidence of man's sin but are useful in that they create rivers. However, Keill in particular makes much of highlighting that the formation of Burnet's world – through vortices of matter settling – 'doth not much differ from the *Cartesian* method of making the earth'; an influence which Burnet himself did not acknowledge explicitly, but which several writers had identified in their critiques of the *Theory*.[36] Scriptural interpretation had therefore become a site of contestation between two rival natural philosophies, as Keill recognized, using his examination of Burnet's *Theory* as an opportunity to assert the legitimacy of Newtonian gravitational attraction above the outmoded Cartesian physics. In the *Principia*, Newton had shown that vortices do not exist because they cannot account for the regular motions of comets, and are also unable to explain the periodic time of the planets.[37] Newton's proofs contribute to Keill's argument that the foundations of Burnet's theory are 'not only precarious, but impossible', meaning that 'his whole Hypothesis must fall with them' (*Examination*, pp. 16–17, 175–76). In his response to Keill, however, Burnet maintains his belief that vortices carry the planets, and rejects universal gravitation as accounting for their motion, requesting Keill to explain whether attraction 'is a Mechanical Principle or no'. Like Newton himself, Keill would wish to leave the question of the cause of gravity unanswered.[38]

Keill compared not only Burnet's method, but also his supposed intellectual arrogance to that of the French philosopher:

> *Des Cartes* [...] has encouraged so very much this presumptuous pride in the Philosophers, that they think they understand all the works of Nature, & are able to give a good account of them, whereas neither he, nor any of his followers, have given us a right explication of any one thing. (*Examination*, p. 12)

The fervent Newtonianism of Keill is at the expense of any recognition of the contribution of Descartes to natural philosophy, which puts him at odds with some of his fellow Newtonians. For instance, Keill criticizes Wotton for arguing that Descartes joined physics and geometry, because 'there is not one demonstration drawn from Geometry, or indeed any demonstration at all' in Descartes' *Principia Philosophiæ* (1644), meaning that Wotton 'either understands no Geometry' or has never read the author concerned.[39] The boldness of Keill's strike seems symptomatic of his support for Christ Church in the Phalaris controversy.

Swift would have certainly agreed with Keill's condemnation of Descartes as a proud and vain builder of reductive systems. The French philosopher is a satiric target in the *Tale*, *Battel* and *Travels*. The materialism implicit in Descartes' idea of vortices brought him disapproval from some, and is possibly the main reason for his inclusion amongst the roll-call of philosophical enthusiasts in the 'Digression on Madness'.[40] The symbol of the vortex, so central to the Cartesian theory of planetary motion, in Swift's hands becomes an appropriate conceit in ridiculing what he sees as Descartes' solipsistic thinking, and dualistic concept of mind and body. In the *Tale*, '*Cartesius* reckoned to see before he died, the Sentiments of all Philosophers [...] rapt and drawn within his own *Vortex*', while in the *Battel*, the point of Aristotle's arrow 'quickly found a *Defect* in the *Head-Piece*' of the book of '*Des-Cartes*', and death 'drew him into his own *Vortex*' (pp. 108, 157). Swift's attacks echo those of Thomas Sprat, which charge Descartes' solitude with being detrimental to his enquiries: 'they, who will onely transscribe [*sic*] their own thoughts, and disdain to measure or strengthen them by the assistance of others, should be in most of their apprehensions too narrow, and obscure'.[41] The Spider's self-imposed seclusion, claiming to be '*spinning out all from [him]self*' (p. 150), is also emblematic of the Cartesian deductive method, which could be accused of reaching conclusions implicitly contained within its first principles.[42]

Verbal echoes in the *Battel* suggest that Swift was aware of the accusation that Burnet owed much of his theory to Descartes. Swift appropriates Keill's nationalistic charge within his satiric allegory, with the Bee accusing the Spider of '*a little foreign Assistance*' in his '*Store of Dirt and Poison*', despite the '*boast [...] of being obliged to no other*' (pp. 150–51). However, the satire can operate in at least two other ways. In a general manner, it attacks what Swift sees as the Moderns' impudent denial of the value of Ancient wisdom, but with Burnet functioning as a suitable archetype. It might also ridicule Burnet's insistence upon the power of human reason and the originality of his own work, whilst he criticized

the Ancients for coming to knowledge not by 'fair Reasoning and observations upon Nature', but 'delivered to them from others by Tradition
and Ancient Fame' (Book I, Chap. 1, p. 3). Despite these broader meanings, the Bee further characterizes the Spider as a Cartesian when referring to his *'Method and Skill'* (p. 152): a phrase which implicates all
Moderns, but particularly Descartes.[43]

Suggesting more indebtedness to Keill's *Examination*, the fable ends
when the Bee 'has grown impatient' and flees 'strait away [...] without looking for a Reply', leaving the *'Spider* like an Orator, *collected*
in himself, and just prepared to burst out' (p. 151). Keill condemns
Burnet's *Theory* as bad natural philosophy which has been blown up
into a system through literary fabrication, with its vivid descriptions of
destruction so loved by prose stylists like Steele:

> His Rhetorical expressions may easily captivate any incautious
> reader, and make him swallow down for truth, what I am apt to think
> the Author himself [...] designed only for a Philosophical Romance,
> seing [*sic*] that an ordinary examination thereof, according to the
> laws of Mechanisme cannot but shew, that he has acted the part
> of an Orator much better than he has done that of a Philosopher.
> (*Examination*, p. 26)

In an ill-advised effort to pre-empt criticism, Burnet had brought this
on himself, remonstrating with 'Men of Wit' who 'call such Theories
as these, Philosophick Romances', because 'such Romances must all
Theories of Nature, and of Providence be', in that they contain 'a *Plot*
or *Mystery* pursued through the whole Work [...] made already by the
Great Author' (Preface, sig. A5ᵛ). For Keill, not only did the *Theory* use
outmoded (i.e. Cartesian) theories, and was not based on mathematical
principles, but also its flamboyant prose was inappropriate for a work of
natural philosophy, and contravened the matter-of-fact style cultivated
by the Royal Society who, according to Sprat, 'indeavor'd, to separate
the knowledge of *Nature*, from the colours of *Rhetorick*, the devices of
Fancy, or the delightful deceit of *Fables*' (*History*, p. 62). Attracted to its
eloquence, the 'incautious reader' can easily become trapped in Burnet's
system, like the 'infinite Numbers of *Flies*' lured into, and 'slain and
devoured' within, the Spider's palace (*Tale*, p. 149). For Swift, Keill's
charges against the *Theory* – that 'never any Book was fuller of Errors
and Mistakes in Philosophy, so none ever abounded with more beautiful Scenes and surprising Images of Nature' (*Examination*, pp. 175–76) –
may have served as further confirmation that Modern writing was mere

oratory, without the truth to substantiate powerful rhetoric. Swift colludes in Keill's condemnation of Burnet's *Theory* as an extravagant work of 'fancy' rather than a work of natural philosophy which describes the 'truth' of things: as 'literature' rather than 'science'.

Keill's conceit that Burnet's theory is an 'Ingenious Romance' (p. 176) goes some way in explaining why Swift initially figures the cobweb, and allegorically Burnet's philosophical 'edifice in the air', as the *'Spider's Cittadel'* (p. 149). The romance trope may have also suggested to Swift the simile used to describe the dead flies: 'like human Bones before the Cave of some Giant' (p. 149). The elaborate structure of a castle is the principal setting of romance fictions, and an appropriate figure for reductive theoretical systems, and is used by both Burnet and Keill. To 'choose out some of the principal heads of the Theory, and having shown them to be false and disagreeable to the laws of Mechanisme, the rest must all fall to the ground' (p. 27) is Keill's design for the *Examination*, while Burnet responds to Keill by boasting that 'you only pick out a loose stone here or there; or strike off a Pinnacle, this will not weaken the Foundation, nor have any considerable effect upon the whole Building' (*Reflections upon The Theory*, p. 3).[44] The romance motif also serves to maintain the connection between Burnet and the Cartesian philosophy. For instance, in the 'Digression on Madness' Descartes' vortices are ridiculed as a *'Romantick* System' (*Tale*, p. 108), possibly following Temple's anecdote that 'Des Cartes, among his friends, always called his philosophy his romance; which makes it as pleasant to hear young scholars possessed with all his notions, as to see boys taking *Amadis* and the *Mirror of Knighthood* for true stories'. This Quixotic trope had a long shelf-life in the eighteenth century, with Charles Boyle's son John, the Fifth Earl of Orrery, describing Descartes as 'a knight errant in philosophy, perpetually mistaking windmills for giants'.[45]

The discursive allusions to the romance genre dramatize the encounter as a social dispute. The Spider's verbal assault on the Bee is characterized by feudal and aristocratic discourse which insists upon his moral and social superiority, and the value of gentlemanly honour and manners: '*Sirrah* [...] *you should have more Respect to a Person, whom all the World allows to be so much your Betters'*, '*What art thou but a Vagabond* [...] *without Stock or Inheritance'* (p. 150). The Ancients had typically been allied with the amateur-gentleman in their battle to avoid displacement by the Moderns, associated with the professional scholar.[46] The social standing of Charles Boyle in comparison to Wotton or Bentley illustrates this dichotomy well. However, Brean Hammond highlights that Swift reverses the terms and class associations of the Ancients and

Moderns quarrel to depict the Spider as a man of property threatened by the Bee.[47] This could be an unforeseen by-product of Swift's adoption of the emblem of the spider, a creature whose characteristics – such as his associations with '*Mathematicks*', and spinning '*wholly from himself*' (p. 152) – are appropriate to the allegory in many ways, but whose webs are associated all too easily with metaphors of property. Whether or not these class connotations are accidental, the allegory of the Ancients and Moderns seems to break down at this point, revealing the limitations of the fable form in maintaining a consistent scheme of correlation. Indeed, John Traugott proposes the opposite social interpretation: that on a 'superficial level' the allegory of the Spider and the Bee 'represents Temple's attitudes – and only slightly below the surface, Swift's idea of himself', with Swift wanting to see himself as the Bee, 'like Temple a gentleman ranging above the vulgar'.[48] However, it is possible that Swift is not intentionally reversing the social associations of the Ancients and Moderns controversy, but alluding to Burnet's response, in which he frequently calls attention to Keill's 'very rude words' and 'fierce and vehement' censures of the thinkers with whom he disagrees, producing 'not usual Language amongst Gentlemen'.[49]

Weaving Webs of Allegory

While Keill feared that Burnet's rhetorical mastery could enchant the unsuspecting reader, the 'incautious reader[s]' of Swift should also be wary of trapping themselves within their own webs of interpretation. Unlike brief occasional allusions, satiric allegories tempt readers to elicit thorough and consistent hermeneutical schemes.[50] Consequently, it is difficult to know where to stop reading the fable allegorically. Could it, on one level, serve as a detailed allegory of the 'Dispute' (p. 148) between Burnet and Keill, considering the number of direct references to Burnet's *Theory* and Keill's *Examination*? Is the Spider's threat to teach the Bee '*better Manners*' a figurative re-enactment of Burnet's accusation that Keill is 'so rude to strangers' (*Reflections upon the Theory*, p. 45)? Does the Bee's obligation to '*Heaven alone for* [its] *Flights*' (p. 150) represent Keill's belief in the reasonableness of the biblical account and in the role of divine intervention?[51] Does its visit to '*all the Flowers and Blossoms*' signify Keill's use of many scholars, Ancient and Modern, in his critique of Burnet? Or does the Bee's sociability and communal work reflect Keill's connection to Christ Church, in contrast to the solitary Burnet? Is the poisonous reasoning at work in the Spider's mind figured as '*Liquor in the Vessel*' (p. 150) in order to refer to the 'oily liquor' in Burnet's Cartesian theory, which combined with 'little earthy particles' to form the first 'firm consistent substance upon the face of the Chaos'?[52] Does the Spider's 'Resolution to be heartily scurrilous and angry, to urge *on* his own Reasons, without the least Regard to the Answers or Objections of his Opposite' (p. 150) allude to Burnet's vehement defence of the *Theory* in his *Reflections* upon them? Such speculations are perhaps symptomatic of a web spun too many times, and they result in an allegory so detailed and obscure that its ideal readership would have only included the Christ Church Wits.

Nevertheless, it is somewhat appropriate that Swift constructs an allegory related to debates about the allegorical reading of scriptural history and prophecy. It is tempting to see this as an intentional correspondence: that Swift's assertion of the possibilities of metaphorical modes of reading is a response to Burnet's enthusiasm for the literal, leaving 'no room' for 'allegorical expositions' (*Theory*, p. 91). This would certainly fit with Swift's techniques elsewhere: Brean Hammond has argued that Swift often 'employs allegory in a way that destroys its own mode of functioning', such as in the 'Tribnia' passage of *Gulliver's Travels* (*PW*, XI, 191–92).[53]

That the allegory of the Spider and the Bee is also a fable offers further modes of interpretation, and ultimately compels the reader, guided by Æsop, to derive a universal, moral meaning from the narrative, as befits the fabulist tradition. The Spider and Bee, therefore, variously become symbols of: the Moderns and the Ancients; of rationalists and empiricists; of solipsistic and eclectic modes of thought; of useless and useful appropriations of knowledge; of proud and humble authors.[54] Swift had made modest claims about his own fable compositions: 'there is no writing I esteem more than Fables, nor any thing so difficult to succeed in, […] which I have frequently endeavoured at in vain'.[55] The multivalent nature of this prose fable of the Spider and the Bee, however, demonstrates that Swift could achieve greatness within the genre. Indeed, Augustan criticism recognized the fable as a literary form specifically designed to involve the reader's engagement to an acute degree. In Joseph Addison's opinion, 'in the reading of a Fable […] the Reader comes in for half of the Performance',[56] but as the narrator of the *Tale* acknowledges, readers may never uncover the author's intended 'moral':

> *Grubæan* Sages have always chosen to convey their Precepts […] within the Vehicles of Types and Fables, […] it has fared with these Vehicles after the usual Fate of Coaches over-finely painted and gilt; that the transitory Gazers have […] fill'd their Imaginations with the

outward Lustre, as neither to regard or consider, the Person or the Parts of the Owner within. A Misfortune we undergo with somewhat less Reluctancy, because it has been common to us with *Pythagoras*, *Æsop, Socrates*. (p. 66)

For the *Tale*-narrator, the 'correct' interpretation of allegorical fables, seemingly more than of any other form of literature, rests on the ability to determine the author's intentions. However, he implies that an inability to achieve this is not always a problem because the precepts revealed may not be to one's taste or sense of morality, as represented by the reputed physical ugliness of the three Ancient writers he cites.[57] The early critical responses to the *Tale*, many of which accused its central narrative of blasphemy,[58] are sure to have made Swift even more aware of the pitfalls of allegorical writing in putting across one's intentions.

For Jayne Elizabeth Lewis, the fable of the Spider and the Bee is central to the *Battel*'s depiction of the Ancients and Moderns debate. Æsop's speech 'shows readers how to sort out the complex figural strategies' in the *Battel* as a whole, harnessing a 'unique potential for representation' otherwise lacking, because the Spider and Bee, unlike the books, are visually distinct from each other.[59] However, one should proceed with caution when judging the overall outcome of the conflict, and especially when equating Æsop's reading with an authorial statement, because of the multiple and self-ironies at work: the fabulist compares the Spider's '*Poison*' to a '*large Vein of Wrangling and Satyr*' (p. 152), making Swift something of a satiric weaver himself. Moreover, the specific allusions to Burnet and Keill add another level to the allegory for readers to decipher, in the form of particular and direct satire, thus complicating the fable's relation to the wider intellectual dispute. Such allusions invite the reader to see the Bee as a representation of Keill, the Modern natural philosopher, although this simple figuration is not the full story. Keill's friendship with the men of Christ Church, and his support of them in debunking various ideas of the self-consciously 'Modern' Burnet (and Wotton and Bentley, as we will see) meant that Keill was, like the Bee, not necessarily an Ancient himself but an '*Advocate, retained by us the* Antients' (p. 152). In addition, Keill's writings suggest that he saw Newtonian natural philosophy as restoring forgotten Ancient knowledge. Keill's complex cultural allegiances, therefore, demonstrate that 'Ancient' and 'Modern' are often equivocal categories. The clear-cut differentiations which Æsop derives from the fable are revealed to be fictions in an intellectual war. This is not to say, however, that there is a structural irony at work. The figurations of the Spider as Burnet (the Modern whose writings resemble the work of Ancient scholiasts) and the Bee as Keill (the Ancient-supporting Modern) do not completely reject the ostensible, literal meaning of the allegory, but destabilize and deconstruct the *'great Skill in Architecture'* (p. 152) behind the very construction of allegorical systems. For what do the Spider's momentary schemes primarily satirize, if it is not the reductive mind-set of a *'lazy Contemplation of four Inches round'* (p. 151)?

It is generally argued that Swift transforms the Baconian simile of Bee-as-Modern natural philosopher and Spider-as-Ancient scholastic rationalist into Bee-as-Ancient and Spider-as-Modern. However, the characteristics of Swift's Bee (who visits *'all the Flowers and Blossoms'*) and Spider (*'with a Native Stock within [its]self'*) imply that the fable reproduces rather than distorts Bacon's argument.[60] The Bee's own precept that *'an universal Range, with long Search, much Study, true Judgment, and Distinction of Things, brings home Honey and Wax'* (p. 151) resembles the 'moral' of Bacon's aphorism:

> The true job of philosophy is not much different [from the way of the bee], for it depends not only or mainly on the powers of the mind, nor does it take the material gathered from natural history and mechanical experiments and store it unaltered in the memory but lays it up in the intellect changed and elaborated.[61]

And we should recall that Bacon himself survives the battle: Aristotle's arrow misses the *'valiant Modern'* and hits Descartes instead (p. 156). Swift's appropriation of Bacon's analogy implies that the self-consciously 'Modern' Burnet reminds him paradoxically of the 'Ancient' scholastic thinkers Bacon was attacking. Burnet criticizes the Ancients for their lack of method: 'their Learning or Philosophy consisted more in Conclusions, than in Demonstrations' (*Theory*, Book I, Chap. 1, p. 3). However, Swift, following Keill, places this charge at Burnet's own work: the Spider is 'fully predetermined in his Mind against all Conviction' (p. 150) and ignores the external findings in Nature which the Bee puts to such good use. In this light, Burnet becomes an arrogant hypocrite, 'swelled' up with a pride unwarranted by his meagre productions, bringing to mind Ralpho's vitriol at 'Learning that cobweb of the brain, / Profane, erroneous and vain' in *Hudibras*.[62] The *Battel*'s borrowing of Bacon's image implies that Burnet is not empirical enough in his approach, because he constructs a 'Philosophical Romance' which relies upon his own conjectures and *'a little foreign Assistance'* from the disproven natural philosophy of Descartes, instead of Scripture and reason. As Keill asserts in the *Examination*, if the evidence is not available then it is best to leave ultimate causes to God, rather than producing empty speculation.

Swift's Bee could be both an Ancient and a Modern. Rather than offering a moment of satiric clarity, the digression proliferates the general uncertainty about which side's forces this mock-heroic chooses as its victors. Æsop's interpretation of the fable shows how the same materials can be appropriated by opposing intellectual approaches, just as Swift adapts the work of a Newtonian natural philosopher for his own ends, using 'Modern' knowledge to attack other Moderns. Readings of science in Swift's works have often identified an anti-Newtonian attitude,[63] but many of the central conceits, imagery and details of satiric attack in the fable of the Spider and the Bee are probably derived from Keill's criticism of Burnet. Swift's theological position towards Burnet's theory could be seen as very similar to Keill's, with both asserting the sufficiency of divine intervention in seeking to explain things, rather than having recourse to determining secondary causes. What is more clear, is that in his satires Swift was often an opportunist, and would utilize whatever conceits and metaphors were relevant to his attack: like the Bee he was a '*Freebooter*' whose 'Curiosity' alone could lead him to reduce his targets 'down to the very Foundation' (pp. 150, 149).

3
Newtonian *Battels* with Rising Stars and Wheeling Moons

The *Tale* and *Battel* (1704) appeared at a time when Low Church Anglicans appropriated the discoveries and theories of Newtonian natural philosophy in their defences of Christianity. These 'physico-theological' writings were associated with, but not exclusive to, the lectures established through the will of Robert Boyle (1691). Designed to prove 'the *Christian Religion*, against notorious Infidels', these sermons reflect fears of an atheistical materialism promulgated by Thomas Hobbes and 'libertine' followers of Epicurus and Lucretius, whose systems explained the workings of the universe through matter and motion alone.[1] The first Boyle lectures were delivered from the pulpit of St Martin-in-the-Fields in 1692 by Richard Bentley, then chaplain to the Bishop of Worcester (Edward Stillingfleet), and soon-to-be Master of Trinity College, Cambridge.

It is thought that Bentley's lectureship had been arranged by the Trustees John Evelyn and Thomas Tenison, but it is possible that Newton was involved in the selection of the young chaplain.[2] Either way, Bentley saw the potential for the discoveries documented in the *Principia*, especially the theory of universal gravitation, to be accommodated within a natural theology, and many of his cosmological and teleological arguments were developed in consultation with Newton himself. The operation of the gravitational forces which Newton had discovered – of all objects of matter attracting each other, with strengths inversely proportional to the square of the distance between them – had become a central concern in the religious controversy. Traditional thought placed the source of all activity in the universe in God's will, and so because Newton had identified gravity as accounting for some principles of motion in both celestial and terrestrial bodies, there was an urgency to recognize this force as a form of God's power rather than a property attributed to matter itself.[3] Bentley therefore made certain to express that gravity was a 'constant energy infused into matter by the Author of all things'. The intricate design of the universe could not have originated in the random movement of atoms but only in the Divine Will through the action of universal gravitation, 'a higher principle' than mechanism and material causes, and the 'regular harmony' of the planetary motions 'must deservedly be ascribed to divine art'.[4]

This conception of the harmonious, Newtonian universe as a reflection of divine power would continue throughout the century as an important image for natural philosophers and poets alike. Bentley's Boyle lectures helped to establish the cultural omnipresence of Newton's *Principia* in the eighteenth century, with physico-theology emerging as the dominant Anglican argument against atheism. Some of the other Boyle lecturers, such as John Harris, Samuel Clarke and William Whiston, continued Bentley's project, and works like John Ray's *The Wisdom of God Manifested in the Works of the Creation* (1691) and William Derham's Boyle lectures of 1711 and 1712 (published as *Physico-Theology*, 1713) used natural history as Bentley had done natural philosophy, viewing the study of the intricate design of earthly phenomena as a celebration of God's power.[5]

Bentley 'the *New* and *Rising-Star*'

Swift, a committed High Churchman, shared the Low Church physico-theologians' concerns about the materialist threat and it has been argued that there are many affinities between his strategies in attacking Epicurus and other materialists in the *Tale* and the 'Ode to the Athenian Society' (1692), and those present in the polemics of Bentley and other Boyle lecturers.[6] However, attempts to identify Bentley's lectures as a specific pretext for the *Tale* and *Battel* have not been conclusive, and it has been a source of debate as to whether Swift was even aware of the lectures or other examples of physico-theological discourse at the time of the *Tale's* composition. Phillip Harth claims that the Anglican rationalist polemics of the latitudinarians and Cambridge Platonists against Catholicism, Puritanism and atheism formed the religious and philosophical context of the *Tale's* satire on abuses in religion. These Anglican divines (including Edward Stillingfleet, John Tillotson, Henry More and Ralph Cudworth), whilst acknowledging the necessity of revelation, upheld 'reason' as the basis of religious belief and practice in the face of Puritans and Catholics, who instead resorted to using the 'inner light' or the unwritten apostolic tradition respectively. In contrast, the physico-theologians, who had included Samuel Parker, John Wilkins and John Ray prior to Bentley, were concerned almost exclusively with writing against the atheist threat, and supported a more empirical theory of knowledge.[7]

Harth's thesis occludes the physico-theologians, despite their already important status as prominent Anglican apologists of the 1690s. This is perhaps because Harth is principally concerned with reconstructing Swift's intellectual background, rather than identifying targets of his satire, which the physico-theologians are more likely to constitute. At the conclusion of his study, Harth contends:

> [Swift's] reading of, and sympathy for, the Anglican rationalist apologetics against atheism seems almost as much a matter of course when we remember that it was between 1691 and 1694 that most of this reading probably took place. Although the arguments of the physico-theologians against atheism had been competing for some years with the Anglican rationalist discourses on the same subject, the ultimate triumph of the former and their success in driving their competitors from the field really dates from the inauguration of the Boyle lectures in 1692 by Wotton's friend Bentley. That the young man reading for ordination in Temple's library at Moor Park should have been completely *au courant* and aware of new trends in religious controversy is hardly to be expected. (*Swift and Anglican Rationalism*, p. 163)

Such a claim appears tendentious when we acknowledge that Bentley, in his career as philologist, was one of the chief opponents of Temple and the Christ Church Wits in the Phalaris controversy, and consequently emerged as one of the chief 'Moderns' targeted in the *Tale* and *Battel*.[8] Bentley was known to Swift as more than merely 'Wotton's friend': these two scholars were equally useful satiric archetypes of all that could be seen as wrong with Modern learning.

Although we can only speculate regarding the date of the *Tale*'s composition due to the rarity of research materials from Swift's time at Moor Park and Kilroot, it has been proposed that Swift completed most of the work on the *Tale* between 1696 and 1699, but continued to revise the work up until its publication in 1704.[9] It seems almost inconceivable that by 1699 or later Swift would have been unaware of at least the existence and central ideas of Bentley's sermons, which had by that time already gone through several editions and reprints.[10] Bentley was such an important target of Swift's early satires that for him to be indifferent to Bentley's non-philological, but arguably more famous, theological and philosophical work would seem unlikely.

Recently the possibility that Swift was alert to Bentley's theological writings at the time of the *Tale* began to receive some critical attention. Objecting to Harth's assertion, A. H. De-Quehen argues that 'the Boyle Lectures should be numbered among the several works of which *A Tale* is in some sense a version'. Within the discursive multiplicity and madness of the *Tale* it is possible to find all manner of writing echoed, but De-Quehen does not provide particularly acute evidence (of either a stylistic or substantive nature) for the allusion to Bentley he suggests.[11] David Bywaters, meanwhile, in his study of clerical satire in the *Tale*, does not claim that Swift intentionally alludes to Bentley's lectures specifically, but asserts that at certain moments Swift ridicules 'not only science in general, but its use by the clergy in support of religion', and traces such theological appropriations of natural philosophy further back into the seventeenth century, to writers such as Samuel Parker, the butt of Andrew Marvell's *Rehearsal Transpros'd*, a satire much admired by Swift. Frank T. Boyle's *Swift as Nemesis* constitutes the most sustained discussion of the *Tale* in relation to the physico-theological appropriation of Newton's discoveries, including in Bentley's sermons. He has even gone so far as to suggest that the phenomenon of 'vapours' in the 'Digression on Madness' is modelled upon Newton's oblique proposal in the *Principia* that a property in the ether is responsible for the action of attractive force. The textual evidence for this is scant, and the argument relies upon the unlikely premise that Swift possessed extensive knowledge of Newtonian philosophy at this time and engaged in a complex close reading of the *Principia*.[12]

Whether Swift actually *read* Bentley's Boyle lectures is uncertain, but he was definitely aware of them indirectly, and this has the effect of increasing the contextual limits of the *Tale* and *Battel* somewhat, although it restricts the nature of Swift's allusions to lampoon and caricature, rather than parody of Bentley's physico-theological discourse. In the Preface to his *Reflections*, which Swift unquestionably read and frequently parodies in the *Tale*, Wotton declared that Bentley's sermons had been an important inspiration during his enterprise. Moreover, the lectures were also referred to in the several Christ Church outpourings against Bentley's work on Phalaris, although they paid only some attention to their *content*. *Dr. Bentley's Dissertations [...] Examin'd* (1698) pointed out what they saw as his audacity in treating a 'Gentleman' (that is, Charles Boyle, the future Earl of Orrery) 'with so much Contempt and Indignity' when Bentley had enjoyed the advantage of the lectures instituted by Charles' great uncle 'and by reason of that Post must be suppos'd to have had a due respect for his Name and Family'. Likewise,

Francis Atterbury's *Short Review of the Controversy* (1701) drew attention to Bentley's 'wonderful respect for the Honourable *Robert Boyle*' and 'more than ordinary regard to his Memory' at a time when he was inhibiting Charles' access to the Phalaris manuscript. Bentley's association with the cosmological is drawn upon in the ironical representation of 'Bentivoglio' in William King's *Dialogues of the Dead* (1699) as '*a Star already,* and if he proceeds in his Learned Labours may become a Constellation. He is Reverenc'd by all for being the *New* and *Rising-Star,* and *the brightest light of Britain*'.[13] This conceit would be borrowed by Swift nearly three decades later in *A Discourse, To Prove the Antiquity of the English Tongue,* where he associates the critic with the great natural philosopher: 'our illustrious modern star, Doctor Richard Bentley, with whom the republic of learning must expire; as mathematics did with Sir Isaac Newton' (*PW*, IV, 231). Swift's hyperbolic assessment that the entire discipline of mathematics has ended seems a fitting ironic riposte to the excessive praise in the many elegies which appeared after Newton's death in 1727.[14] The ironic appellation 'star' suggests that Swift connects Bentley with Newton not only because they are each celebrities in their respective fields.

Centers, Tombs and Moons

The mock-heroic *Battel* is principally concerned with allegorizing the conflict between the Ancients and Moderns, and is appropriately set in St James's Library, where Bentley resided and apparently hampered Charles Boyle's access to the King's MS. While Bentley's status as royal librarian and *Phalaris* critic has been emphasized in many approaches to the *Battel*, his role as Boyle lecturer has been somewhat overlooked.[15] This chapter will highlight the moments in the satiric allegory which appear to allude to Bentley's physico-theology, and explore the significance of these to our present knowledge of Swift's intellectual background and allegiances. It will build upon the previous chapter in exploring John Keill's *An Examination of Dr Burnet's Theory of the Earth* (1698) as an important source of inspiration and encouragement for the *Battel*'s assault on Bentley, revealing that Swift exploited fault-lines within the developing Newtonian community.

Although the *Battel*'s attacks on Bentley were undoubtedly provoked by his quarrel with Christ Church, its first description of the (Book of) Bentley unequivocally identifies him as not only the *Phalaris* critic but also the Boyle lecturer. Bentley is a 'fierce Champion for the *Moderns*' who sought to 'knock down two of the *Antient* Chiefs' (Phalaris and

Æsop) but 'endeavouring to climb up, was cruelly obstructed by his own unhappy Weight, and tendency towards his Center' (p. 147). Both R. J. Dingley and Frank T. Boyle have rightly argued that Swift is associating Bentley with the *Principia*.[16] The phrase 'tendency towards a Center' is a circumlocution of Newton's centripetal forces. Any type of force can act centripetally, but at the time of the *Principia* it was particularly associated with, and used synonymously for, gravitation, as we find in Swift's lampoon.[17] The inward direction of the force highlights the pride and vanity with which Swift characterizes the Modern enterprise. The royal librarian, scholar, chaplain and Boyle lecturer assumes masterful understanding of many different disciplines, and so is aptly figured as 'Tall, but without Shape or Comeliness' (p. 160), but in Swift's satiric vision this knowledge is all directed towards the self. Swift presents Bentley as using knowledge as a means of self-promotion and self-aggrandizement, rather than to increase collective human achievement. Bentley's fitting comeuppance associates him with the pursuit of systems of knowledge which are inherently solipsistic and reductive: 'being light-headed, they have in Speculation, a wonderful Agility, and conceive nothing too high for them to mount; but in reducing to Practice, discover a mighty Pressure about their Posteriors and their Heels' (p. 147). Swift's representation of Bentley is therefore similar in satiric strategy and effect to a long line of Moderns looking only within themselves, with the Spider '*engendering on it self*' (p. 151), Descartes drawn 'into his own *Vortex*' (p. 157), and the Laputians, with 'one of their Eyes turned inward' (*PW*, XI, 159).

After disagreements with many of his fellow Moderns, the Book of Bentley withdraws from the general assembly and, accompanied by his 'beloved *W—tt-n*', attempts a night-time raid on 'some neglected Quarter of the *Antients* Army'. Before encountering the 'Enemy's Outguards', Bentley and Wotton come to '*Aldrovandus*'s Tomb, which they pass'd on the side of the declining Sun' (p. 161). In his *Reflections*, Wotton claims that unlike the authoritative natural histories of Conrad Gesner (1516–65) and Ulisse Aldrovandi (1522–1605), the writings of the Ancients Ælian and Pliny are '*Rhapsodies* of Stories and Relations partly true, and partly fabulous' (p. 272).[18] The Italian professor Aldrovandi is therefore a key 'champion' of the Moderns with regard to knowledge of natural history, and would be chosen as a distant relative of Martinus Scriblerus (*Memoirs*, p. 96). What Swift may have found laughable is that Wotton's specific discussion of Aldrovandi's work is only in relation to the knowledge of insects (*RAML*, pp. 264–65), a subject ironically celebrated for its 'great Usefulness' in Section V of the *Tale* (p. 83).

Swift's association of Bentley's and Wotton's works with Aldrovandi's volumes is perhaps best explained through reference to the Preface to the *Reflections*. Here Wotton places his work within the emerging physico-theological tradition, with Bentley's Boyle lectures as his principal model:

> I thought it might be Labour exceeding well spent, if, whilst I enquired into what was anciently known, and what is a new Discovery, I should at the same Time furnish my Mind with new Occasions of admiring the boundless Wisdom and Bounty of that Almighty and Beneficent Essence, in and by whom alone this whole Universe, with all its Parts, live, and move, and have their Being.
>
> I had also a fresh Inducement to this Search, when I found to how excellent purpose my most learned and worthy Friend, Mr. *Bentley*, has, in his late Discourses *against Atheism*, shewn what admirable Use may be made of an accurate Search into Nature, thereby to lead us directly up to its Author. (sig. A13^v–A14^r)

The emphasis on personal fulfilment through the contemplation of the Book of Nature resembles Boyle in his *Occasional Reflections*. Wotton presents the composition of his book as an experiment upon the self, as well as an assertion of the superiority of Modern learning and a defence of Christianity against the supposedly growing tide of atheism. The reference to Paul's repudiation of the Epicurean thinkers of Athens, that 'in him [the Lord] we live, and move, and have our being' (Acts 17.28), is a characteristic of opponents of deism, including Bentley.[19] But what is most significant is that, according to Wotton, Bentley has demonstrated the usefulness of 'an accurate Search into Nature'. Swift's correlation of Aldrovandi with Wotton and Bentley appears to equate the discipline of natural history with the practice of physico-theology, apparently engendered by Wotton's misleading description of Bentley's work. This is possibly a symptom of the limited number of sources through which Swift was made aware of scientific ideas at this time: this single mention of Bentley's Boyle lectures is its only occurrence in Wotton's *Reflections*. Whatever Swift's rationale for connecting the two contemporary scholars with this sixteenth-century natural historian, its satiric effect is to equate their work with the study of merely the minute and inconsequential.

Whilst the works of all other authors alluded to in the *Battel* are "alive and well" at the beginning of this mock-heroic narrative, Aldrovandi's have a unique status in that they are terminally out of action. Swift may be making reference to Aldrovandi's publication history, with the majority of the volumes of his *Works* appearing in print posthumously.[20] The 'Tomb' is a fitting addition to the gothic imagery within this paragraph, as well as providing an irresistible opportunity for some half-homonymic punning (tomb/tome). Moreover, it suggests that Wotton and Bentley are re-visiting 'dead' knowledge of the Moderns, which lasts only momentarily and is 'apt to suffer so much in the Carriage' (*Tale*, p. 27), whereas Ancient works have endured for centuries, and go on to survive the small skirmish this 'Full and True Account' describes.

Following this venture past the tomb of Aldrovandi 'on the side of the declining Sun', Bentley and Wotton continue on their way to raid a stronghold of the Ancients. The *Battel*'s narrator employs an extended simile which persists in satiric form the Christ-Church Wits' class-based attack on the two professional scholars:

> As when two *Mungrel-Curs*, whom *native Greediness*, and *domestick Want*, provoke, and join in Partnership, [...] nightly to invade the Folds of some rich Grazier; They, with Tails depress'd, and lolling Tongues, creep soft and slow; mean while, the conscious *Moon*, now in her *Zenith*, on their guilty Heads, darts perpendicular Rays; Nor dare they bark, though much provok'd at her refulgent Visage, whether seen in Puddle by Reflexion, or in Sphear direct. (p. 161)

The natural philosopher, or natural philosophy as a discipline, is portrayed as a 'rich Grazier' who has found much wealth in exploiting Nature; Bentley and Wotton are ravenous and lowly scavengers who wish to voraciously devour the bountiful livestock of natural knowledge to aid their social advancement. The 'bestial diminution' (as John M. Bullitt might call it) at work attaches their intellectual desperation to a concrete image, and a variation upon this is employed in the *Tale*'s 'Apology', where Wotton is compared to a sluggish ox (p. 12).[21] This simile does not account for their sense of both shame and rage in the presence of the Moon, however. To explain this, one must turn to Bentley's sermon on the *Origin and Frame of the World*:

> Without [the Earth's] diurnal rotation, one hemisphere would lie [...] in perpetual darkness and frost, and the best part would be burnt up [...] It is better, therefore, that the earth should often move about its own centre, and make these useful vicissitudes of night and day, than expose always the same side to the action of the sun. But how came it so to be moved? Not from any necessity of the laws of

motion, or the system of the heavens: it might annually have compassed the sun, and yet have always turned the same hemisphere
towards it. This is matter of fact and experience in the motion of the
moon, which [...] always shews the same face to us, not once wheeling upon her own centre. [...] That the earth, therefore, frequently
revolves about its own centre, is another eminent token of the divine
wisdom. (*Works*, III, 182–83)

By 1692, when Bentley delivered his lectures, it was known that the
Moon did turn upon its own axis. In Book III of the *Principia* Newton
had demonstrated that this was so, but explained that because the lunar
day is equal to the time of its periodic revolution in its orbit about the
Earth, 'the same face of the moon will always very nearly look in the
direction of the further focus of its orbit', with minimal deviation.
Newton had corresponded on this matter with the German mathematician Nicolaus Mercator (Kaufmann) (c. 1620–87) in the 1670s, and
Mercator had published hints in his astronomical compendium of
1676.[22] Unaware that the lunar day was equal to its terrestrial orbit,
Bentley supposes that the Moon 'always shews the same face to us'
because it does not rotate.

The Earth's diurnal rotation had been hypothesized for centuries,
but was demonstrated beyond refutation in the *Principia*.[23] Despite its
erroneous astronomy, Bentley's argument regarding this motion could
be cited as a characteristic piece of physico-theological discourse, and
typical of the Newtonian attempts to accommodate an active divine
providence into a mechanical system of nature.[24] Bentley posits the
usefulness of the existence of a particular natural phenomenon, with
diurnal rotation regulating the Earth's exposure to the Sun, and he
believes he is using an observation based in empirical science (that it is
a 'matter of fact and experience' that the Moon does not rotate upon its
own axis, because it 'always shews the same face to us') to provide evidence of the limits of man's knowledge. The Moon's apparent inactivity
shows that the Earth's daily revolution cannot be accounted for using
the laws and systems that man has discovered at work in the universe.
For Bentley, marvels such as this prove that mechanical explanations
of the universe cannot provide all the answers, countering Cartesian
philosophies, which many seventeenth-century English thinkers had
found appealing, but were concerned had rendered God inactive.[25]
More importantly, the exclusive nature of this motion to mankind's
terrestrial abode demonstrates God's active providence in the world,
contradicting the deist contention that the Creator is remote from his

creation. The passage ends with what would become a conventional need to provide proof of the wisdom and goodness of God, and is in answer particularly to Hobbes' claim that such attributes could not be discovered.[26]

Bentley's example of divine providence drawn from the Earth's axial motion may have been inspired by Newton himself. Writing to Bentley about the incorporation of his natural philosophy in the sermons, Newton comments: 'ye diurnal rotations of ye Sun & Planets [...] could hardly arise from any cause purely mechanical, [...] they seem to make up that harmony in ye system wch [...] was the effect of choice rather then [sic] of chance'. If Newton had included 'satellites' within this remark, perhaps Bentley might not have fallen into trouble. The cause of diurnal motion had apparently concerned Newton for some time. Corresponding with Thomas Burnet, Newton admitted he knew 'no sufficient naturall cause' of the Earth's rotation, and hypothesized that its speed had gradually accelerated over the six days of the Creation, thereby allowing the literal account of Genesis to be a true representation.[27] Following Newton, Bentley believed that the phenomenon of the Earth's diurnal rotation was another example of God's providence, but his effort to prove this led him into astronomical inaccuracy.

It now becomes apparent why Swift figures Wotton and Bentley as slyly attempting to attack the Ancients but exposed and distracted by the Moon's 'refulgent Visage'. Swift was somehow aware of Bentley's error and alludes to this to compound the attack on the scholar. While R. J. Dingley has proposed the relevance of the Moon error to Bentley's 'tendency towards his Center', the *Battel*'s subsequent scene in which the 'conscious *Moon*' illuminates the 'guilty Heads' of Wotton and Bentley addresses the Boyle lecturer's error more acutely, and situates it within the extended theme of his over-reaching of knowledge beyond his specialism.[28] The Moon is personified as 'conscious' in the figurative sense that it is privy to the actions and deficiencies of Bentley and Wotton (transposing the conventional trope of the 'conscious Muse').[29] This works on two levels, in terms of the military campaign of the 'Books' of Bentley and Wotton within the narrative of the *Battel*, and allegorically, with regard to Bentley's astronomical blunder in his Boyle lectures. Appropriately, the light of the Moon itself illuminates Bentley's mistake. The Moon is presented as consciously at her brightest, positioning herself directly overhead at the highest point, with her enlightened hemisphere turned fully towards the Earth. The horizon is at ninety degrees to the Moon in order for her to 'dart' her perpendicular and, therefore, most dazzling rays.[30]

Swift's very specific reference might suggest that he had first-hand knowledge of Bentley's printed sermons. However, it has been difficult to prove that Swift was echoing the Boyle lectures at any other point in the *Tale* or *Battel*, and more importantly, it would be a stretch of the imagination to consider that Swift had identified this astronomical error himself. A far more probable source is John Keill's *An Examination of Dr Burnet's Theory of the Earth* (1698). There seems to be no other work from the period which highlights Bentley's mistake and, as identified in Chapter 2, there are detailed parallels between the attacks on the Cartesian Earth-theorist Burnet in Swift's *Battel* and Keill's work, suggesting that Swift had indeed read the *Examination*. The following section contends that Swift's appropriation of Keill's criticism of Bentley grants significant insight into the satiric technique and purpose of the *Battel*, and Swift's attitudes toward natural philosophy in the 1690s and early 1700s, if not beyond.

The Politics and Theology of 'Dilating on *Matter* and *Motion*'

Keill's *Examination* critiqued Burnet's interpretation of the creation, fall, flood and conflagration, from the position that the literal descriptions in the scriptural account are sufficient to provide explanation because of the miraculous nature of divine providence. As a Newtonian, contesting Burnet's Cartesian-influenced system was Keill's priority, but it was also necessary to answer the Newtonian William Whiston's response to Burnet, *A New Theory of the Earth* (1696), which used the imaginary possibilities opened up by Newtonian physics to propose that a comet passing close to the Earth caused the Deluge and would be responsible for bringing about Judgement Day.[31] The ensuing debate between Keill and Whiston revealed a tension within Newtonianism regarding the proper appropriation of Newton's discoveries, and it has been asserted that this resonated particularly along religious and political lines, between High Church Tories (thought to include Keill), and Low Church Whigs like Whiston and Bentley.[32] Chapter IV of the *Examination* illustrates the two-fronted attack in which Keill was engaging. Here he assesses Burnet's natural explanation for the perpetual Spring of the Garden of Eden: that the Earth's axis was inclined in a perpendicular position to the plane of the ecliptic, resulting in equal days and nights throughout the year.[33] Keill digresses in his evaluation of Burnet to take a shot at Bentley, who is

> not very well skilled in *Astronomy*; for [...] he confidently saies, that [...] *the Moon alwaies shews the same Face to us, not once wheeling*

about her own Centre, whereas 'tis evident to any one who thinks, that
the Moon shews the same face to us for this very reason, because she
does turn once, in the time of her period, about her own Centre. But
it were to be wished, that great Criticks would confine their Labours
to their Lexicons, and not venture to guess in those parts of Learning
which are capable of demonstration. (p. 70)

It is easy to argue that Keill publishes this insulting reproof because he
wishes to prevent the dissemination of erroneous astronomical knowledge, especially by someone who purports to be a Newtonian but is
apparently ignorant of details within the *Principia*. However, the sheer
venom with which he condemns Bentley might not only originate in a
need to preserve and assert empirical truth, but could also be related to
Keill's political, social and institutional allegiances, specifically his High
Church values, and his connections with Christ Church, which would
result in his move there in 1703. His attack on Bentley's knowledge of
natural philosophy, which was appropriated by Swift in satiric form,
seemed to be a means of supporting the more general assault by the
'Wits' of his future college, subsuming any commitment to the growing
Newtonian community. Keill was elected to the Royal Society in 1700,
meaning that the most recent, English version of the quarrel between
the Ancients and Moderns, which began as a clash between Temple and
the Royal Society (represented by Wotton), spilled over into a disagreement between Society members.

All combatants knew cultural and institutional factors were at work
in the controversy. Wotton replied directly to Keill in *A Defense of the
Reflections upon Ancient and Modern Learning* (1705), scolding him for
unscholarly rudeness in an echo of Keill's broadside on Bentley: '*it were
to be wished*, that Men that endeavour to deserve well of Religion and
Learning, might be treated with Candor and Decency'. For Wotton,
'It is no want of Judgment, not to know all of Sir *Isaac Newton's*
Discoveries; especially when they [...] are so thick crouded as they
are in his Incomparable Book'.[34] Wotton's argument seems to miss,
or intentionally obscures, the real point. Bentley sought to legitimate
his Boyle lectures through their connection to the Newtonian natural
philosophy, and so it is embarrassing to say the least, and seriously
negligent at its worst, to be ignorant of one of Newton's discoveries.
Wotton explains that Bentley 'will not persist in an Error' and so left
out the phrase 'not once wheeling about her Center' in the 1699 edition of his lectures (p. 9). However, to merely leave out this phrase does
nothing to alter the fundamental problem with the passage, in that it

seeks to demonstrate the providence of the Creator through proving the uniqueness of the Earth's diurnal rotation, which cannot be shown to be the case.

Deflecting attention away from Bentley's mistake, Wotton finishes his rejoinder by arguing that 'there is scarce one single Instance' urged by Bentley which George Cheyne 'has not urged in the same way', but that 'Dr. *Cheyne's* Authority will pass with Mr. *Keill*, because his book was approved by Dr. *Freind* of *Christchurch*, and by two excellent Mathematicians, my very worthy friends, Dr. *Arbuthnot*, and Mr. *Craig*' (p. 10). Wotton refers to Cheyne's *Philosophical Principles of Natural Religion* (1705) which, as its title suggests, is another exercise in physico-theological argument, but one that he suspects Keill will endorse because of its High Church Tory support. Wotton supposes that Keill is attacking Bentley's physico-theological approach, when in fact Keill's *Examination* itself uses natural philosophy to support an argument from design. For instance, Keill states that his own explication of the inclination of the Earth 'cannot but lead us into a transcendent admiration of the divine wisdome', and 'if the rest of the works of nature were well observed, we should find several advantages which accrue to us by their present constitution which are far beyond the uses of them that are yet discovered'.[35] Keill's second comment is within a page of exposing Bentley's error, so it seems reasonable to argue that he had this particularly in mind.

Other members of the Christ Church circle would also approve of the general argument of Bentley's sermons, but found errors in his method. *A Short Account of Dr. Bentley's Humanity and Justice* (1699), perhaps written by William King, found 'much good Learning and some good Argument' in his lectures, but expresses concern that

> every sort of Proof does not immediately commence Demonstration; and I shall never be easily persuaded to believe, that it is necessary to confute the Atheist to affirm as a Theological Truth, That *every Star is a World, and every one of those Worlds inhabited*; which, though I think, may be true, yet I do not think infallibly so.[36]

The theory of the plurality of worlds attracted particular interest after Fontenelle, although John Wilkins had earlier sought to popularize such ideas.[37] Bentley, almost paradoxically, uses the possibility of life on other planets to counter atomistic models of creation:

> would it not raise in us a higher apprehension of the infinite majesty and boundless beneficence of God, to suppose that those remote and

vast bodies were formed, not merely upon our account, [...] but for different ends and nobler purposes? [...] as the earth was principally designed for the being and service and contemplation of men, why may not all other planets be created for the like uses, each for their own inhabitants which have life and understanding? (*Works*, III, 175)

As with the consequences of his Moon error, Bentley's argument could be seen as also contributing to the erosion of the traditional conception of man's unique place in the universe, rather than serving his intention of demonstrating divine providence.

Unlike Keill and the author of *Dr. Bentley's Humanity and Justice*, Swift is suspicious of the very mode of reasoning that characterizes the Boyle lecture project, perhaps because of the implications outlined above. *A Letter to a Young Gentleman, Lately Entered into Holy Orders*, thought to have been written in 1707 and generally attributed to Swift, argues that 'the frequent Custom of preaching against *Atheism, Deism, Free-Thinking*, and the like' seems to 'perplex the Minds of well-disposed People with Doubts, which probably would never have otherwise come into their Heads' (*PW*, IX, 77–78).[38] For Swift,

Some Gentlemen [...] are apt to fill their Sermons with philosophical Terms, and Notions of the metaphysical or abstracted Kind; which generally have one Advantage, to be equally understood by the Wise, the Vulgar, and the Preacher himself. [...] Others again, are fond of dilating on *Matter* and *Motion*, talk of the *fortuitous Concourse of Atoms*, of *Theories*, and *Phænomena*; directly against the Advice of St. *Paul*, who yet appears to have been conversant enough in those Kinds of Studies. (*PW*, IX, 76–77)

Paul had encountered Epicurean philosophers in Athens (Acts 17.18), but Swift is most probably referring to Paul's warning to the Colossians: 'Beware lest any man spoile you through Philosophie and vaine deceit, after the tradition of men, after the rudiments of the world, and not after Christ' (Colossians 2.8). In his *Sermon upon the Excellency of Christianity*, Swift again alludes to the passage in Colossians, but also mentions how Paul advised Timothy to 'avoid prophane and vain babblings, [...] that is, not to introduce into the Christian doctrine the janglings of those vain philosophers, which they would pass upon the world for science' (*PW*, IX, 242). When *A Letter to a Young Gentleman* was composed, the Boyle lectures of Bentley and others were well known, and certainly the most famous sermons containing physico-theological forms of argument, so it is a strong possibility that Swift's censure has them specifically in mind.

Bentley makes it explicit from the beginning of his first sermon that to use the Scriptures to defend Christianity would be 'improper now, when we are to argue and expostulate with such persons as allow no divine authority to our text', and so his methodology instead involves turning to 'other books extant, which they must needs allow of as proper evidence; even the mighty volumes of visible nature, and the everlasting tables of right reason' (*Works*, III, 1–2). Of Bentley's many opponents, he is perhaps thinking particularly of Hobbes, who denied that Scripture gives credence to the belief in the incorporeal nature of the spirit, and also of Spinoza, who challenged the authority of Scripture more fundamentally, arguing that knowledge of the authorship and transcription of the text is 'not so much imperfect as untrustworthy'.[39]

The absence of scriptural reference in Bentley's lectures is perhaps indicative of the general shift in mainstream forms of Anglican theology, not just physico-theology, in the late seventeenth century. However, at the start of the eighteenth century there appears to be a realignment of intellectual forces, with the argument from design and the new natural philosophy – discourses which had aided Anglicans previously – appropriated into free-thinking.[40] In Swift's opinion, for physico-theologians like Bentley to reject arguments from revealed religion is a concession too far towards the atheist camp, when they should be defending the Christian faith on its own terms. As Michael DePorte observes, Swift appears to ignore his own advice to the 'Young Gentleman' in his parody of the writings of the deist Anthony Collins, *Mr. C—ns's Discourse of Free-Thinking* (1713).[41] Likewise, on several occasions, the narrator of *An Argument against Abolishing Christianity* (1708) adopts atheistical terminology in referring to the 'System' of the Gospel, and treats it correspondingly as he might an 'antiquated and exploded' philosophical theory (*PW*, II, 27). It can be argued, however, that as parodic works which attack through ridicule, *Mr. C—ns's Discourse* and *An Argument against Abolishing Christianity* give less legitimacy to the views they oppose than a serious condemnation which gives its target undue credence.

For Bentley to call upon only the 'Book of Nature' to demonstrate the existence and wisdom of God could be seen as a movement towards the pantheistic ideas of Spinoza. The appropriation of natural philosophy within theological discourse was therefore a highly contested issue, and could be associated with the promulgation of heterodox ideas. Moreover, Bentley follows this system of Anglican apologetics whilst the methodology of his textual scholarship could be used to challenge the legitimacy of Scripture, thereby assisting the claims of Spinoza and other deists. This was a paradox not lost on the Christ Church Wits, who wonder

> Whether [Bentley] thinks, that his *Philosophical Lectures* serve more to the establishment of Religion, than his *Criticisms* do to overthrow it? For is he not Positive, that the Idioms of the Letters prove them to be *a Thousand Years later than* Phalaris? And are not some of these very Idioms frequently to be met with both in the *Gospels* and *Epistles?* (*Dr. Bentley's Dissertations [...] Examin'd*, pp. 67–68)

Later, the Wits develop the conceit that the Boyle lectures and *Dissertation* on Phalaris must have been written by two different men called Bentley, contrasting the 'Learned Doctor' chosen by the 'then Fathers of the Church, as a fit person to vindicate the Truth of Religion' with the 'Sophist' whose 'Arguments to disprove the Epistles of *Phalaris*' are of 'Equal weight to prove the Writings of *Moses* and the New Testament to be of much Later date' (pp. 200–201). Wotton recognized that the purpose of Peter's conjectural interpretation of the Will was 'seemingly perhaps to laugh at Dr. *Bentley* and his Criticisms' (*Defense*, p. 53). However, Wotton was probably unaware that rather than a simple barb at Bentley's classical scholarship, Swift (following the Christ Church Wits) was perhaps highlighting the dangerous implications of Bentley's methods if applied to Scripture.

It is likely that Bentley's blunder about the Moon's diurnal motion not only provided Swift with proven and public evidence of incompetence which he could use as satiric ammunition in an increasingly personal feud, but also would have illustrated to him the danger of using scientific ideas within the construction of natural theologies. Bentley's Boyle lectures initiated the association of the Newtonian philosophy with providentialism.[42] Many of Bentley's demonstrations of God's hand in the continuation of the universe were underpinned by specific examples from natural philosophy. It is perhaps strange to find Swift in the position of chastising a self-proclaimed Newtonian for his poor knowledge of Newton's work, but Swift is highlighting the problem with Bentley's scheme: if evidence of individual examples of God's wisdom and benevolence are based on natural knowledge later proven to be incorrect then this contributes to a slow erosion of belief in divine providence, and hands easy arguments to atheist or deist thinkers. In Swift's opinion, Bentley's method seems to prove what Wotton had attempted to argue against: 'That Studying of Natural Philosophy and Mathematicks, was a ready Method to introduce Scepticism at least, if not Atheism into the World' (*RAML*, p. 357). The 'physico-logic' (as the *Tale*-narrator might call it) of Bentley's enterprise, from which the spiritual has been removed, leaves Christianity more, not less, vulnerable to its atheistic opponents.

Bentley's error (and its inadequate correction) was, of course, an easy subject for satiric attack, but for Swift it also functioned as an emblem of the impermanence of, and false pride in, Modern knowledge. Perhaps it is of no wonder that Swift emphasized the ephemerality of Aldrovandi's work, and chose to associate it with the productions of Bentley and Wotton. Likewise, when Gulliver visits Glubbdubdrib, the island of necromancers, the ghost of Aristotle is summoned and in conversation acknowledges his 'own Mistakes in Natural Philosophy, because he proceeded in many things upon Conjecture, as all Men do', whilst remarking that: 'new Systems of Nature were but new Fashions, which would vary in every Age' (*PW*, XI, 197–98). '*Aristotle*' associates Ancient learning with a modesty that recognizes the limitations of scientific knowledge, leaving Modern learning teeming with arrogance.[43] Whether Ancient or Modern, all 'Systems of Nature' seem subject to transience because they are the productions of man, restricted in his capacity for knowledge (although Lord Monboddo found it crucial to assert the longevity, nay eternity, of the Newtonian philosophy in explicit defiance of the ghost of Aristotle's charge).[44] It is likely that in Swift's opinion, for Christianity to demonstrate its truth through alignment with one particular and potentially short-lived natural philosophy would run the risk of itself going 'out of Vogue'.

The Moon's 'refulgent Visage' in the *Battel* indicates that Swift was acquainted with the details of a particular dispute involving the appropriation of incorrect natural knowledge, and allegorizes it through particular episodes within the main narrative. However, does this familiarity translate into successful satire? The use of such specialized scientific knowledge has the potential to produce a level of signification too obscure for the *Tale* and *Battel*'s readers to decipher, unless they are *au fait* with the many twists and turns within the Phalaris quarrel of Temple, the Christ Church Wits, and Keill, versus Bentley and Wotton, which raged for more than a decade and through numerous publications. The mock-heroic conceit that underpins and pervades the *Battel* would surely have had a wide appeal to Swift's readers, but this episode suggests that particular sections of the *Tale* volume were more intended for the enjoyment of an exclusive and intimate circle of thinkers who wheeled upon the centre of Christ Church College. It is small wonder then, that Jean Le Clerc remarked that 'an odd game goes on throughout the book, where we often do not know whether the author is making fun or not, nor of whom, nor what his intention is'. This is not to say that Swift's most ideal audience were any wiser: while Atterbury found the *Tale* to be 'full of wit, humour, good sense, and learning', King thought the *Tale*-author's aims included: 'to be profane', 'to shew how great a proficient he is [...] at cursing and swearing', and 'to exceed all bounds of modesty'.[45] Swift's 'Apology' certainly had much work to do.

'*Bantring*' with '*Newton*'s Mathematicks'

For Bentley and Wotton, Newton was a key champion of the Moderns.[46] Then why does the *Tale*-proper make no reference to Newton specifically? Surely the *Principia* would qualify Newton as one of the 'great Introducers of new Schemes in Philosophy' in the 'Digression on Madness' (p. 107)? Or, more sympathetically, why does Newton not feature as a hero, or even as one of the '*Bowmen*' (p. 152) of the Moderns in the *Battel*? It is possible that this is related to the alliance with Christ Church that Temple and Swift had forged. Gregory, Keill and Freind were all early supporters of the Newtonian philosophy, and Temple and Swift needed to keep as many precious comrades as possible in their quarrel with Bentley and Wotton. Descartes and Gassendi were fair game, but to bring 'The great Philosopher of this age, the most Ingenious and Incomparable Mr. *Newton*', as Keill described him (*Examination*, p. 16), specifically into the dispute would fracture their coalition, revealing the ideological fault-lines between this varied group of friends and colleagues who had been united in their condemnation of the presumptuous Bentley. The general assault on Bentley had benefited greatly from Keill's skirmish: to alienate such an asset would be very foolish. Natural philosophy in itself may well have provoked Swift to dismiss it as encouraging an obsession with the physical world, but its appropriation by Anglican apologetics was a more worrying by-product because it challenged where authority should be placed.

By 1710, however, Swift would be happy to mention Newton in his defence of the mode of satire employed in the *Tale*. In the 'Apology' appended to the fifth edition, the 'Author' (who may or may not be Swift in his own voice)[47] remarks:

> *the great Part of those who have no Share or Tast of either* [Wit or Humor] *lay themselves bare to the Lashes of Both, think the Blow is weak, because*

they are insensible, and where Wit hath any mixture of Raillery; 'Tis but calling it Banter, *and the work is done. This Polite Word of theirs was first borrowed from the Bullies in* White-Fryars, *then fell among the Footmen, and at last retired to the Pedants, by whom it is applied as properly to the Productions of Wit, as if I should apply it to Sir* Isaac Newton*'s Mathematicks, but, if this* Bantring *as they call it, be so despisable a Thing, whence comes it to pass they have such a perpetual Itch towards it themselves? To instance only in the Answerer already mentioned; it is grievous to see him* [...] *at every turn going out of his way to be waggish.* (*Tale*, p. 14)

Frank T. Boyle contends that Swift is writing in response to the chaplain, friend and translator of Newton, Samuel Clarke (1675–1729), whose second set of Boyle lectures, delivered in 1706, attacked the *Tale* as the example of a work by authors who take 'profane, impure, filthy' things and represent them as 'harmless and indifferent' in order to 'laugh Men out of their natural shame and abhorrence of them; nay, even to recommend them with their utmost Wit'. However, Clarke's *Discourse* is not addressed to them, because '*Banter* is not capable of being answered by *Reason*'.[48] Swift would not have taken kindly to his work being addressed as Deist '*Banter*', one of two words he confessed 'I have done my utmost for some Years past, to stop the Progress of' (*The Tatler*, 230, in *PW*, II, 176). Of unknown etymology, as a noun 'banter' seemed to originate only in the 1690s, and as a verb it came into usage only just before, in the 1670s.[49] The general meaning of the word was therefore still a site of contestation. More importantly, Swift would have been exasperated by Clarke's lack of wit and his inability to read the *Tale*'s ironies.

However, it is not clear that Swift had Clarke's response in mind when writing the 'Apology'. The 'Answerer already mentioned' was in all likelihood Wotton, whose *Defense of the Reflections*, appended to the third edition (1705), included his *Observations* upon the *Tale*. In his *Observations*, Wotton quickly dismisses the *Tale*'s attacks upon Bentley and himself, remarking that 'the rest of the Book which does not relate to us, is of so irreligious a nature, is so crude a Banter upon all that is esteemed as Sacred' (p. 48).[50] By those who are 'insensible' to the blows of the *Tale*'s wit, Swift is probably referring to his chief opponents Wotton and Bentley, and countering Wotton's flippant rejoinder regarding the success of the *Tale*'s satire and his accusatory glance at the dangerous implications of the religious allegory. Swift responds to Wotton by placing satire and science side by side: neither the '*Productions of*

Wit' nor *'Sir* Isaac Newton*'s Mathematicks'* warrant dismissal as mere 'Banter'. Swift is perhaps suggesting how easily Newton's mathematics can be rejected as nonsense by those ignorant of its workings, with an ironic nod to Wotton's (and perhaps Bentley's) 'expert' knowledge of the *Principia*. As a characteristically 'Modern' production, the *Defense* tries to keep abreast of all recent contributions to knowledge, as well as bolstering the *Reflections* against the assaults of Temple, Keill and the Christ Church Wits, and the two strategies were of course connected. That 'the Stock of Knowledge still encreases' even 'since the Second Edition of the Reflexions came out' is for Wotton evidence of the fruitfulness of Modern enquiry (p. 36). Of the two works he names, one of them is, appropriately, Newton's *Opticks*, which he proceeds to summarize (pp. 36–37). Wotton also supplements his account of astronomy by noting that Newton and Gregory 'know vastly more of the System of the Heavens [...] than *Hipparchus* or *Ptolemee*' (pp. 19–20).

The *Opticks* had consolidated Newton's reputation, which had been steadily building through the 1690s (partly due to the efforts of men like Gregory and Keill), and since the first and second editions of the *Reflections* Newton had become a crucial example of the superiority of Modern knowledge. So it is no wonder then, that by the time of the *Defense* Wotton would make much of this, and Swift would appropriately respond in the 'Apology' through reference to Wotton's foremost champion. This is not to say that Swift was attempting to belittle Newton's mathematics here: even the most ironic interpretation of the passage would find the satiric barb particularly blunt. Swift's attitude at this time might be attributable to the posthumous influence of Temple, who singled out mathematics as a useful discipline.[51] Moreover, when the 'Apology' was published, Swift had been friends with Catherine Barton (c. 1680–1739), Newton's step-niece, for around three years, and often dined at Newton's house on Jermyn Street, where Barton lived. It is perhaps most appropriate, therefore, to take the 'Apology' at face value here. The 'Author' of the 'Apology' freely admits his ignorance of Newton's mathematics in order to satirize Wotton's poor knowledge of the true workings of the *Tale*. This un-mocking allusion to Newton can be viewed as more evidence of the occasional basis of much of his satiric work. But by 1726, no longer needing to aid Christ Church in its intellectual battles, out of touch with Barton, and more aware of Newtonian ideas through reading his copy of the second edition of the *Principia* (1713), Swift subjects Newton to the full venom of his satire in the 'Voyage to Laputa', for reasons we will soon explore.

4
Laputian Newtons: Science, the Wood's Halfpence Affair and *Gulliver's Travels*

It was almost inevitable that *Travels into Several Remote Nations of the World* (1726), now known as *Gulliver's Travels*, would be permeated with the ideas, discoveries, practices and language associated with natural knowledge, given the changes in European culture brought about by the so-called 'scientific revolution'. The travelogue form, which parodically structures its narrative, had become increasingly influenced by empirical modes of observation during the seventeenth century, and reports of voyages and field-trips were often found within the pages of the Royal Society's *Philosophical Transactions*, gratifying a readership fascinated by exotic and prodigious specimens of nature. Indeed, Barbara M. Benedict has argued that as a product of and response to this culture of enquiry and wonder, *Gulliver's Travels* 'brims with satiric targets that embody curiosity'.[1]

Whilst Gulliver describes farfetched cultures and events that make the reader question his truthfulness, stylistically the narrative insists upon its factuality and simplicity (*PW*, XI, 291).[2] The pedantic focus on quantity and measurement imitates discursive modes that gave primacy to mathematical explanation and matter of fact, and were infiltrating the developing genre of the novel. In applying numerical precision to objects that challenge realism or social decorum, Gulliver's narrative simultaneously satirizes and draws imaginative power from the impulse for authenticity. In substance as well as style, the concepts and technologies of the sciences were important satiric devices for Swift, perhaps most compellingly illustrated in the moments of microscopic perspective in Book II, which parody Robert Hooke's descriptions in *Micrographia* (1665).[3] But in the 'Voyage to Laputa', Swift's allusions to the sciences are far greater in number and magnitude as Gulliver, himself a 'Sort of Projector' in his youth (*PW*, XI, 178), encounters a royal court of introverted men obsessed with mathematics on an island propelled through the air by magnetic forces, and pays visit to an institution engaged in scientific, technological, and medical research of dubious merit.

Kings of Inattention

In the 1710s, between the *Tale* and *Travels*, Swift wrote very little on his own concerned with experimental philosophy or other 'Modern' forms of learning, and it is unclear how much he was involved with the collaborative 'Scriblerian' satires that made reference to the varieties of scientific curiosity. But during this time Swift's life intersected with those of several people who were practitioners or at least admirers of mathematics and the new natural philosophy, from whom he would have learnt much about Newtonianism and its surrounding culture, as well as ways of incorporating such material into his writing. The close friendships he developed with these men and women perhaps indicate that readings of 'science' in the *Travels* should look beyond ideological dichotomies.

The most important of these friendships was probably with John Arbuthnot (1667–1735), the mathematician, physician, antiquarian and Scriblerian satirist, whom Swift once called the 'King of inattention' because of his Laputian-esque absent-mindedness.[4] Swift recognized that Arbuthnot, FRS from 1704, had a special 'Vein' which no other 'Man alive possesses' to turn the latest developments in natural knowledge into conceits with satiric and comic power, remarking that 'all that relates to the Sciences' in the *Memoirs* must come from him.[5] While the Scriblerian works often adopt satiric strategies Swift had used in the *Tale*, they were themselves a source of inspiration when writing the *Travels*. *The Humble Petition* (1716), for instance, probably by Arbuthnot (perhaps with some assistance), imagined a project that would have been welcome in the Academy of Lagado. Other works, such as *God's Revenge Against Punning* (1716), anticipated the Laputians' 'continual Disquietudes' (*PW*, XI, 164) in that they drew upon anxieties about apocalyptic destruction caused by celestial phenomena (changes in the Sun's orbit, eclipses or comets), as found in the works of Burnet, Halley, Whiston and William Derham (among others), and reminded readers of the total solar eclipse, observable nova and spectacular aurora borealis that had captivated people in 1715–16.[6] Both Arbuthnot and Swift use these narratives of astronomically induced panic to satirize the millenarian theories of William Whiston (1667–1752) in particular, seemingly concerned that his appropriations of the new natural philosophy were fostering new or variant forms of superstitious credulity, rather than extinguishing unenlightened views of the cosmos, running into the 'same Temper that Boys discover, in delighting to hear terrible Stories of Sprites and Hobgoblins' (*PW*, XI, 165).[7] However, in reply to an unrecovered letter in which Swift laments the political changes wrought by the death of Queen Anne, Arbuthnot half-teases:

> I should have the same concern for things as yow, were I not convinc'd that a comet will make much more strange revolutions upon the face of our Globe, than all the petty changes that can be occasiond by Goverts & Ministrys, and yow will allow it to be a matter of importance to think of Methods to save ones self & family in such a terrible shock when this whole earth will turn upon new poles & revolve in a new orbite. (6 August [1715], in *CJS*, II, 142)

In one sense, after the Queen's death Arbuthnot's life did turn upside down: he lost his role as physician-in-ordinary, and the influence and houses accompanying that position.[8] But in adopting the theories of Whiston and Halley, and sounding a lot like a Laputian, Arbuthnot attempts to put Swift's fears into perspective. The celestial metaphor was particularly appropriate, given that months previously Swift had attributed his epistolary silence to 'that eclypse which happen'd on the first of August' (Swift to Pope, 28 June 1715, in *CJS*, II, 133).

When Swift returned to Ireland at the fall of Harley's ministry, one of the men who made his time in Dublin more tolerable was his personal physician, Richard Helsham (1683–1738). Not only a distinguished man of medicine who in 1733 was appointed Regius Professor of Physic at Trinity College Dublin, in 1724 Helsham became the first holder of the Erasmus Smith professorship of natural and experimental philosophy. In a letter to Pope, Swift described Helsham as 'an ingenious good-humour'd Physician, a fine gentleman, an excellent scholar, easy in his fortunes, kind to every body, hath abundance of friends, [...] is not this the true happy man?' (13 February 1728[–9], in *CJS*, III, 210). This sounds little like the Laputians, abstracted from the social world, each having 'one of their Eyes turned inward, and the other directly up to the Zenith' (*PW*, XI, 159), and forever worried about stellar or cometary catastrophe. Ehrenpreis detects some irony in Swift's description of Helsham, but when suffering from the effects of Ménière's disease in 1733, Swift told Charles Ford that Helsham was 'the best' of his physicians, 'is very kind and visits me constantly', and the Dean later appointed him one of his executors, although Helsham died before acting in that capacity.[9]

Around 1717, Swift began a lasting and close friendship with the Dublin schoolmaster Thomas Sheridan (1687–1738) who, as Ehrenpreis suggests, was perhaps a more appropriate model for the Laputians' evasion of the real world, despite Swift finding him 'doubtless the best instructor of youth in these kingdoms, or perhaps in Europe'. Whilst they shared a love of ludic punning and word-play, were both High Churchmen (and suspected Tories), and collaborated on *The Intelligencer* (1728–29), Sheridan was a scholar whom the Dean called 'a Man of intent and abstracted thinking, enslav'd by Mathematicks', had a tendency for absent-mindedness, and 'was altogether ignorant in worldly management'.[10] Swift spent much of 1725 at Sheridan's estate at Quilca, in county Cavan, 'reading books twice over for want of fresh ones', and 'finishing correcting, amending, and Transcribing my Travells'.[11] Sheridan's library included a number of books on contemporary natural philosophy and natural history, including William Derham's *Physico-Theology* and Whiston's summaries of Newton's *Principia* and Halley's cometography, and it is possible Swift consulted such works whilst finishing Book III. Perhaps significantly, Sheridan owned Boyle's *Experiments and Considerations Touching Colours*, which included the story of the man born blind who could discern colours by feeling them, burlesqued in the Academy of Lagado.[12]

Appointed vicar of Laracor in 1700, and staying in nearby Trim, Swift became the friend and customer of Joseph (Joe) Beaumont, a local linen draper and general merchant.[13] Like Gulliver, Beaumont was a bit of a 'Projector', proposing improvements to Dublin harbour, publishing geometrical tables for textile manufacture, and speculating on how to calculate longitude.[14] Swift's poem on Archdeacon Thomas Walls's vestry begins with a reference to their mutual friend's interest in natural philosophy:

> WHOEVER pleaseth to enquire,
> Why yonder Steeple wants a Spire,
> The gray old Fellow Poet *Joe*
> The Philosophic Cause will shew.
> Once, on a Time a Western Blast,
> At least twelve Inches overcast,
> Reckoning Roof, Weather Cock and all,
> Which came with a prodigious Fall;
> [...]
> For by the Laws of Gravitation,
> It fell into its proper Station.[15]

It is uncertain whether the lines beginning 'Once, on a Time', with their juxtaposition of fairy tale-like storytelling and mathematical precision, adopt Beaumont's voice, but in any case, the poem lightheartedly suggests that the 'Philosophic Cause' merely states the obvious. Tragically, Beaumont experienced mental health problems from around 1716, and in 1724 committed suicide. This illness is sometimes attributed to his growing fixation with mathematics, and particularly the longitude problem, and for Swift perhaps served as evidence for the psychological dangers of speculative learning, reflected in the Laputians' introspection and anxieties.[16]

When Swift came to write the *Travels*, therefore, he knew very well several natural philosophers and mathematicians, which may have informed his Laputian caricatures. The solipsistic existence of the flapper-needing philosophers might also hint at Descartes, whom Swift had twice before trapped in 'his own *Vortex*' (*Tale*, pp. 108, 157). But more than any other man, over several decades of celebrity, Newton had established himself as the archetypal natural philosopher, as well as President of the Royal Society and Master of the Mint, and rumours about his eccentricity proliferated, especially because many could not believe a man of such genius could be 'normal'. Swift might have heard, for instance, that when Arbuthnot visited Paris in 1699, the mathematician Guillaume François Antoine, Marquis de l'Hôpital asked him 'every particular about Sir I. even to the colour of his hair said does he eat & drink & sleep is he like other men?'[17]

Swift probably encountered stories of Newton's aloofness and introspection from an important but overlooked friend: Catherine Barton (c. 1680–1739), the daughter of Newton's half-sister, Hannah Smith. Barton lived with Newton in Jermyn Street from the early 1700s until his death, and in August 1717 she married John Conduitt (1688–1737), who succeeded Newton as Master of the Mint and who, with Barton's assistance, attempted to write a biography of his predecessor.[18] Reputedly the mistress of Newton's friend Lord Halifax at one time, Barton would be immortalized in Kit-Kat Club toasting verses that praised her beauty through Newtonian-tinged imagery:

> Stampt with her Reigning Charms the Standard Glass,
> Shall current thro' the Realms of *Bacchus* pass.
> Full fraught with Beauty shall new Flames impart,
> And Mint her shining Image on the Heart.[19]

Swift dined with Barton on many occasions during his time in London in the reign of Anne, perhaps as early as 1707. Indeed, Swift told Stella that 'I love her better than any body here', and Stella apparently teased Swift about the closeness of this friendship: 'I'll break your head in good earnest, young woman, for your nasty jest about Mrs. Barton'.[20] The Tories even used this relationship to threaten the Whig Newton's position at the Tower, with Bolingbroke apparently sending Swift to Barton to let Newton know 'he thought it a sin his thoughts should be diverted by his place at the Mint & that the Queen would settle upon him a pension'. Swift also found her a great source of political gossip: 'Mrs. Bart[on] is still in my good Graces; [...] the best Intelligence I get of Publick Affairs is from Ladies, for the Ministers never tell me any thing'.[21] It is probable that Barton told Swift much about the step-uncle whose domestic affairs she attended to, and in Laputa such stories were later appropriated and deployed in satiric form. Newton would sometimes, for instance, let his dinner stand for hours, and eat his supper cold for breakfast, because he was so engrossed in his studies, and would have benefited from a flapper or two by his side.[22] Indeed, Walter Scott states that 'the Dean's friends' (who precisely is unclear) believed that 'the office of flapper was suggested by the habitual absence of mind of the great philosopher' Newton.[23]

Whilst the perceived solipsisms of many natural philosophers are worthy of satiric censure, or at least comedy, it is generally accepted that the attack on mathematicians in the 'Voyage to Laputa' is to some degree a form of revenge against Newton for his involvement in the assay of William Wood's Irish halfpence.[24] The specific circumstances of Swift's animosity have surprisingly been little studied, however, despite their implications regarding the interpretation of Gulliver's third voyage and Swift's attitude to science in general. Newton is not the all-encompassing target, but this chapter's exploration of some key passages within this context may contribute to an understanding of the 'miscegenation' of satiric objects in Book III.[25]

Newton, Wood and the Drapier

In July 1722, the English manufacturer William Wood was granted a patent by the Crown to coin for Ireland 360 tons of copper money (with a face value of £108,000) over 14 years. Ireland had a poor currency system and gravely lacked small change, with many copper pieces being either below their intrinsic value or counterfeits, and as the country had no national mint, it was usual for private minters to provide smaller coinage.[26] However, Wood had obtained permission through bribing Ehrengarde Melusina, Duchess of Kendal (George I's mistress), and the corruption involved was widely rumoured.[27] The Irish feared that the market would be flooded with debased coinage, which would cause severe inflation and be easily forged. Alerted to this situation by Archbishop William King, Lord Abercorn and Lord Chancellor Midleton, Swift was worried about the coin's intrinsic value, but his main concerns were the political circumstances under which the patent was granted to a non-native minter and forced upon the Irish without their consent, as neither the Irish Parliament nor the Commissioners of the Revenue in Dublin had been consulted.[28] Motivated by 'perfect hatred of Tyran[n]y and Oppression', Swift interrupted the composition of *Gulliver's Travels* in order to write five letters in the persona of a draper in which he set out arguments against what he saw as a colonial imposition, and a reminder of the country's dependent status, in an attempt to encourage a boycott of the new currency and a more general atmosphere of protest within the Irish popular imagination.[29]

As Master of the Mint (a position he had held since 1699), Newton was requested by the Royal Treasury to examine the quality of Wood's coinage. Newton's assay, held at the Tower of London on 27 April 1724 (but not officially communicated for over 3 months), used specimens 'which have from time to time been taken from the several parcels coined & sealed up', and discovered that the coins were all of full weight but varied widely (a fact neglected in the Privy Council Committee's Report). However, Newton found the copper to be 'of about the same goodness & value' as that used in English coins, and a vast improvement on the Irish coins produced in the reigns of Charles II, James II and William III.[30] The Dublin *Postboy* (31 July 1724) consequently reported that 'Mr. Wood had in all Respects perform'd his Contract' (*PW*, X, 189). Swift's second *Drapier's Letter* was vehement in its reply: 'His Contract! With whom? Was it with the Parliament or People of *Ireland*? [...] they detest, abhor, and reject it, as Corrupt, Fraudulent' (*PW*, X, 16).

The second *Letter* was not only a broad constitutional protest but also examined the conditions of Newton's 'impudent and insupportable' assay. Wood had been permitted to select the coins for testing, and Newton himself had insisted that the sample be brought to London rather than sending men to Bristol.[31] Swift was therefore suspicious of the sampling procedure: '*Wood* takes Care to coin a Dozen or two Half-pence of good Metal, sends them to the *Tower* and they are approved, and these must answer all that he hath already Coined, or shall Coin'. Common sense, expressed in language to appeal to the common Irishman, is used by the Drapier to debunk the 'scientific' investigation of the renowned Newton:

if I were to buy an hundred Sheep, and the Grazier should bring me one single Weather, fat and well fleeced by way of *Pattern*, and expect the same Price round for the whole hundred, without suffering me to see them before he was paid, [...] I would be none of his Customer. (*PW*, X, 17)

Swift points out that Newton reported the samples were taken from batches produced from 'Lady day 1723 to March 28th 1724', whereas it was known that the coins sent to Ireland were minted in 1722.[32] Swift was not alone in his criticism. David Bindon found a discrepancy between the Privy Council's report and Newton's assay concerning the dates of coinage, meaning that 8 months were unaccounted for, while Sir Michael Creagh, the former Lord Mayor of Dublin, observed:

how Visible and Plain must it appear to all the World, That Mr. *Wood* and his Friends have Imposed upon Sir *Isaac Newton*, Mr. *Southwell*, and Mr. *Scrope*, by bringing them Specimens of said Coyn, and Tryal-Pieces so different in Value and Weight from what is daily seen in *Ireland*.[33]

Creagh's suspicions were confirmed by the assay of several parcels of Wood's coin carried out by William Maple, a Dublin chemist, and produced as evidence for a committee of the Irish House of Commons. According to the Drapier, this 'very skilful Person', who Swift probably knew personally, found halfpence of four kinds, three being 'considerably under Weight' (*PW*, X, 31).[34] Swift uses Maple's results to put forward an alternative mathematical case which augments the later accusations of Newton's partiality. The Drapier manipulates Maple's 'exact Computation' of the weight difference between the four sorts to show that 'the Publick will be a Loser' of £82,168.16s. For every halfpenny in a pound exceeding the number set out in the patent, Wood could allegedly make £1680 profit more than allowed (*PW*, X, 32–33). While it has since been identified that Maple did not include Wood's costs of production in his calculation, it still meant that a sizeable excess profit would be achieved.[35]

In Swift's opinion, there is also another problem with the investigation. In the third *Letter*, he argues that comparison of Wood's coins with those produced for Ireland in the previous century proves nothing, because at times of war, rebellion or insurrection 'the Kings of *England* were sometimes forced to pay their Armies here with mixt or base Money' (*PW*, X, 33). For Swift, Newton's letter presents the minutiae of the results of his assay as experientially proven 'facts' (p. 278) even though the test procedures are fundamentally flawed. Swift and Creagh imply that Newton is either complicit in Wood's act of deception or has made methodological errors unworthy of his reputation.

For Swift, it is appalling to see apparently empirical methods used to justify a scheme that evinced English tyranny, and astonishing that Newton's work at the Mint was perhaps not so 'scientific' at all, either intentionally or through gross error, particularly because the Royal Treasury used Newton's reputation as the greatest natural philosopher and Royal Society President to assert their authority in the whole affair. For example, the 'Report of the Privy Council Committee' (24 July 1724) stated that Newton:

> was Consulted in all the Steps of settling and adjusting the Terms and Conditions of the Patent; and after mature deliberation, your Majesty's Warrant was sign'd, directing an Indenture in such Manner as is practised in your Majesty's Mint in the Tower of London. (*PW*, X, 198)

The third *Letter*, 'Some Observations upon' this Report, recounts a story regarding a competition for the patent, apparently refereed by 'Sir *Isaac Newton*', that took place six years previously between Wood and three other men. Wood had made the worst offer, revealing it to be 'plain with what Intentions he sollicited this Patent; but not so plain how he obtained it' (*PW*, X, 29). Swift uses this story to suggest that Newton, who was 'consulted in all the Steps', had been dealing in an underhanded manner from the very beginning. For the Drapier, what the report said of the circumstances of sampling was no longer relevant, 'Since it is now plain, that the Biass of Favour hath been wholly on [Wood's] side' (*PW*, X, 31). Herbert Davis could find no record of this particular trial, but discovered in the Calendar of Treasury Papers that in December 1717 Wood was offering to provide copper to the Mint. No matter whether the information was false (and Newton's corruption is very unlikely), it contributed to Swift's sense of Newton's misconduct, or was at least fuel for the Drapier's propaganda, which often exploited the difficulty in judging fact from fiction.[36] The severity of Swift's animosity is also evident in *Doing Good: A Sermon, On the Occasion of Wood's Project* (1724). According to Swift, 'the meanest instruments often succeed in doing public mischief [...] by deceiving us with plausible arguments, to make us believe, that the most ruinous project they can offer is intended for our good' (*PW*, IX, 237). The assay is one such 'plausible argument', presenting matters of fact apparently based in empirical modes of thought.

Bowing to the immense political and cultural pressure, the patent was eventually surrendered in August 1725, and Swift received much of the credit for this (and, despite his anonymity, had already been awarded the freedom of the City of Dublin). But he clearly harboured resentment, and long after the Wood affair (and even Newton's death), would continue to question Newton's integrity. For instance, in 1729, on the occasion of James Maculla's proposal to circulate notes stamped on copper, Swift compared the weights of various coins himself. Finding the halfpenny of Charles II's reign to be 'of the finest kind', he concludes that 'it is probable, that the officers of the Mint were then more honest' (*PW*, XII, 97). Swift was not the only author to seize upon the rumours about Newton's motives. For instance, an anonymous poem on Wood's halfpence, *A Letter from a Young Lady, to the Revd. D–n S—t* (1724) states that:

> The *Principles* by which Men move,
> Are private Interest, base Self-Love;
> So far their Love or hate extends
> As serves their own contracted Ends.[37]

In this intricate conceit, rather than external forces acting upon a body to change its current state of rest or motion (as explained in Newton's first law), the speaker proffers self-interest as an inherent motivation in man. While the power of gravity as it 'extends' is dependent upon the proximity of attracting objects, the nature of a man's actions towards others is determined by their own 'Ends'. The poem presents the great writer of the *Mathematical Principles of Natural Philosophy* as possessing no moral principles at all.

The association of Newton with Wood as a satiric strategy is perhaps confirmed in the third *Letter*. After discussing the '*Small Circumstantial* Charge for the Purchase of his Patent' which the Crown will receive, the Drapier wonders whether Wood has 'discovered the *Longitude*, or the *Universal Medicine*? No; but he hath found out the *Philosopher's Stone* after a new Manner, by *Debasing* of *Copper*, and resolving to force it upon us for *Gold*' (*PW*, X, 35–36). By the Longitude Act of 1714, Commissioners were appointed to judge all relevant projects, and could award up to £2000 to experimenters and pay up to £20,000 if a practical method for determining longitude at sea gave a correct result to within 30' or 30 geographical miles. In July 1714, following the introduction of a reward to assist finding the Pretender, Swift joked to Arbuthnot about the state's recent (and misplaced) generosity: 'They had better Put out a Proclamation that whoever discovers the Pretender or the Longitude shall have 100000^{ll}' (*CJS*, I, 630). Parliament took the advice of Newton (as President of the Royal Society) when it established the Board of Longitude, and he became one of its first commissioners.[38] It is no wonder, therefore, that the Drapier associates Wood's financial success with another instance of state remuneration.[39]

The *'Universal Medicine'* provides a logical link to the Drapier's principal conceit, which posits Wood's halfpence as a bogus form of transmutation. The association of minting with scientific (or pseudoscientific) experiment is obvious but effective, and given further impetus considering Newton's involvement in the Wood affair. The use of alchemical metaphor continues in Swift's poetry on the halfpence. In 'Prometheus, A Poem', normally attributed to Swift, Wood's fraudulent behaviour is emphasized several times in the description of the coins' production:

> Together mingl'd in a Mass
> Smith's *Dust*, and *Copper*, *Lead* and *Brass*,
> The Mixture thus by Chymick Art,
> United close in ev'ry Part.
> In Fillets roll'd, or cut in Pieces,
> Appear'd like one continu'd Spec'es,
> And by the forming Engine struck,
> On all the same IMPRESSION stuck. (ll. 3–10, in *Poems*, I, 344)

The coins are of very poor quality (containing even 'Smith's *Dust*'), and so the reference to 'Art' can be read ironically. However, 'Chymick Art' also has the effect of connecting the coins' manufacture with the deceit and artifice of the alchemist. Likewise, the overwrought elisions of 'Appear'd like one continu'd Spec'es' embody the deception Swift sees at work: the coins may 'appear' to be of a single substance, but actually contain several unseen constituent parts. The agent of the final stage of production ('forming Engine') associates the process with mechanized, unnatural violence, and the prominence given to deception continues in the capitalized stress on 'IMPRESSION'.

In 'A Simile, on Our Want of Silver, and the only Way to remedy it' Swift constructs an allegory of the affair by means of the identification of silver with the Moon in alchemical discourse.[40] Due to the scarcity of small silver in Ireland, the value of gold fell in comparison, resulting in the devaluation of the guinea (which contained gold).[41] The poem argues that what is needed is not '*Wood*'s Copper', but for 'Our Silver [to] appear again' (ll. 27, 32, in *Poems*, I, 354). However, a 'Feminine

Magician' and '*brazen* Politician' (the Duchess of Kendal and Robert Walpole) have hidden the silver moon with 'A Parchment of prodigious Size' (Wood's patent) (ll. 19–21). Upon hearing the Drapier's 'Counter-Charm of Paper' the parchment will shrivel, and 'drive the Conj'rers to the Devil' (ll. 26, 29–30), drawing upon a typology of political wizardry that Swift had exploited previously.[42] The 'Conj'rers' perhaps represent not only the Duchess of Kendal, Walpole and Wood, but also Newton. For in Swift's *A Compleat Collection of Genteel and Ingenious Conversation*, known as *Polite Conversation* and published in 1738 (but composed over the course of at least thirty years), the narrator 'Simon Wagstaff', jealous of Newton's fame, states that the great man 'was thought to be a Conjurer, because he knew how to draw Lines and Circles upon a Slate' (*PW*, IV, 123). This lampoon exploits the long-held superstition that Swift mentions in 'To Dr D–l—y, on the Libels Writ against Him': 'as of old, Mathematicians / Were by the Vulgar thought Magicians' (ll. 95–96, in *Poems*, II, 503).[43] To dismiss the eminent natural philosopher using the insulting term 'Conjurer' is an immense slur, particularly in the time following Newton's death, when faith in Newtonianism was at its zenith.

Whether Swift thought that the Master of the Mint had been intentionally deceitful or not, as a rhetorical strategy the Drapier suggests that Newton was complicit in Wood's deception. Swift was clearly disappointed by the conclusions of the assay of the halfpence and, as the remainder of the chapter outlines, his brutal satiric assaults on Newton in the 'Voyage to Laputa' and *Polite Conversation* suggest that Swift felt compelled to seek revenge for the Mint's approval of the patent.

'Taylor', Astrologer and 'Workman in the Mint'

In *A Social History of Truth*, Steven Shapin argues persuasively that late seventeenth-century natural philosophers presented themselves as gentlemen to invoke the associations of gentility with truthfulness and honour in order to increase the authority of their knowledge-claims. In contrast, the mercantile classes were frequently viewed with suspicion. By the early eighteenth century, however, networks of patronage and investment which sought the validation, dissemination, and commodification of natural knowledge were in full force. As Larry Stewart has shown, a new market associated with natural philosophy arose within the world of prospectors, financeers and engineers. A deluge of schemes and inventions claimed to transform human mastery of nature into the means of public improvement, although it was thought that there were many unscrupulous and opportunistic projectors exploiting the grow-ing belief in the benefits of new technology.[44] Indeed, several critics have suggested that the impractical designs of the Lagadan Projectors are not only aimed at the Royal Society but also, and perhaps more, at economic speculators and inventors, including Wood, whom Swift often refers to as a 'PROJECTOR' in *The Drapier's Letters* (*PW*, X, 35).[45] While one could take issue with the degree of this, given the resemblance of many Lagadan experiments to those described in the *Philosophical Transactions*, Newton's involvement with Wood's halfpence might have confirmed for Swift a suspicion that the new sciences could be used to support 'projects' for individual commercial gain and the exercise of imperial power at the expense of the welfare of the people. But the con-nections between Newton, natural philosophy and the cultures of credit and invention were also vulnerable sites that a satirist could manipulate to spread charges of duplicity and vulgarity.

Additionally, in asserting the legitimacy of their representations natu-ral philosophers would consequently seek to disqualify other knowl-edge systems and practices. Such conflicts would ultimately take place in the cultural field, making use of political and moral resources in order to distinguish between 'bogus' and 'credible' forms of knowledge.[46] The following pages show that in his caricatures of Newton, Swift was able to exploit (for his own, opposing, ends) the same discourse of gentility employed by the natural philosophers themselves, and also took advan-tage of the disciplinary proximity between astronomy and astrology, presenting Newton as a deceitful tradesman of low birth and spurious learning.

In *Polite Conversation*, Wagstaff attempts to create a 'System' of eloquence for men and women of gentility to artificially follow (*PW*, IV, 104). His mechanical scheme physicalizes words, reminiscent of a conceit in the *Mechanical Operation* and Section I of the *Tale*:

> there is hardly a polite Sentence in the following Dialogues, which doth not absolutely require some peculiar graceful Motion in the Eyes, or Nose, or Mouth, or Forehead, or Chin; or suitable Toss of the Head, with certain Offices assigned to each Hand; and in Ladies, the whole Exercise of the Fan, fitted to the Energy of every Word they deliver. (*PW*, IV, 103)[47]

Polite Conversation is a work of irony not only in that Wagstaff seeks to promote sophisticated utterance through the accumulation of verbal cliché, but also because his own sense of importance results in literary conduct which is far from genteel. It soon becomes apparent that this sizeable ego is a useful vehicle of social satire, giving Swift licence to create provocative caricatures. Significantly (and appropriately, given the mechanistic theory of oral expression he outlines), the person who Wagstaff fears will vie with him for future fame is 'one Isaac Newton', whose celebrity status he seeks to diminish through equating him with the lower classes. Newton's position at the Royal Treasury is highlighted specifically, but reduced to simply 'Workman in the Mint'. Newton's mathematics and natural philosophy perhaps come off even worse: he is identified as a mere 'Instrument-Maker' who 'it seems, was knighted for making Sun-Dyals better than others of his Trade', and his complex diagrams are facetiously described as 'Lines and Circles upon a Slate, which no Body could understand' (*PW*, IV, 122–23).

Wagstaff also suggests that Newton's chief 'Skill' involves 'making Pot-hooks and Hangers, with a Pencil; which many thousand accomplished Gentlemen and Ladies can perform as well, with a Pen and Ink, upon a Piece of Paper, and in a Manner as little intelligible as those of Sir *Isaac*' (*PW*, IV, 123). Swift not only belittles Newton's mathematical accomplishments as a riposte to the many celebrations of the eminent natural philosopher's unique 'genius', but also ridicules the cultural fascination with the new sciences as a means to refinement, promoted by periodicals like Addison's *Spectator*. Natural philosophy had recently entered the drawing rooms of the polite classes and was encouraging the fashionable consumption of books and instruments by 'many thousand accomplished Gentlemen and Ladies'. By implication, Swift makes parallels between the assimilation of the Newtonian philosophy into genteel culture, and Wagstaff's pompous endeavour to promote civilized behaviour through the 'great Compass of real and useful Knowledge' in his 'Science' (*PW*, IV, 103).

Swift's satiric diminution also serves to expose an intellectual tension regarding the appropriate role of the natural philosopher. Newton had apparently 'first proved his inuentions by Geometry & only made use of experiments to make them intelligible & to convince the vulgar'.[48] Swift highlights a real problem of communication which blighted the dissemination of the Newtonian philosophy: 'no Body could understand' Newton's concepts, and yet to make his work accessible (by becoming a measly 'Instrument-Maker') would constitute a "dumbing down" for the sake of the lay person.[49] According to Barton and Conduitt, even Newton's own students at Cambridge would tease him, saying 'there goes the man who has writt a book that neither he nor any one else understands' ('Miscellanea', f. 2r).

Wagstaff's invective also attempts to devalue Newton by calling him an 'obscure Mechanick': a phrase recalling *The Drapier's Letters*, in which Wood the Wolverhampton businessman is goaded as 'a *poor, private, obscure Mechanick*' (*PW*, X, 41). The repetition of this derogatory epithet is unlikely to be a coincidence. Swift not only forges a connection between Newton's studies and the productions of vulgar manual workers as a rhetorical strategy, but also brings to mind the Wood's halfpence affair, through which (in Swift's satiric vision) the Master of the Mint has become socially and morally tainted. Sprat's *History of the Royal-Society* made great egalitarian claims that the newly formed institution would admit men of all religions, countries and professions. Although the Society in reality remained a high-class club of '*Gentlemen*, free, and unconfin'd' for many years, in ideological terms the precious realm of knowledge reserved for the gentleman-amateur began to erode, as natural philosophy itself became a profession.[50] The association of Newton with Wood might suggest to the reader that knowledge was drifting away from the confines of the aristocratic elite who had previously controlled the nature of its boundaries.

The intertextual echo of 'obscure Mechanick' demonstrates that Swift was barely able to conceal his anger at Newton for his role in the assay of Wood's halfpence. However, in *Gulliver's Travels*, published twelve years earlier, Newton is subtly caricatured rather than brazenly lampooned, although the strategies of diminution, especially through social class, are deployed against him here also. It is thought that the first and second voyages were written in 1721 and 1722, the fourth voyage mainly in 1723, and the third during 1724 and up to the autumn of 1725.[51] Composing the 'Voyage of Laputa' in the aftermath of the halfpence affair, what may have been conceived as a broad assault on the cultural obsession with the new sciences, and the ubiquity of the Newtonian philosophy, became for Swift an opportunity to also carry out savage attacks upon a man with whom he was deeply disappointed.

The royal court of Laputa, obsessed with mathematics and music, and hovering at a distance far above its imperial subjects on Balnibarbi, is usually read as a satire upon the ruling Hanoverian house and Whig regime, and there are numerous identifiable political parallels.[52] Among the many topical references, the most critically accepted allusion to Newton involves the 'Taylor' commanded by the Laputian King to measure Gulliver for a suit of clothes, although the episode can also be read more generally as an attack on the impractical nature of mathematical studies. After taking Gulliver's measurements by quadrant, rule and compasses, the 'Taylor' produces clothes 'very ill made, and quite out of Shape, by happening to mistake a Figure in the Calculation' (*PW*, XI, 162). Walter Scott claims that this passage refers to the printer's error in Newton's calculation of the distance between the Earth and the Sun, a correction of which appeared in the *Amsterdam Gazette*. This suggestion is accepted by most critics, although Nicolson and Mohler argue that Swift is also satirizing the interest in determining altitude.[53] If Scott's identification of the 'Taylor' as Newton is correct, it is at least worth bearing in mind that the most significant and publicly embarrassing error in the *Principia*'s first edition actually concerned resisted motion. Discovered by Johann Bernoulli, the French mathematician and friend of Leibniz, and publicly declared by his nephew Nikolaus whilst visiting London in September 1712, Newton realized that the mistake was due to a more fundamental flaw in his reasoning, and would involve extensive work, especially because the proof of the new result would need to exactly fit the space allotted in the *Principia*'s second edition (1713), which was already printed.[54]

The context of Bernoulli and Leibniz as Newton's philosophical opponents may also go some way towards accounting for Gulliver's explanation that the Taylor 'did his Office after a different Manner from those of his Trade in *Europe*' (*PW*, XI, 162), offering an alternative (or supplement) to the usual suggestion of the Newtonian/Cartesian dichotomy. The Leibniz-Newton controversy concerning the discovery of calculus was a more direct source of opposition between British and continental thought at this time: a dispute which readers may have brought to mind when Gulliver mentions the 'Custom of our Learned in *Europe* to steal Inventions from each other' (*PW*, XI, 185). Despite the death of Leibniz in 1716, it is clear that the severe animosity had not subsided by the time of the *Travels*.[55] Meanwhile, presenting Newton in this lowly occupation would not only be appropriate in relation to his publication and calculation difficulties, but also pour scorn on him through diminishing his professional status and superior mathematical ability to the level of a mere artisan, anticipating the strategy at work in *Polite Conversation*. Furthermore, that the 'Taylor' is commanded by the King of Laputa directly may imply Newton's biased role in the Wood affair, or more generally, his patronage by the Whig administration (which rewarded him for acting as an advisor in mining, navigational and astronomical affairs).[56]

Confirming that class prejudice was a well-used satiric weapon in Swift's arsenal, the attack on John Partridge in the *Bickerstaff Papers* and its related poems makes much of the astrologer's previous profession as a cobbler. In the first paper, Bickerstaff laments how wretchedly the 'noble

Art' of astrology is treated by 'a few mean illiterate Traders between us and the Stars' (*PW*, II, 141). For Bickerstaff, Partridge's mercantile origins function as a metonym for his whole approach to this discipline of knowledge. In 'An Elegy on Mr. *Partrige*, the Almanack-maker', Swift condemns judicial astrology through mock-heroically transforming it into an empirical science, and uses Partridge's lowly status to confirm the absurdity of this exaggeration. The speaker wonders 'How *Partrige* made his *Opticks* rise, / From a *Shoe Sole* to reach the Skies' (ll. 21–22, in *Poems*, I, 98), and makes several attempts to demonstrate 'the near Alliance / 'Twixt *Cobling* and the *Planet Science*' (ll. 29–30):

> A Scrap of Parchment hung by *Geometry,*
> A great Refinement in *Barometry,*
> Can like the Stars foretel the Weather;
> And what is *Parchment* else but *Leather*? (ll. 41–44)

Astrology is not only an artificial product manufactured specifically for the marketplace, but developments in natural knowledge (in this case, '*Barometry*') render it obsolete and explode its authority.

Whether intentional or otherwise, Partridge, the astrologer and 'cobbler', is linked intertextually with Newton, the illustrious natural philosopher and now miscalculating 'Taylor'. Moreover, in *Polite Conversation* Wagstaff describes Newton's geometrical diagrams as a series of 'Pot-hooks and Hangers' (*PW*, IV, 123): a conceit Swift previously employed in *Predictions for the Year 1708*, where Bickerstaff complains of 'common Astrologers' whose charts use 'a few Pot-hooks for Planets to amuse the Vulgar' (*PW*, II, 149). Swift seeks to belittle the work of both Partridge and Newton through equating dependence upon the market economy with poor 'scientific' proficiency, and the occupational similarity implies a short practical distance between their disciplines (whilst concealing a vast conceptual difference). The verbal echoes and discursive similarities which resonate across and between these texts, if not revealing intentional moments of association, at least show that the ostensible affinity of astrology and astronomy (in their 'trading in the stars') suggested to Swift that similar strategies of deflation could be pursued in relation to both forms of celestial knowledge in order to pierce the overblown cultural images of Partridge and Newton.

After meeting with the 'Taylor', Gulliver's account of the Laputians goes on to observe that 'Most of them, and especially those who deal in the Astronomical Part, have great Faith in judicial Astrology, although they are ashamed to own it publickly' (*PW*, XI, 164). This is also often read as a joke at Newton's expense but the reasons why have not been expounded. While the association of astronomy and astrology might have a broader aim – to associate natural philosophers in general with cultural deception and outmoded beliefs – the possibility that Swift is taking another swipe at Newton is at least worth considering. Swift may have been simply creating a rumour from scratch. For instance, Edmond Halley (1656–1742) was the victim of such a slur in the *Bickerstaff Papers*:

> in the Year 1686, a Man of Quality shewed me, written in his *Album*, that the most learned Astronomer Captain *Hally*, assured him, he would never believe any thing of the Stars Influence, if there were not a great Revolution in *England* in the Year 1688. (*PW*, II, 149)

This perhaps glances at how Partridge predicted James II's death in late 1688, and justified its non-fulfilment through an allegorical reading.[57] Halley had no interest in astrology, and it is suggested that Swift is merely 'perpetrating a bit of gratuitous mischief' by obliquely referring to the feud between Halley and John Flamsteed (1646–1719), the Astronomer Royal, which was at its height in the year Swift was writing as Bickerstaff.[58] For satiric purposes, the predictive element of Halley's cometary calculations is equated with divine forecasts. Flamsteed receives similar treatment in 'The Progress of Beauty' (c. 1719), where his 'Skill' (with all its lower class connotations) in telescopic observation is associated with the horoscopes of Partridge and his rival astrologer and personal and political enemy, the High Church Royalist John Gadbury (ll. 85–100, in *Poems*, I, 228–29).[59]

Newton's case is slightly different to that of Halley or Flamsteed, however, in that Newton confessed to an early interest in astrology, although his cometography would ultimately lead to the downfall of celestial divination.[60] According to Conduitt, in 1663 Newton acquired an astrological book at Sturbridge fair. Newton's urge to understand the book's mathematical explanations inspired him to study mathematics seriously and he was 'soon convinced of the vanity & emptiness of the pretended science of Iudicial astrology'.[61] This might be another occasion upon which Barton had been a useful source of biographical knowledge. Nevertheless, associating Newton with astrological quackery attempts to move a figure of status, power and celebrity into the intellectual and social margins. It is now thought that Swift attacked Partridge principally because his almanacs reflected his radical Whig Protestantism: his astrology *per se* was merely an easy target.[62] Highlighting Newton's alleged belief in astrology in the 'Voyage to Laputa' perhaps follows a comparable satiric method.

If it is accepted that the reference to the 'hypocrisy' of the Laputian astronomers (in their public proclamations of enlightened progress but private 'Faith' in occult disciplines) is another attack on Newton, then the rest of the paragraph could be explained in a similar fashion, and confirms why it is 'judicial' rather than 'natural' astrology which the Laputians secretly practise, tallying with their political aspirations. That the Laputian mathematicians are 'perpetually enquiring into publick Affairs, giving their Judgments in Matters of State' finds parallels in Newton's assay and perhaps also in the 'Political arithmetick' of John Graunt and (especially) Sir William Petty. An anatomist, founder fellow of the Royal Society, and inspirer and President of the Dublin Philosophical Society, Petty (1623–87) argued that all affairs could be expressed in 'Terms of *Number, Weight,* or *Measure*'.[63] Crucially, Petty applied this methodology to Ireland in a number of topographical and demographical studies, most notoriously in what became known as the Down Survey: the Cromwellian settlement that reallocated the forfeited Irish property of the Civil War rebels (over 8 million acres) to English (and usually Protestant) soldiers and investors.[64] Petty's impulse to value human beings, particularly the Irish, in merely financial terms was clearly parodied in *A Modest Proposal* (1729),[65] but the moral extremes to which the approach could be taken are also exploited in a much earlier piece, *An Argument against Abolishing Christianity* (1708), which responds to the claim 'there are, by Computation, [...] above Ten thousand Parsons; whose Revenues added to those of my Lords the Bishops, would suffice to maintain, at least, two Hundred young Gentleman of Wit and Pleasure, and Free-thinking' (*PW*, II, 30).

An emphasis on narrative credibility through quantification is a common trope in the *Travels* – Gulliver weighs and measures the gigantic hailstones in Brobdingnag, for instance – yet in that same country 'Political arithmetick' becomes an object of direct satire when the King laughs at the 'odd Kind of Arithmetick [...] in reckoning the Numbers of our People by a Computation' (*PW*, XI, 117, 131). In Laputa, the target is broadened to encompass interventions such as Newton's assay, when Gulliver, this time as a satiric mouthpiece, remarks:

> I could never discover the least Analogy between the two Sciences [mathematics and politics]; unless those People suppose, that because the smallest Circle hath as many Degrees as the largest, therefore the Regulation and Management of the World require no more Abilities than the handling and turning of a Globe. (*PW*, XI, 164)[66]

Unlike Plato's *Republic*, which argues (in the words of Arbuthnot) that 'whoever is to be educated for magistracy, or any considerable post in the commonwealth, may be instructed first in arithmetic, then in geometry, and thirdly in astronomy', the 'Voyage to Laputa' implies that power is placed in the hands of even the greatest (natural) philosopher at one's peril.[67] The specularly disadvantaged Laputians are responsible for the political subordination and financial exploitation of Balnibarbi through literally 'turning a blind eye'.

While Swift's caricatures of Newton often rely upon occupational and social diminution for their satiric effect, there seems to be a paradox in this line of attack, for what is often missing from Laputian society is the practical application of their knowledge. As well as hearing the 'Musick of the Spheres' (*PW*, XI, 162), the Laputians also exhibit the extreme idealism associated with the Pythagoreans.[68] Even their food is served in geometrical form, such as 'a Shoulder of Mutton, cut into an Æquilateral Triangle' (*PW*, XI, 161): a joke shared with the *Memoirs*, where Martinus's 'disposition to the Mathematicks was discover'd very early, by his drawing parallel lines on his bread and butter' (pp. 107–108). However, despite the Laputians' attention to culinary detail, they fail to address current problems or make provision for future needs. The citizens of Balnibarbi are generally in poverty (*PW*, XI, 175), and their houses

> are very ill built, the Walls bevil, without one right Angle in any Apartment; and this Defect ariseth from the Contempt they bear for practical Geometry; which they despise as vulgar and mechanick, those Instructions they give being too refined for the Intellectuals of their Workmen. (*PW*, XI, 163)

Laputian mathematics is in stark contrast to the Brobdingnagian, which is 'wholly applied to what may be useful in Life; to the Improvement of Agriculture and all mechanical Arts' (*PW*, XI, 136). Swift's satiric norm suggests that it is only through the *appropriate* application of mathematical knowledge in the external world, in which theorists work with labourers and 'Mechanick[s]', that real 'Improvement' can be achieved. Many of the Lagadan experiments imply that science must be in accordance with common sense and inductive reasoning, with natural philosophers validating their methods through experience. For instance, extracting 'Sun-Beams out of Cucumbers' (*PW*, XI, 179) might be theoretically possible, but the absurdity of this pursuit arises from its impracticality (the mismanagement of available resources). Lord Munodi, with his 'magnificent, regular and polite' properties, possessions and conduct (*PW*, XI, 175), similarly makes explicit that Swift gives value to learning which usefully assists in everyday experience, rather than knowledge that only seems advantageous to scientific experiment.[69]

For Swift, the futile experiments of the Lagadan Academy and the flawed sampling in Newton's assay of the halfpence, as well as Petty's 'Political arithmetick', each constitute significant misuses of 'Modern' learning. However, Swift is not (or not *only*) making a distinction between pure and applied disciplines, or between abstraction and common sense, although Swift was certainly suspicious that natural philosophers may not fulfil their utilitarian claims.[70] Instead, Swift argues that when the new sciences are employed in practical projects political, social, and moral choices are inevitably involved. This argument goes some way towards confirming that the caricatures of Newton in the 'Voyage to Laputa' and *Polite Conversation* are not attacks upon the culture of natural philosophy *per se*, but perhaps the result of Swift's continued vengeance against the Master of the Mint.

The Occasion of Lindalino

The political and moral dimensions of applying natural knowledge are thrown into stark relief when Gulliver divulges more about the flying island itself. The Laputians as a population are barely able to socially interact, let alone find practical uses for their speculations, and yet the island's magnetic properties have been exploited for military purposes. The King uses the advanced technologies of Laputa to keep control of his kingdom below, and it has been argued that the island's operation draws upon not only William Gilbert's *De Magnete* (1600), but also pseudoscientific and mystical speculations on magnetism and voyages to the Moon.[71] In addition, there are elements in Gulliver's report which burlesque accounts of magnetic experiments and geographical surveys that Swift might have come across in the *Philosophical Transactions*.[72]

By ordering the island to be hovered above Balnibarbi, the King can even deprive his subjects of the sun and rain, consequently afflicting them with 'Dearth and Diseases' (*PW*, XI, 171): probably a reference to England's repressive laws of trade against Ireland.[73] Most significantly we are told that 'This Load-stone is under the Care of certain Astronomers, who from Time to Time give it such Positions as the Monarch directs' (*PW*, XI, 170), a statement which brings to mind Newton's involvement with Wood's patent: a scientist commanded by the government to aid the continued oppression of the provinces. The island itself may allude to one of Newton's discoveries. Gulliver mentions that Laputa has a diameter of 7837 yards (*PW*, XI, 167), and if one substitutes miles for yards, as Nicolson and Mohler suggest, it gives a figure almost exactly like Newton's estimate of the Earth's diameter.[74] In the proportion of its spatial dimensions, the magnetic island is therefore literally a *terrella* ('little earth'), as Swift continues to play with scale in lands far beyond Lilliput and Brobdingnag.

It is also unlikely that Swift arbitrarily decided that the great load-stone would be 'in Shape resembling a Weaver's Shuttle' (*PW*, XI, 168). By domesticating this technology of the foreign 'other' through direct comparison with European invention, Gulliver's description resembles the rhetorical strategies of many essays published in the *Philosophical Transactions*.[75] More importantly, however, this detail confirms that the magnet and the elevated land mass which it controls act in part as a symbol of Britain's economic grip over Ireland. Indeed, Corolini's *Key* (1726), published by Edmund Curll, identified the load-stone as 'a just Emblem of the *British* Linen and Woollen Manufactures'.[76] The Navigation Acts of the Restoration designated Ireland the status of a colony, meaning that its exports had to be loaded in English ships at English ports, with heavy duties placed on Irish livestock. This dire economic situation was compounded by the Woollen Act (1699) which, by banning the export of Irish manufactured woollen garments, and permitting the export of raw wool to only a few specified English ports, decimated the country's most thriving industry.[77] Swift, for whom the 'woollen manufacture of this kingdom sate always nearest [his] heart' (*PW*, XIII, 90), thought the Irish themselves were making the situation worse: in several tracts supporting Dublin weavers he appealed to the fashionable classes to purchase 'home-manufactures' rather than appearing to desire to wear only imports. In 'A Letter to the Archbishop of Dublin, concerning the Weavers' (c. 1729) Swift even misogynistically jokes: 'if the Virtuosi could once find out a world in the Moon, with a passage to it, our women would wear nothing but what directly came from thence' (*PW*, XII, 67). The Laputians' skill in harnessing this natural power, by placing a 'very strong Axle of Adamant' through the middle of the load-stone, means that it is 'poized so exactly that the weakest Hand can turn it'. The potential physical frailty of the controller emphasizes acutely how technical expertise can offer immense political and military power and, furthermore, how this authority is wielded by those of a higher class and more delicate disposition (and it is tempting to suggest that this corporeal feebleness also seeks to imply moral failings).

There are other topical allusions one might consider, although they range in their determinacy. The Laputian astronomers have, for instance, produced a 'Catalogue of ten Thousand fixed Stars' (*PW*, XI, 170). As Paul Turner argues, their success invites comparison with Flamsteed's catalogue of 2935 stars (the publication of which had instigated a feud between the Astronomer Royal and Newton), and Corolini's *Key* thought the rarities in the '*Astronomers Cave*' resembled those present at Flamsteed's observatory at Greenwich.[78] The operators of the load-stone have also 'observed Ninety-three different Comets, and settled their Periods with great Exactness'. Gulliver hopes that 'If this be true', the astronomers would make their work public so that the 'Theory of Comets, which at present is very lame and defective' in Europe would be 'brought to the same Perfection with other Parts of Astronomy' (*PW*, XI, 171). Halley was the most famous cometographer, publishing calculations of orbits in *Astronomiae Cometicae Synopsis* (1705), but in highlighting the difficulty of predicting cometary motions Swift might have in mind a passage he would have come across in the *Principia*, where Newton admits his cometographical work needs more data:

> because of the great number of comets, and the great distance of their aphelia from the sun, and the long time that they spend in their aphelia, they should be disturbed somewhat by their gravities toward one another [...]. Accordingly, it is not to be expected that the same comet will return exactly in the same orbit, and with the same periodic times. (Book III, Proposition 42, pp. 936–37)

Given such problems, Newton might have indulged in Gulliver's fantasy of immortality in Luggnagg: 'What wonderful Discoveries should we make in Astronomy, by outliving and confirming our own Predictions; by observing the Progress and Returns of Comets' (*PW*, XI, 210).

It is tempting to find irony at work in Swift's allusion to the 'Perfection' of Laputian/Newtonian astronomy. Swift would be suspicious of any system of knowledge claiming absolute truth, but in *Thoughts on Various Subjects* he admits that 'The Motions of the Sun and Moon; in short, the whole System of the Universe, as far as Philosophers have been able to discover and observe, are in the utmost Degree of Regularity and Perfection' (*PW*, IV, 245). This ideal cosmology, however, reflects the wisdom and power of its Creator, not of its observers. Gulliver's account also raises questions of scientific and narrative authority. He acknowl-edges that he cannot confirm if the astronomers really have observed this number of comets and correctly calculated their periods of orbit, but only report the 'Confidence' with which they make these assertions. Moreover, whilst the operators of the loadstone claim to have achieved exceptional cometographical knowledge, Gulliver earlier learnt that the Laputians have calculated that in 31 years' time a comet 'will probably destroy us':

> if in its Perihelion it should approach within a certain Degree of the Sun, (as by their Calculations they have Reason to dread) it will conceive a Degree of Heat ten Thousand Times more intense than that of red hot glowing Iron; and in its Absence from the Sun, carry a blazing Tail Ten Hundred Thousand and Fourteen Miles long; through which if the Earth should pass at the Distance of one Hundred Thousand Miles from the *Nucleus*, or main Body of the Comet, it must in its Passage be set on Fire, and reduced to Ashes. (*PW*, XI, 164–65)

Despite the numerical precision and elaborate nomenclature contained within the Laputians' predictions, the conjectural nature of their theories is made plain. Even if the knowledge of such catastrophes could be acted upon, there are far too many conditionals in their projections to take these anxieties seriously. Meanwhile, the simple astronomy of the Houyhnhnms, able to 'calculate the Year by the Revolution of the Sun and the Moon, but use no Subdivisions into Weeks [...] and understand the Nature of *Eclipses*' (*PW*, XI, 273), prevents unnecessary panic.

In Gulliver's account of the load-stone, connections between the officer-astronomers and Newton, and the flying island and British imperial power, are clearly suggested. In the episode involving Laputa and Balnibarbi's second city of Lindalino, these links are fundamental to its satiric integrity. Gulliver tells of the Laputians' discovery that Lindalino, assumed to represent Dublin, had devised a form of resistance against the flying island which (ironically) attracts the great load-stone of the flying island towards the city:

> the Inhabitants [...] erected four large Towers, one at every Corner of the City (which is an exact Square), equal in Height to a strong pointed Rock that stands directly in the Center [...] Upon the Top of each Tower, as well as upon the Rock, they fixed a great Loadstone, and in case their Design should fail, they had provided a vast Quantity of the most combustible Fewel, hoping to burst therewith the adamantine Bottom of the Island, if the Loadstone Project should miscarry. (*PW*, XI, 309)

After informing the King 'a general Council was called, and the Officers of the Loadstone ordered to attend', at which

> One of the oldest and expertest among them obtained leave to try an Experiment. He took a strong Line of an Hundred Yards, and the Island being raised over the Town above the attracting Power they had felt, He fastened a Piece of Adamant to the End of his Line which had in it a Mixture of Iron mineral, of the same Nature with that whereof the Bottom or lower Surface of the Island is composed, and from the lower Gallery let it down slowly towards the Top of the Towers. The Adamant was not descended four Yards, before the Officer felt it drawn so strongly downwards, that he could hardly pull it back. He then threw down several small Pieces of Adamant, and observed that they were all violently attracted by the Top of the Tower. The same Experiment was made on the other three Towers, and on the Rock with the same Effect. (*PW*, XI, 309–10)

The magnetic 'Experiment' itself, and Gulliver's impartial recording of it, resemble accounts given in the *Philosophical Transactions* and, perhaps crucially, in his friend Helsham's Trinity College Dublin lectures (which had contradicted Newton's account of the ratio between magnetic attraction and distance).[79] Gulliver states the length of the line and the particular chemical composition of the adamant used. After the initial investigation the astronomer carries out a control test without the 'strong Line', and then repeats the first test on 'the other three Towers, and on the Rock'.

Arthur E. Case's allegorical interpretation of the episode, in which the 'four large Towers' signify the Grand Jury, the Irish Privy Council, and the two Houses of the Irish Parliament, does not identify this 'officer of the loadstone', and merely states that the unsuccessful experiment represents the bold resistance of the Irish institutions.[80] However, it can be of no coincidence that in a passage which seems to allude to the attempted introduction of Wood's halfpence, an experiment takes place using a sample of material in order to determine the magnetic force at work, 'assaying' the adamant below the flying island. That it is the 'oldest and expertest among them' hints at the elderly Newton as Master of the Mint, conducting the assay of Wood's coinage for the Privy Council. Swift depicts the assay as an experiment on attractive forces (although magnetic rather than gravitational) in order to reinforce the allusion to Newton. Like the assay, the officer's experiment does nothing to relieve the situation. The King's response to the rebellion to command 'all the

Inhabitants of the Island to cast great Stones from the lower gallery into the Town' (*PW*, XI, 309) – bombardment with projectiles that makes use of gravity – is at the very least a coincidence when one considers that the Royal Treasury's answer to Irish concerns about Wood's coinage was to engage the efforts of Newton.

The Lindalino episode was not published during Swift's lifetime, and until the 1890s existed only in manuscript in Ford's interleaved copy of the first edition. The passage was probably one of many additions composed by Swift in early 1727. For the first edition, the publisher Benjamin Motte had requested Andrew Tooke to draft alternative passages for the more controversial materials, and for Motte's next edition Swift had hoped to use his own substitutes and bridging passages for the 'mangled and murdered Pages'. However, these additions, including the Lindalino episode, were too late to be included, and Swift could not locate this fragment when preparing George Faulkner's 1735 edition.[81] Given the rebellious action it depicts, this passage would have been just as unlikely to receive publication even then.

While Michael Treadwell has convincingly related the circumstances which prevented the episode's publication, F. P. Lock once suggested that its continued omission was intentional on Swift's part, not due to its potentially controversial nature, but for aesthetic reasons: 'It is really a rejected idea [...] Its narrative mode is quite unsuited [because] it invites detailed allegorical interpretation in a way that most of *Gulliver's Travels* does not'. Lock is particularly critical of Case's interpretation involving the 'four large Towers' because he finds it strange that such different institutions are represented identically. Moreover, the passage 'contains nothing and no one that can stand for either the Drapier, Wood, the halfpence, or the Duchess of Kendal'.[82] Lock overlooks the role played by Newton in the affair, neglects the way in which *The Drapier's Letters* conflate Wood, Walpole, George I and the Privy Council as a rhetorical strategy, and defines allegory in a way that is probably too restrictive for the *Travels'* complex symbolic matrix of satiric referents. Whatever the 'Towers' of Lindalino specifically represent (if anything), it is clear that Swift composed the adamant experiment with Newton's assay in mind. Swift emphasizes the importance of Newton's role in the halfpence affair, showing how 'science' has aided colonial oppression, literalized in the island's downward force. And this fragment was probably drafted at a time very close to the scientist's death, which his friend Pope marked in a very different way, with the famous celebratory, hagiographic 'Epitaph. Intended for Sir Isaac Newton, In Westminster Abbey' (1730) brilliantly associating the *Opticks* (1704) with God's first act of creation.[83]

Some critics contend that few episodes in the *Travels* can be read allegorically because fully consistent schema cannot be found.[84] However, as Ehrenpreis has shown, even traditional allegories are works of multiple meanings that disrupt conventional modes of signification. Brean Hammond, moreover, suggests that Swift's awareness of the instability of allegory is present within the *Travels* itself, in that it functions as an 'allegorigenic' text which generates possibilities of allegorical reading, but also undermines the reader's attempts to interpret in such a way.[85] The identification of the 'oldest and expertest' astronomer with Newton is clearly made, but there is no developed characterization. Like the other possible references to Newton in the voyage, only certain aspects of his life or personality are drawn upon where necessary. The text resists a fully allegorical interpretation because other events in the whole affair are omitted. Gulliver states a wish 'to dwell no longer on other Circumstances' (*PW*, XI, 310), thereby suppressing the satiric allegory. The *Travels'* self-conscious concern with genre permits only a tantalizing glimpse of an allegorical narrative, but the reader is left with enough clues.

It is sometimes assumed that allegories are a symptom of artistic weakness, and that allegorical readings belie the complexity of the many modes of representation Swift used. One of Swift's supreme achievements is his ability to fulfil the demands of general and particular satire simultaneously. Swift often has a specific satiric object in mind, but from it he generates universal, ahistorical targets and implies general conclusions. Inconsistencies with the intricate details of the objects of representation will inevitably occur: the early readers Pope spoke to apparently thought the *Travels* 'rather too bold, and too general a Satire: but none that I hear of accuse it of particular reflections'.[86] However, it cannot be doubted that many topical allusions and allegorical schemes of some sort or another are present in Gulliver's narrative, and attempts to explicate them have been undertaken since the many 'Keys' which greeted the work soon after its arrival in the marketplace. Swift accommodates his specific objects to suit more general ends, but this does not mean that particular components must remain unidentified. It is in the strange blend of the specific with the general where the significance of these episodes lies. Allegorical readings should not be dismissed as the result of critical naivety, but accepted as a powerful way of intercepting *one* layer of a text's multivalent meaning.

Whatever the reason for the Lindalino episode's omission from editions during Swift's lifetime, the fragment nevertheless offers an insight into Swift's intentions during the mid-1720s, going some way in explaining the problems of satiric coherence many readers have encountered in Gulliver's accounts of Laputa and Balnibarbi. Critics have wondered, for instance, why Irish affairs become a central concern, but the state of the country is blamed upon both scientific and commercial projects.[87] Perhaps more than any other passage composed for the voyage, the episode demonstrates the reason these elements are connected. In this light, the satire on mathematics and other scientific disciplines in this book is less the result of a clash between two world-views and more a personal vendetta against the country's leading natural philosopher.

According to Edward Said, too many claims are made for viewing Swift as a 'moralist and thinker who peddled one or another final view of human nature, whereas not enough claims are made for Swift as a kind of local activist, a columnist, a pamphleteer, a caricaturist'. There are inconsistencies in Swift's ideological values because he was primarily engaged in 'particular struggles of a very limited sort'.[88] Discussing the preparation of Faulkner's edition with Ford, Swift himself acknowledges that many of his works were 'temporary occasional things, that dye naturally with the Change of times' (20 November 1733, in *CJS*, III, 709). Swift reacts to events in an immediate fashion and therefore the intentions of his 'local performances' (such as *The Drapier's Letters*) exist in the temporal sphere. The Lindalino episode, probably composed in early 1727, attempts at only a short temporal remove to write the history of this particular 'local performance' and its context.

The 'Voyage to Laputa' was finalized in the aftermath of the Wood affair and consequently much of the spirit of *The Drapier's Letters* is continued in this book, going some way in accounting for the particularly ferocious attack on science which many have found in Book III, and for its reputation as the least successful voyage of the *Travels*. Yet, as Gay and Pope reported, the differences between the voyage and the other three had led some to go so far as to question its authorship: 'they think the flying island is the least entertaining; and [...] 'tis agreed that part was not writ by the same hand' ([7] November 1726, in *CJS*, III, 47–48). Swift would reply that he himself found in the second volume (i.e. Books III and IV) 'several passages which appear to be patch'd and altered, and the style of a different sort' (17 November 1726, in *CJS*, III, 56), probably due to the interference of Motte and Tooke.[89] The reason for Book III's difference to the other voyages will never be truly known, and probably lies somewhere between these personal and textual circumstances.

It is perhaps no coincidence that the first dissenting voice regarding the voyage came from Arbuthnot, telling Swift that 'the part of the projectors is the least Brilliant' (5 November 1726, in *CJS*, III, 44). Although a fellow of the Royal Society, Arbuthnot was not averse to addressing aspects of scientific learning in a similarly fervent way in his own satires. What Arbuthnot may have found to his dislike is the very open personal attack upon a great natural philosopher he knew well. Arbuthnot had served on two Royal Society committees under Newton: his diplomatic skills were instrumental in arranging the publication of Flamsteed's catalogue, and he also worked on the inquiry that investigated John Keill's accusation that Leibniz's system of calculus plagiarized Newton's. Arbuthnot even appended an assay of modern foreign coins by 'that accurate person' Newton to his *Tables of Ancient Coins* (1727).[90] As one would expect given Arbuthnot's control over the scientific materials, Newton did not come under fire in the Scriblerian writings and, by implication, is actively supported in the *Memoirs*: one of Martinus's impractical schemes is to 'pierce the first crust or *Nucleus* of this our *Earth*, quite through, to the next concentrical Sphere [...] chiefly to refute Sir Isaac Newton's Theory of *Gravity*' (p. 168). Arbuthnot's criticism of the 'Voyage to Laputa' may also be due to disappointment that Swift had not consulted him for supplementary materials for Laputa when 'he could have added such abundance of things upon every subject', and had apparently ignored the advice to become 'aquainted w[t] some new improvements of mankind that have appeard of late'.[91]

While the 'Voyage to Laputa' is permeated with moments of particular satire, elsewhere in the *Travels* there appears to be more general reflection upon the vanity and impracticality of natural philosophy. In Houyhnhnmland, when Gulliver explains 'our several Systems of *Natural Philosophy*', his master laughs that 'a Creature pretending to *Reason*, should value itself upon the Knowledge of other Peoples Conjectures, and in Things, where that Knowledge, if it were certain, could be of no Use': an opinion that Gulliver compares to the 'Sentiments of *Socrates*', who prized ethical over natural knowledge (*PW*, XI, 267).[92] Likewise, in Gulliver's account of Glubbdubdrib, the island of necromancers, the events suggest that Swift the moralist and thinker rather than 'local performer' is responsible. Through the creation of a historical panorama of natural philosophy the text is explicit in its claims for offering an authoritative view. The ghost of Aristotle predicts that '*Attraction*, whereof the present Learned are such zealous Asserters' will be soon 'exploded', as his own system, and those of Gassendi and Descartes had been, because: 'new Systems of Nature were but new Fashions, which would vary in every Age; and even those who pretend to demonstrate them from Mathematical Principles, would flourish but a short Period of Time' (*PW*, XI, 198). Pope would offer a similar perspective in his *Imitations of Horace*:

> Sages and Chiefs long since had birth
> E're Caesar was, or Newton nam'd,
> These rais'd new Empires o'er the Earth,
> And Those new Heav'ns and Systems fram'd [...].[93]

It is difficult to untangle Pope's shades of irony in this quatrain, which threaten to characterize the great natural philosopher as the latest in a long line of mystics who make grand claims about the way of things; although, unlike Newton himself, his predecessors 'had no poet' (l. 14). Meanwhile, despite the universal and gnomic wisdom apparently on offer in Swift's often-quoted aphorism, the specificity of the ghost of Aristotle's comment cannot be ignored. The narrative situation gives the impression of detachment and objectivity, but it is clear that the Newtonian philosophy as outlined in the *Principia*, and distinguished above other 'Systems of Nature' by its basis in 'Mathematical Principles', is the target. In terms of its motivation, this assault is just as occasional as the Lindalino episode, but its specificity and vindictiveness is shrouded in a voice of common sense and moral dictum. This is not to say that Swift did not hold firm philosophical and theological principles with regards to the limits of human knowledge, but that in the 'Voyage to Laputa' these are often subsumed by more immediate concerns.

It is clear that Swift held Newton partly responsible for the attempt to impose Wood's coinage upon Ireland, and placed the scheme in the culture of commercialism that made use of the authority of Newtonian natural philosophy. In *The Drapier's Letters*, Swift therefore attempted to question Newton's reputation as the greatest mathematician. The 'Voyage to Laputa' sustains Swift's indignation, suggesting that any interpretation of his 'attack on science' in this instance must appreciate the specific political and economic motives behind it. In this satiric onslaught, Swift called upon various methods of deflation, including associating Newton and natural philosophy with discredited pseudosciences and the lower classes. Through identifying the oldest 'officer of the loadstone' as Newton, this chapter has shown how the Lindalino episode helps to increase the satiric coherence of the voyage. The general satiric targets of the 'Voyage to Laputa' – mathematics, natural philosophy and the Royal Society – were all intensely associated with Newton in early eighteenth-century public perception. In *A Discourse, To Prove the Antiquity of the English Tongue*, apparently written in the late 1720s, the narrator even remarks (ironically) that the entire discipline of mathematics expired at the time of Newton's death (*PW*, IV, 231). Any attack upon Newton 'the man' would undoubtedly also fall metonymically upon Newton 'the natural philosopher', and the institutions and philosophy he represented. It is sometimes argued that some scholars do not distinguish between the 'real' Newton and the fictional one imagined by his contemporaries.[94] However, Newton himself made use of his cultural persona, as Swift was well aware. Correspondingly, to unleash his full fury at Newton, the mathematician, natural philosopher, President of the Royal Society, and – most importantly in this case – Master of the Mint, Swift drew upon all the rhetorical strategies, scientific knowledge, even idle gossip, at his disposal.

5

Socinians and Queens: Samuel Clarke and 'Directions for a Birthday Song'

> The world is wider to a Poet than to any other Man, and new follyes and Vices will never be wanting any more than new fashions. Je donne au diable the wrong Notion [tha]t *Matter* is exhausted. For as Poets in their Greek Name are called Creators, so in one circumstance they resemble the great Creator by having an infinity of Space to work in.[1]

While Swift was always open to the figurative potency of philosophical notions, he made it plain he was no fan of metaphysics. He received *male* in the third-year examination on Aristotelian physics, and whilst writing to his cousin Thomas about their studies at Trinity College, declared: 'to enter upon causes of Philosophy is what I protest I will rather dy in a ditch than go about'.[2] This attitude did not alter with age. In 'The Dean's Reasons for Not Building at Drapier's Hill' (1730?), Swift maintains his anti-metaphysical pose. The poem appears to be Swift's last from the twenty-eight month period in which he stayed at the Gosford Estate with Sir Arthur and Lady Anne Acheson.[3] As the title implies, Swift had purchased land there with a view to erecting a house, but his relations with Sir Arthur had apparently become increasingly frosty, although he claimed to Pope that his change of mind was the result of having 'neither years, nor spirits, nor money, nor patience for such amusements'.[4] The speaker associates Acheson's aloofness with his philosophical interests, which are characterized as an unhealthy obsession:

> Still rapt in speculations deep,
> His outward senses fast asleep;
> [...]

> Beyond the skies transports his mind,
> And leaves a lifeless corpse behind. (ll. 45–46, 49–50,
> in *Poems*, III, 900)

This is a relatively cheap shot, relying upon the various meanings of 'rapt'. But this bed of meditation quickly becomes a tomb, and the dreaming philosopher a mummified carcass. Swift's neat octosyllabics and simple alliteration enact this sense of coolness and enclosure, and belie the meditative 'transportation' the subject seeks. Lying behind Swift's easy joke, however, is the empirical assumption that our 'outward senses' should be our guides, and must lead the way on this earth, not 'Beyond the skies'.

There is then an abrupt turn in thought, allied with a change in metre, with the speaker (who we assume is Swift himself) offering his personal perspective:

> But, as for me, who ne'er could clamber high,
> To understand Malebranche or Cambray;
> Who send my mind (as I believe) less
> Than others do, on errands sleeveless;
> [...]
> My spirits with my body progging,
> Both hand in hand together jogging,
> Sunk over head and ears in matter,
> Nor can of metaphysics smatter;
> Am more diverted with a quibble
> Than dreams of worlds intelligible;
> And think all notions too abstracted
> Are like the ravings of a crackt head; (ll. 51–54, 57–64)

Swift owned works of Nicolas Malebranche (1638–1715), and this poem suggests that he had also attempted to read the philosopher's adversary François de Salignac de La Mothe-Fénelon (1651–1715), Archbishop of Cambrai, perhaps whilst staying with Sheridan.[5] The mental action of contemplation is figured ironically as strenuous but purposeless physical activity, as 'clamber[ing]', 'progging', 'jogging', with an appropriate emphasis on the body: 'hand in hand', 'head and ears'. The poem highlights what Swift sees as the paradox within much philosophical discourse of the time: of retreating into the mind to contemplate the nature of matter. The confession of being 'more diverted with a quibble' is not surprising, coming from the writer of *A Proposal to Correct the*

English Tongue, but the Hudibrastic polysyllabic rhyme of this couplet was probably too tempting for Swift to resist. As one might also suspect, the poem says more about Swift's fickleness than Acheson's true character: less than two years before, the Dean told Pope that 'Sir A. is a man of sense, and a scholar'.[6]

Contemporary discourse with regards to the nature of matter (as well as other metaphysical subjects, such as cosmology, necessity, determinism, the nature of space), would inevitably have recourse to take into account the arguments of the Newtonian philosophy. There were many 'crackt head[s]' appropriating Newton's discoveries, especially in the production of physico-theologies. Such applications became more and more sophisticated, none more so than in the writings of Samuel Clarke (1675–1729). This theologian soon came to Newton's attention, and he would go on to defend and help shape the Newtonian philosophy in reaction to the attacks of Newton's great continental rival, Gottfried Wilhelm Leibniz (1646–1716), in a correspondence mediated through Caroline of Anspach, Princess of Wales (Queen from 1727). However, Clarke was a controversial thinker, and his heterodoxy became associated with Newtonian ideas. This chapter argues that allusions to atomism in the poem 'Directions for a Birthday Song' (c. 1729) suggest that Swift was aware of the Leibniz-Clarke debates and the potentially materialist implications of Newtonian metaphysics. At a time when Court Whig discourse often employed natural philosophy to legitimate the Hanoverian succession, Swift uses scientific tropes to condemn the court of George II and Caroline. 'Directions' is revealed to be a damning assault upon Clarke's theology, connecting the increasingly politicized Newtonianism to the growth of heretical ideas that challenged both church and state.

Socinians and Queens

Clarke was one of the first to grasp the Newtonian philosophy, with his Latin translation of the *Opticks* appearing in 1706. Chaplain to the Bishop of Norwich, Clarke came to prominence when he was invited to deliver the Boyle lectures of 1704. The success of these sermons resulted in his promotion to Chaplain in Ordinary to Queen Anne, and from 1709 he was granted the rectorship of St James's, Westminster (which included Newton as a trustee).[7] His lectures, published as *A Demonstration of the Being and Attributes of God* (1705), returned to the Newtonian-influenced approach of Bentley, basing his initial proofs of God's existence in cosmological argument. It is believed that Clarke was responding in particular to the deist John Toland's misappropriations of the Newtonian philosophy, which included identifying gravity as a quality inherent in all bodies rather than superadded by God.[8] While Clarke used the traditional *a posteriori* argument to prove God's intelligence (that the order and beauty of the universe must have been created by a wise being), he also introduces more original demonstrations, derived from our conceptions of the infinity of space and time. Clarke shows that infinity and eternity must exist because we cannot remove these concepts from our minds, and the substance which possesses such attributes must be God.[9] For Clarke, appeals to reason are most successful when they appropriate the firm logic of mathematics, and his arguments abound in mathematical principles and analogies.[10]

His lectures were well received generally and he was asked to deliver a second set of sermons the following year, published as *A Discourse Concerning the Unchangeable Obligations of Natural Religion* (1706). Clarke's focus in these lectures moved from targeting atheism to arguing with deism, as he sought to demonstrate the intrinsic nature of morality and the necessity of the Christian revelation. For Clarke, his opponents included the author of the *Tale*, a work which turned 'every thing [...] into ridicule and mockery'.[11] If Swift did become aware of Clarke's view of the *Tale*, this personal grievance would have compounded more significant concerns. In 1712 Clarke published *The Scripture-Doctrine of the Trinity*, which argued from metaphysics that the Father and Son could not be of one substance, meaning that '*absolutely Supreme Honour* is due to the Person of the *Father* singly'. Contradicting the Nicene and Athanasian Creeds, Clarke's beliefs resemble those of Arius, the early fourth-century priest, whose opinions are known through three orations against his followers by Athanasius of Alexandria.[12] The Arianistic character of *The Scripture-Doctrine* was quickly seized upon by several High Churchmen. In 1713 Clarke was dismissed as one of Anne's chaplains and in June the following year he became subject to a formal complaint from the Lower House of Convocation.[13] Although he was not prosecuted, his advancement in the church was severely damaged. There is evidence to suggest that Clarke's heterodoxy became a hot topic in the Scriblerian circle at this time: in a letter to Thomas Parnell, Gay mentions that 'Esdras Barnivelt' complains of 'Dr Clarke's Book of the Trinity'.[14] 'Barnivelt' is the pseudonym Pope uses for *A Key to the Lock* (1715), and Pope's later attacks on Clarke suggest that Gay is indeed referring to his Scriblerian friend.

Clarke's acquaintance William Whiston had been more open about his heterodox beliefs. Like Clarke, Whiston was an early supporter

of Newton's ideas and in *A New Theory of the Earth* (1696) used them
to propose that a comet's close proximity to the Earth brought about
the Deluge and would cause the Apocalypse (a theory satirized in the
'Voyage to Laputa' and numerous Scriblerian pieces).[15] Whiston succeeded Newton as Lucasian Professor of Mathematics at Cambridge in
1703 and popularized the Newtonian philosophy through his coffee-
house lectures of the 1710s, some of which were attended by Pope.[16]
However, in 1708 Whiston was formally charged with heresy following
his Boyle lectures of the previous year (published as *The Accomplishment
of Scripture Prophecies*), reaching trial in July 1713, and in the mean-
time lost the Lucasian chair. His *Primitive Christianity Reviv'd* (1711)
confirmed any suspicion of Arianism, and in the preface he mentions
discoursing with 'an excellent Friend of mine whom I have not liberty
to name, [...] and another Person of great Eminence [...] particularly
about the then so much disputed Doctrine of the Trinity', likely to be
Clarke and Newton. Buoyed by Whiston's comments, rumours began to
surface that Newton shared similar beliefs to his follower.[17]

Of course, we now know with certainty that Newton did question
the authenticity of the doctrine of the Trinity, which depended upon
I John 5.7 and I Timothy 3.16. Despite keeping his most explicit anti-
Trinitarian writings in manuscript, Newton himself did not help matters
regarding the rumours. The General Scholium of the *Principia*'s second
edition (1713) appeared to support Clarke's *Scripture-Doctrine* of the
previous year: '"god" is a relative word and has reference to servants,
and godhood is the lordship of God, not over his own body [...] but
over servants'.[18] Could Newton be describing Christ and the Holy Spirit
as the 'servants' of God who are not of the same 'body'? According
to Larry Stewart, the heterodox conclusions of the General Scholium
were 'utterly transparent' by the end of Anne's reign, as is evident in
the many High Church attacks on Newton's philosophy. Whiston and
Clarke (and by implication, Newton) were perceived to be reviving the
Arian heresy, and Newtonian metaphysics itself was by some accused to
be the foundation of such unorthodox views.[19]

Swift was certainly aware of Whiston's anti-Trinitarian beliefs. In
Mr. C—ns's Discourse of Free-Thinking (1713), Swift groups Whiston with
'free-thinking' deists like the eponymous Anthony Collins. The narrator, 'a Friend' of Collins, laments that rather than prosecuting him,
'why might not poor Mr. *Whiston*, who denies the Divinity of Christ,
be allow'd to come into the Lower House of Convocation, and convert
the Clergy?' (*PW*, IV, 31). There is some exaggeration at work here, in
that Whiston did not deny Christ's divinity explicitly, but is given the

epithet of 'Socinian' (*PW*, IV, 34). Unlike Arians, Socinians did deny the divinity of Christ, believing that it was through his act of sacrifice on the Cross that he was exalted to the right hand of God. Socinians also rejected the immortality of the soul and God's foreknowledge of future events. Neither denials tally with Whiston's views, but both 'Arian' and 'Socinian' were used interchangeably as terms of abuse for those accused of questioning Christ's status or of interpreting Scripture too radically, and Swift's categorizations follow this trend.[20] Indeed, Swift's satire makes little differentiation between various philosophical or theological positions: '*Atheists, Deists, Scepticks* and *Socinians*' are all condemned together, and their challenge to church and state is associated with a Whiggish impulse. Swift's amplification of the specific nature of Whiston's heterodoxy forms part of the work's general hyperbolic vision of attacks on Christianity.[21] For Swift, it is not only that such heterodox writings exist, but also that there are so many of them in print. The narrator notes that Whiston has produced 'several Tracts' questioning the Trinity, leading to the proposition that 'If Ten thousand Free Thinkers thought differently [...] they would be all Duty bound to publish their Thoughts [...] though it broke the Peace of the Church and State, Ten thousand times' (*PW*, IV, 36). As the irony of this passage implies, Swift was in favour of censoring works which denied the shared doctrines of Christianity.[22]

In his sermon *On the Trinity*, Swift is particularly critical of the incursions of logic into the re-interpretation of Christian doctrine, appearing to refer explicitly to Clarke's method:

> Since the World abounds with pestilent Books, particularly written against this Doctrine of the Trinity; it is fit to inform you, that the Authors of them proceed wholly upon a Mistake: They would shew how impossible it is that *Three* can be One, and *One* can be Three; whereas the Scripture saith no such Thing, at least in that manner they would make it. (*PW*, IX, 167)

These considerations of the Trinity 'by Rules of Philosophy [...] have multiplied Controversies to such a Degree, as to beget Scruples that have perplexed the Minds of many sober Christians' (*PW*, IX, 160). Of all the contemporary attacks upon Christianity, Swift found the questioning of the Trinity to be the most serious, and such speculation receives another damning assault in *Thoughts on Religion*: 'the proceedings of the Socinians are both vain and unwarrantable; because they will be never able to advance their own opinion, or meet any other success than breeding doubts' (*PW*, IX, 261). For Swift, there is no difference between Arian or Socinian beliefs and atheism, since Christ's divinity is an essential Christian doctrine. Although he is here considering 'Socinianism' as a historical phenomenon, it is likely that he also has some contemporary targets – including Whiston, and perhaps Clarke – in mind.

According to Joseph Spence, Pope had similarly complained that metaphysicians 'from Clarke down to Jacob Behman, have all (almost equally) platonized and corrupted the truth' that 'is to be learned only from the Bible, [...] without the wresting of commentators or the additions of schoolmen'. It is normally assumed that Pope gave vent to his concerns about Clarke's philosophy in the fourth book of *The Dunciad*, which includes a 'gloomy Clerk' who has rejected reasoning *a posteriori*:

> Let others creep by timid steps, and slow,
> On plain Experience lay foundations low,
> By common sense to common knowledge bred,
> And last, to Nature's Cause thro' Nature led.[23]

Instead, the Clerk takes 'the high Priori Road', deducing the being and attributes of God by 'reason[ing] downward' from first principles and ignoring experience (ll. 471, 472), resembling the *a priori* method in Clarke's first Boyle lecture, *A Demonstration of the Being and Attributes of God*. Pope had already condemned such an approach in *An Essay on Man*:

> Say first, of God above, or Man below,
> What can we reason, but from what we know?
> [...]
> Thro' worlds unnumber'd tho' the God be known,
> 'Tis ours to trace him only in our own.

Pope told Spence that the rule of reasoning laid out here will 'go a great way toward destroying all the school metaphysics' and what is advanced by the 'church-writers' who have 'introduced so much of those metaphysics into their systems'.[24] Clarke had himself admitted that *a posteriori* argument using the 'Temporary phenomena of nature' was 'by far the *most generally* useful', but was forced to argue *a priori* because 'Atheistical Writers have sometimes opposed the Being and Attributes of God by such *metaphysical* Reasonings' and thought it necessary to dispute with them using the same methods.[25] This was, of course, similar to Bentley's strategy in his own Boyle lectures, of fighting the atheists on their terms.

Pope seems to imply, however, that Clarke's metaphysics have led him to 'doubt of God' (*Dunciad*, IV, l. 472). As a 'Sworn foe to Myst'ry' who 'damns implicit faith, and holy lies' (ll. 460, 463), the Clerk has many deist characteristics, which could suggest that Pope has free-thinkers like Toland and Matthew Tindal more in mind than the Latitudinarian Clarke. However, as James Noggle argues, it can be inferred that Pope sees Clarke as 'someone who tries to believe in God in the wrong way' and becomes an atheist unintentionally.[26] For Pope, Clarke's public questioning of the Trinity, and the metaphysical method used to pursue this line of reasoning, would have done nothing but confirm his atheism. In *The Dunciad*'s mock-apocalyptic vision, the rationalization of theology using (apparently) mathematical methods forms part of the poem's climax: 'See *Mystery* to *Mathematics* fly! / In vain! they gaze, turn giddy, rave, and die' (ll. 647–48). Pope's indictment of his culture associates all forms of 'dulness' – including metaphysics – with its Queen. And the 'gloomy Clerk' is not only a pedantic dunce, but someone far more dangerous: an atheist with 'strong impulsive gravity of Head' who is 'by sure Attraction led' to Dulness's throne to be appointed to public office (ll. 75–76).

While Pope, Swift, and the other Scriblerians were no doubt suspicious of the incursions of metaphysics and mathematics into theological discourse, their collaborative satires were often open to the comic possibilities of such speculations. *The Memoirs*, for instance, devotes almost a whole chapter to burlesquing in pedantic detail Clarke's lengthy dispute with Collins concerning the nature of consciousness and the soul (pp. 137–42). As Christopher Fox has lucidly shown, on this occasion the Scriblerians seem in unison with Clarke, in that they both consider a human's identity to be an evolving thing, but not in the continual flux Collins argues. Whilst the Scriblerians are no doubt satirizing Collins' materialist ideas when they compare the changes of individuality through experience to the darning of stockings (p. 140), this not only allows them to explore complex philosophical problems through parody, but also bestows them with a certain comic licence.[27] Despite the Scriblerians' parodic flirtations (and perhaps philosophical agreement) with Clarke's substantialist position here, it is apparent that on other issues (such as the Trinity) they diverged profoundly.

What Swift may have found most disturbing about Clarke and his beliefs was the important position this heterodox theologian enjoyed in the Hanoverian Court. Taught by Leibniz at the Court of Berlin, Princess Caroline had an 'ardent love of learning, and fondness for metaphysical knowledge' and frequently corresponded with her former tutor after moving to England. She made the acquaintance of Clarke when seeking a translator of Leibniz's *Theodicy* (1710), but soon realized that Clarke was 'too much of Sir Isaac Newton's opinion' to endorse the work of his European rival.[28] In a letter to the Princess, Leibniz criticized Newton's work from a philosophical and theological perspective. Caroline presented this extract to Clarke and invited him, as a Newtonian, to reply. Subsequently, both philosophers each exchanged five letters via the Princess, who quickly reversed her intellectual allegiance from Leibniz to Clarke and Newton. It became well known that 'The divine' by whom 'she was most instructed, was Dr. Clarke', and she reportedly declared his writings to be the 'finest Things in the World'.[29] Although Clarke acted as Newton's representative, it is thought by some scholars that Newton himself contributed to the replies.[30] This possibility aside, Clarke's letters still grant significant insight into the theology underpinning the Newtonian philosophy. Leibniz's death in November 1716 cut short their correspondence, but Clarke published the letters in one volume, which has been celebrated as a significant work within the history of ideas. Some contemporaries, however, including Swift's friend Matthew Prior, were critical of the solipsism and prejudice seemingly inherent in the philosophers' squabble.[31]

Leibniz was aware of Clarke's controversial beliefs, and used part of the exchange to demonstrate the theological dangers which he associated with Newtonianism. Hence, one of the most important discussions of the correspondence concerned God's intervention in the universe. The Newtonians, following the General Scholium to the *Principia*, adopted the idea that at the Creation God established a frame of nature subject to natural laws, but that God's providence was still active and could alter that mechanism at will.[32] This was because Newton discovered minor irregularities in the planetary motions which would require God's 'continual government and inspection' (as Clarke puts it) to maintain the stability of his system of the universe (*LCC*, p. 14). For Leibniz, the belief that God was active because he had not created a perfect cosmos was of a Socinian nature because it denied God's foreknowledge of future occurrences (*LCC*, p. 19). Leibniz considered the Newtonians' God to lack perfect wisdom, whilst Clarke and Newton saw God's providential care as a sign of his power. Meanwhile, the Newtonians condemned Leibniz's conception of self-active matter as potentially atheistic, because for them only the will of God could superimpose motion upon matter.[33]

The Newtonians' idea of a voluntarist deity who continued to regulate his creation had political resonance. As Steven Shapin has pointed out, Court Whigs often employed theology and natural philosophy to legitimate the succession of the Hanovers,[34] and could be seen most obviously in John Theophilus Desaguliers' poem *The Newtonian System of the World* (1728). In Clarke's Dedication 'To Her Royal Highness the Princess of Wales' in the published correspondence he makes clear connections between the Newtonian natural philosophy, the truth of natural religion, and the present ruling house. Pre-empting suspicions from more conservative thinkers, Clarke asserts that 'Natural philosophy [...] so far as it affects religion, [...] concerning the extent of the powers of matter and motion, and the proofs from phenomena of God's continual government of the world; is of very great importance' (*LCC*, p. 6). For Clarke, only the Newtonian philosophy had shown the true nature of God's providence, and this 'continual government' through the law of universal gravitation could be seen at work metaphorically on earth. The freedom of the Divine Will in the cosmos suggested that constitutional interventions, including the appointment of monarchs (under the rules of the Bill of Rights, 1690), were justifiable:

By the Protestant succession in the illustrious house of Hanover having taken place, this nation has now, with the blessing of God, a certain prospect [...] of seeing government actually administered, according to the design and end for which it was instituted by providence, [...] of seeing learning and knowledge encouraged and promoted, in opposition to all kinds of ignorance. (*LCC*, p. 7)

In Clarke's opinion, Caroline embodies these values because she possesses 'an impartial love of truth, and a desire of promoting learning', and has 'herself also attained to a degree of knowledge very particular and uncommon, even in matters of the nicest and most abstract speculation' (*LCC*, p. 6).

In one of his papers for *The Examiner*, Swift almost satirizes this physico-political analogy proleptically, by comparing the Copernican heliostatic transformation of cosmology to the crowning of William and Mary:

The *Revolution* of the *Sun* about the *Earth* was formerly thought a necessary Expedient to solve Appearances, although it left many Difficulties unanswered; until Philosophers contrived a better, which is that of the *Earth's Revolution* about the *Sun*. This is found upon

Experience to save much Time and labour, to correct many irregular Motions, and is better suited to the Respect due from a *Planet* to a *fixed Star*. (No. 18 [7 December 1710], in *PW*, III, 34)

This description is, no doubt, intentionally ambiguous: the Copernican and Glorious Revolutions correct 'many', not all irregular motions, and are 'better suited' rather than offering perfect systems. The matter-of-fact tone suggests that neither change does much to alter man's everyday existence. *The Examiner* piece demonstrates that for rhetorical purposes Swift exploited the tendency to correspond celestial events with sublunary affairs, which was ultimately derived from 'mundane' astrology. However, the increasing politicization of Newtonianism became a concern for Swift. In 'Directions', Swift draws attention to the constitutional problems caused by the intense association of heterodox beliefs with the Newtonian philosophy and consequently the royal house it helped to support ideologically.

Beams and Blows

Whilst Swift was disaffected to the Hanoverian regime after 1714, and wrote about the new dynasty with some satiric ferocity,[35] he was not averse to courting their favour or, at least, did not refuse their requests for audience. During his visit to England in 1726, Swift met with Caroline on a number of occasions, and when he returned to Dublin, Arbuthnot would write to him about 'your freind [*sic*] her Royal Highness'. However, relations between the Dean and Princess quickly frayed when Swift never received a settlement in England as promised, nor some medals he wanted in exchange for the 'Piece of Irish Plad' sent to Henrietta Howard (mistress to George II, and woman of the Bedchamber to Caroline), but which ended up in the hands of the Princess. In *Verses on the Death*, Caroline was described ironically as 'so Gracious, Mild, and Good' (l. 181), and the accompanying footnote reported that Swift was 'under her Majesty's Displeasure' (*Poems*, II, 559). Swift also sniggered at his friend Thomas Sheridan's attempt to write an ode for Caroline's birthday in 1729.[36]

In 1732 Caroline commissioned William Kent to erect a pavilion (subsequently known as 'The Hermitage') in Richmond Gardens. Inside her grotto Caroline placed five busts by the Italian sculptor Giovanni Guelfi – of Newton, Locke, Boyle, William Wollaston, and Clarke – which served to cement her reputation as a queen of learning. A competition organized by the *Gentleman's Magazine* resulted in many poems greeting the building of the rural retreat: Pope wrote to Gay that 'Every man, and every boy, is writing verses'.[37] Swift himself received two mock-epigrams on the Hermitage, with the second lamenting that a bust of the Dean was not included in the pantheon of worthies: 'I wonder, good Man, that you are not envaulted: / Prithee, go, and be dead, and be doubly exalted'.[38] Swift's hyperbolic response was to joke that 'Her Majesty never shall be my Exalter / And yet she would raise me I know,—by a halter' (*Poems*, II, 664). Pope, who had alluded to Caroline's bust of Clarke in the *Epistle to Burlington*, teased that he had fashioned his own grotto into a symbolic alternative: 'Few philosophers come here but if ever Fortune, Fate, or Providence bring Dr. Oliver Mr. Borlase and Mr. Allen hither I shall not envy the Queen's Hermitage either its natural or moral philosophers'.[39] The pavilion generated immense public interest, becoming an iconic construction which provoked sneers and envy in equal measure (and, it seems, from the very same people).

Swift considered Caroline's patronage of Clarke more directly in 'Directions for a Birthday Song', thought to have been written on the occasion of George II's birthday on 30 October 1729, but which remained unpublished until 1765. Ridiculing the insipid and sycophantic occasional odes produced by the poet laureate Laurence Eusden (1688–1730), and perhaps by his acquaintance Matthew Pilkington, this outspokenly anti-Hanoverian poem is written in the form of a set of ironic instructions to a poet wishing to compose a royal panegyric. It begins by poking fun at George II through a number of mock-heroic similes, and alludes to various scandals and rumours in the court, before the speaker advises: 'with joy proceed / To praise your Empress, and her Breed' (ll. 151–52, in *Poems*, II, 465).[40]

George II's lengthy visits to Hanover, including one in 1729, did nothing for his popularity amongst the English public. Caroline acted as Regent when the King was absent from the country, which in 'Directions' Swift figures through allusion to the reflection of light:

> Now see her seated on her Throne
> With genuin lustre all her own.
> Poor Cynthia never shone so bright,
> Her Splendor is but borrow'd light;
> And only with her Brother linkt
> Can shine, without him is extinct.
> But Carolina shines the clearer
> With neither Spouse nor Brother near her,

> And darts her Beams or'e both our Isles,
> Tho George is gone a thousand miles. (ll. 173–82,
>   in *Poems*, II, 465–66)

Caroline's status as Queen may have been obtained through marriage, but her royal radiance is of her own making. In one sense, that her 'lustre' is 'all her own' is somewhat paradoxical: the word often refers to shining by reflected light, rather than luminosity *per se*. But the Hanoverians' claim to 'genuin' power in England is problematic for Swift, and the emphasis on the origin of authentic monarchical power functions ironically.[41] The internal half-rhyme, alliteration and assonance at work in 'Carolina shines the clearer' serve to intensify the hyperbolic contrast with the Moon's 'borrowed light'. Whilst the King earlier 'become[s]' the sun-god Apollo (l. 58), here it is the royal consort who is figured as a light-producing body 'dart[ing] her beams' over Britain and Ireland.

How ironically we should read this celebration of Caroline's power is uncertain, for the satiric focus is clearly George's absence by 'a thousand miles', rather than the nature of the Queen's influence. What can be suggested with more confidence, however, is that Swift chooses to allude to the propagation of light not only because of the mock-heroic association of the King with Apollo, and the common odic use of celestial tropes, but also because of its appropriateness to Caroline herself. Any poetic reference to light in 1729 would be sure to bring to mind Newton's *Opticks* (1704). Desaguliers draws upon a similar metaphor in *The Newtonian System of the World*, but for the contrasting reason of asserting the monarch's popularity, with George's 'diffusive Rays' kindling 'Zeal in all the *British* Hearts'; whilst Sheridan's ode compared Caroline to the 'Queen of light' who 'gives Lustre to this Day'.[42] By this time, Caroline's interest in Newtonianism was well known, not only through the Leibniz–Clarke correspondence, but also because of the dedication in Newton's posthumous *Chronology of Ancient Kingdoms* (1728), recognizing this Queen's encouragement of the great natural philosopher and their mutual chaplain Clarke. Using astronomical methods of dating, Newton disputed the chronologies of secular and sacred history put forward by the majority of orthodox writers. Critics noted that his conclusions could undermine scriptural authority and authenticity, and concerns increased regarding the possible heterodox nature of his beliefs.[43] 'Directions' does not name Newton explicitly, but several further allusions to Caroline suggest that Swift associates the Queen with metaphysical speculations that encourage atheism.

After celebrating Caroline as 'Queen of Rhymes' (l. 221) because of the lyrical qualities of her name ('So soft, so sliding, and so sweet', l. 226), the speaker suggests that this will ensure her poetic immortality:

> May Caroline continue long,
> For ever fair and young—in Song.
> What tho the royal Carcase must
> Squeez'd in a Coffin turn to dust;
> Those Elements her name compose,
> Like Atoms are exempt from blows. (ll. 233–38,
> in *Poems*, II, 467)

Swift demonstrates his great comic timing by holding back the relative clause 'in Song' to the end of the couplet, aided by the use of the dash. The speaker wishes for Caroline's continued beauty and youth in the literary, not real, world. It is also less than complimentary that the hypothesized 'royal Carcase' is of such bulk that it must be 'Squeez'd in a coffin'. And while her body becomes particles of dust, the 'Elements' of her name will possess the strength and solidity of 'Atoms'.

This atomic simile hints that Swift was aware of arguments within the Leibniz–Clarke debate. After Caroline witnessed several pneumatic experiments, she wrote to Leibniz to ask him about the notion of the vacuum.[44] In a private reply, but printed as a postscript to his fourth paper to Clarke, Leibniz attacked atomic doctrine (for the ideas of atoms and void are usually linked). Leibniz denies the existence of atoms, preferring to see them as hypotheses constructed by the limited human mind:

> Men [...] fancy, they have found out the first elements of things, [...] We would have nature to go no farther; and to be finite, as our minds are: but [...] The least corpuscle is actually subdivided *in infinitum*, and contains a world of other creatures. (*LCC*, pp. 43–44)

Caroline passed this section of the letter on to Clarke, who responded by maintaining that Leibniz's argument is a 'manifest absurdity':

> if there be no such perfectly solid particles, then there is no matter at all in the universe. For, [...] carrying on the division *in infinitum*, you never arrive at parts perfectly solid and without pores; it will follow that all bodies consist of pores only, without any matter at all. (*LCC*, p. 54)

Leibniz and Clarke clash over the 'Principle of the Best'. For Leibniz, the divine creation of the universe means that there is as much variety as possible, with all matter as heterogeneous and no two particles the same: each particle is divided into further parts, so there are no essential building blocks and therefore no atoms (*LCC*, p. 62). Clarke takes Leibniz's argument to its *reductio* to infer that poreless solid particles must exist, but if every pore is full of matter as Clarke suggests, there can be no void in the universe. In his unambiguous support for atomism Clarke publicly diverges from his mentor. In the *Principia*, Newton refers to particles and corpuscles, but he does not see them as absolutely dense atoms (although few contemporaries took these denials seriously). Newton hypothesizes the existence of atoms for the purpose of following general laws within his mathematics, while Clarke is emphatic about their reality.[45]

Another reason why Leibniz denies the existence of atoms is because they contradict the laws of dynamics, and this is where the meaning of Swift's 'blows' becomes clearer. In one of the queries to the *Optice*, Newton suggests that God formed matter in 'solid, massy, hard, impenetrable, moveable particles'. These particles had no pores, were indestructible, and possessed very little elasticity, making them unable to rebound when hitting each other.[46] Clarke argues that as hard and inelastic, atoms would not conserve the kinetic energy: 'Two bodies, void of elasticity, meeting each other with equal contrary forces, both lose their motion' (*LCC*, p. 52). For Clarke, this proved that there was a diminution of force in the universe which required God's providence to supply new motion to his mechanistic system. In contrast, Leibniz believed in the conservation of motion: that the same amount of force was always present. For kinetic energy to be conserved all matter must be elastic, enabling 'force' (mv^2) to be stored internally (Leibniz's system of energy mechanics therefore corresponded with his belief in motion as inherent within matter). Newton and Clarke's definition of atoms as hard and inelastic would therefore contradict the principle of conservation, as head-on collisions between such particles 'with equal and contrary forces' would run down the total amount of force in the universe.[47] And, according to Leibniz, as God had made a perfect universe then his intervention would not be necessary to sustain his creation. For Newton, this was not a problem, because his idea of the workings of nature was grounded in a voluntarist doctrine of divine omnipotence.[48]

Following Newton's suggestion in the *Optice* of the existence of atoms 'so very hard, as never to wear or break in pieces' (*LCC*, p. 178), in 'Directions' Swift seems to use the simile of 'atoms exempt from blows' in order to draw further attention to Caroline's interest in the

Newtonian philosophy via her patronage of the controversial theologian Clarke. Swift's allusion highlights the theological issues at stake within the Leibniz–Clarke debates. In Leibniz's opinion, atoms do not exist in reality, only within the Newtonian system, whose principles resemble those of the Socinians. The atomic simile in 'Directions' therefore associates the Queen herself with Socinian beliefs.

Moreover, Swift is perhaps hinting at an even more serious, theological consequence of atomism: the potential for belief in materialism. The atomic philosophy was associated with Epicurus, for whom 'the whole of being consists of bodies and space', motion is inherent in matter, and divine providence is absent.[49] The French natural philosopher and Catholic priest Pierre Gassendi (1592–1655) had attempted, in the words of Gulliver, to make the 'Doctrine of *Epicurus* as palatable as he could' (*PW*, XI, 197), by acknowledging God's act of creation and continued omnipotence, explaining motion in matter as the result of superadded divine energy, and allowing for the soul's incorporeality.[50] Boyle had also sought, in the words of Bentley, to show 'how friendly' the 'mechanical or corpuscular philosophy' is to the 'immateriality of human souls, and consequently to the existence of a supreme spiritual Being'.[51] Despite these efforts, atomism was indelibly related to atheism, and 'Directions' emphasizes this through a Lucretian echo. The speaker asserts that the 'elements' of Caroline's name will survive while her body turns to dust, but makes no mention of the whereabouts of the Queen's soul after death, implying its mortality. In Book 3 of *De rerum natura*, called a 'compleat System of Atheism' in *Mr. C—ns's Discourse* (*PW*, IV, 37), Lucretius contrasts the eternal existence of atomic 'seeds' of things with the temporal life of the human soul, which Epicurus believed dies with the body. For the materialist Epicurus

> tis folly to believe
> They [*Mind* and *Soul*] can be made without the limbs, or live.
> Well then, the *Soul* spread o're the limbs must fail,
> And dye with those, as years and death prevail.

When the body decomposes, the soul (which is dispersed through it) loses its consciousness. The body and soul can then be separated into 'scatter'd parts' and so 'can *dye*'. In contrast, atomic 'seeds' are solid and cannot be divided; they repel all blows and so cannot be destroyed:

> [...] what is *immortal*, must be so,
> Because tis *Solid*, above the power of *blow*;

> Whose parts no Wedge divides, which knows no Pore,
> And such are *Seeds*, as I explain'd before:[52]

While Caroline's name might be 'exempt from blows', Swift's allusion to Lucretius suggests that her soul will not survive her bodily extinction. Swift is being a little disingenuous, in that far from being a Christian Mortalist, Clarke defended the immaterial and immortal nature of the soul in his debate with Collins, as at least one of the Scriblerians well knew, although Clarke's views certainly became more radical on a number of issues in the years following this intellectual scuffle. Swift's atomic simile functions to associate the Queen not only with the Newtonians' Socinianist beliefs, but also with materialism and consequently atheism. Following from this, there is something ironic about the survival of Caroline's 'name'. For 'name' can refer to reputation, and the adjective 'good' is notably absent from the line.[53] Caroline's association with atomism – and hence atheism – instead leaves her notorious.

Hell and Hanover

While the suggestion of atheism is only implicit at this point of the poem, at the climax it becomes overt and is identified with Caroline's chaplain specifically. The speaker advises the royal panegyrist to:

> Reject with scorn that stupid Notion
> To praise your Hero for Devotion:
> Nor entertain a thought so odd,
> That Princes should believe in God:
> But follow the securest rule,
> And turn it all to ridicule:
> 'Tis grown the choicest Wit at Court,
> And gives the Maids of Honor Sport.
> For since they talk'd with Doctor Clark,
> They now can venture in the dark.
> That sound Divine the Truth has spoke all
> And pawn'd his word Hell is not local.
> This will not give them half the trouble
> Of Bargains sold, or meanings double. (ll. 261–74,
> in *Poems*, II, 468–69)

Clarke, who died early in 1729 (the likely year of the poem's composition), is accused of propagating atheism within the court. One 'Maid'

Swift might have in mind is Charlotte Clayton (later Lady Sundon), who was Caroline's Lady of the Bedchamber, a patron of Clarke herself, and is reported to have agreed with Clarke that the Athanasian Creed was open to debate.[54] Presumably the maids 'now can venture in the dark' because they think that the soul is mortal and so no longer believe in the existence of spirits. Venturing 'in the dark' may also suggest figuratively that they have turned away from the light of God. It is implied that there is a sense in which Clarke's 'atheism' is appropriate for the contemporary court. While Clarke's dedication to Caroline defends the succession of her husband and father-in-law through allusion to theology and natural philosophy, Swift highlights what he sees as the paradox within this validation strategy.

The ironic epithet of 'sound Divine' emphasizes the heterodoxy of Clarke's opinions and undercuts 'the Truth' which he speaks. However, the meaning of 'pawn'd his word Hell is not local' is less certain. Swift seems to be using 'pawn' in several ways: to refer to Clarke's 'pledge' that his doctrines are the truth; to suggest Clarke's trickery or deception in making these claims (although the *OED* gives 1763 for the first usage in this sense); and to emphasize Caroline's patronage of the chaplain (that he is paid for his words of assurance). The rest of the line is perhaps even more ambiguous. By 'not local' Swift is possibly suggesting that Clarke thinks Hell does not have the attribute of 'place' or a spatial position: in other words, it does not exist in physical reality, which would contradict St Paul's belief that 'every one may receive the things done in his body' (II Corinthians 5.10). This interpretation would be appropriate to the mortality of the soul implied through the Lucretian reference and the maids' new confidence to 'venture in the dark'. Further evidence to support this reading can be found in *Polite Conversation*, where the narrator 'Simon Wagstaff' discusses 'Blasphemy or Free-Thinking': 'some scrupulous Persons [...] are afraid of Sprights. I must however except the Maids of Honour, who have been fully convinced, by a famous Court-Chaplain, that there is no such Place as Hell' (*PW*, IV, 108). It is surely Clarke of whom 'Wagstaff' is speaking, but the ambiguity of 'Directions' is transformed into an emphatic accusation here. In the prose and poetic pieces Swift covers his tracks in different ways. In 'Directions', which remained unpublished during Swift's lifetime anyway, 'Doctor Clark' is named but there is some ambiguity as to the precise nature of his opinion of Hell, while in *Polite Conversation* the denial of Hell is clearly alleged but Clarke is not named explicitly, and is instead present through the euphemism of 'famous Court-Chaplain'.

Why would Swift have been given the impression that Clarke denied the existence of Hell? Swift is perhaps equating the denial of the eternal torture of evil souls and their bodily vehicles with the rejection of Hell as a real place. The idea that the 'fire' of Hell was a metaphor, 'figured to us by corporeal things' to accommodate human understanding of the 'severity of the divine vengeance', had been expounded by lots of thinkers in the Renaissance period, including Calvin, and during the seventeenth century Hell increasingly came to be viewed as both a psychological condition and a physical space.[55] In the early eighteenth century, the doctrine of eternal punishment came under mounting attack from those more liberal theologians we broadly call 'Latitudinarians' because they saw it as inconsistent with the notion of a compassionate God.[56] It was also condemned by deists who saw the threat of eternal torment as another example of the superstition employed by priests to maintain social order. In *Mr. C—ns's Discourse*, Swift draws attention to the similarity between the Latitudinarians and the deists on this issue. The narrating 'Friend' claims the Latitudinarians Henry More and John Tillotson are both '*Freethinkers*', and argues that if both 'deny the Eternity of Hell Torments, a *Free Thinker* may deny all future Punishments whatsoever' because they prefer to reject 'not only that particular Point, but the whole Article to which it relates' (*PW*, IV, 35). The satiric conflation of the two (admittedly already heterogeneous) groups may go some way in elucidating why Swift depicts Clarke as a 'free-thinker' in *Polite Conversation*. Obviously, Clarke would not have seen himself in this way, as his quarrel with Collins proves.

While 'Atheists' argue that belief in 'future Happiness and Pain' is 'A mere Contrivance of the Brain' used to 'entice, / And fit their Proselytes for Vice' ('Stella's Birth-Day' [1727], ll. 19–22, in *Poems*, II, 764), in Swift's opinion the threat of eternal punishment (and expectation of divine reward) was very real, and one which man was obliged to take seriously, especially in order to preserve the social order.[57] This is apparent in his *Sermon upon the Excellency of Christianity*, which criticizes the Ancient heathens because their 'notion of rewards and punishments in another life [...] seems to have rather served as an entertainment to poets, or as a terror of children, than a settled principle' (*PW*, IX, 245). However, Swift was not averse to responding light-heartedly to the denial of the reality of Hell. In 'The Place of the Damn'd', Swift uses the conceit of damnation being a state of consciousness (most famously expressed by Mephistophilis in *Dr Faustus*)[58] in order to condemn contemporary society:

> ALL Folks who pretend to *Religion* and *Grace*,
> Allow there's a *HELL*, but dispute of the Place;

> But if *Hell* by *Logical* Rules be defin'd,
> The Place of the *Damn'd*,—I'll tell you my Mind.
>   Wherever the Damn'd do Chiefly abound,
> Most certainly there's the *Hell* to be found, (ll. 1–6,
> in *Poems*, II, 575)

The speaker then proceeds to list the many professionals in whom Hell may be located, including 'Damn'd *Poets*, Damn'd *Criticks*' and 'Damn'd *Lawyers* and *Judges*' (ll. 7, 9).[59] So whilst 'Directions' condemns Clarke's heterodox conception of Hell, 'The Place of the Damn'd' imaginatively relies upon such a re-interpretation. The poem challenges this notion of Hell through taking it to its *reductio* and thus trivializing its premise.

Evidence of Clarke's concern with the duration of divine punishment can be found in several places. In 1730, the year following Clarke's death, Whiston published a biographical account of the court chaplain. Whilst mentioning his own writings against 'the Eternity of the Torments of Hell', Whiston ventures to add that 'Sir *Isaac Newton* and Dr. *Clarke* [...] were both of the same Sentiments. Nay, Dr. *Clarke* thought that "few or no thinking Men were really of different sentiments in that Matter"'.[60] The deaths of his allies allowed Whiston the opportunity to bolster the credibility of his disbelief in eternal torment through his public revelations. Swift may have heard Whiston's rumour, but several of Clarke's own publications (some of which were owned by Sheridan and therefore accessible to Swift) were also indicative.

In their discussions immortalized parodically in the *Memoirs of Scriblerus*, Clarke had attacked Collins' notion that human identity is in temporal flux because it removed man's moral responsibility for previous actions, making 'a Future State of Rewards and Punishments not only *Improbable*, but *Impossible*'.[61] In his second set of Boyle lectures, similarly, there is little trace of Clarke's heterodoxy, and he argues that the doctrine of everlasting happiness or punishment is 'in it self very credible, and reasonable to be believed' (*Unchangeable Obligations of Natural Religion*, p. 331). Soon after the lectures, however, Clarke became embroiled in an intellectual quarrel with the non-Juror Henry Dodwell, whose *Epistolary Discourse* (1706) claimed that at baptism a person's soul is immortalized, but that those who have not been baptized will be rendered immortal by God at the point of death so that they can endure eternal punishment.[62] Clarke's reply argues that if the soul naturally dies, some people might find it hard to believe that God will make some souls immortal just in order to punish them, and so accuses Dodwell's argument of promoting the removal of the fear of divine judgement. For Clarke, 'the real difficulty of the Question lies in this, how it is reconcileable with the Goodness of God, to put *any Persons at all* upon a necessity of making such an *Option*, wherein if they choose amiss, the Misery they incur must be irrecoverable', suggesting that this is answered by 'supposing the Souls of Men to be naturally immortal; so that they who render themselves uncapable of Happiness, must consequently fall into remediless Misery'.[63] While Clarke does provide a reason why God forces man to make a choice of eternal consequence, his acknowledgement that there is 'difficulty' suggests some equivocation upon this matter, as Philip C. Almond notes.[64]

Clarke's ambiguity with regards to the nature of Hell was also reflected in his etymological analysis of patristic writings. In the preface to *The Scripture-Doctrine of the Trinity*, he argues that it is not of importance what the words may 'vulgarly and carelessly be understood to mean', but in 'what Sense they can be consistent Expositions of those Texts' (p. xxii). As an example, he considers the meaning of the word 'Hell' in the Apostles' Creed. 'Hell' in English 'signifies always, *the place or state of the damned*', but the Greek word 'does not signify *Hell*, but in general only *The invisible State of Those departed*' (p. xxiii). Significantly, he repeats this argument in *The Exposition of the Church-Catechism*, a book owned by Sheridan.[65] Clarke seems to suggest that those who had lived before the time of Christ, and so were ignorant of the Gospel through no fault of their own, were not sent straight to Hell for punishment they did not deserve. For Clarke, therefore, the apostolic narrative of Christ's 'Harrowing of Hell' (based on I Peter 3.18–20) is of questionable authenticity. He was not the first to suggest this, certainly, but what was distinctive about Clarke was that he would also "remove" the meaning of 'Hell' as the 'place or state of the damned' from the Gospel. In *A Paraphrase on the Four Evangelists* (1722), Clarke reads Christ's denunciation of Capernaum as 'thrust downe to hell' (Luke 10.15) allegorically, suggesting that Christ means the city will be 'laid level with the Ground, by a strange and unparalleled Desolation'.[66] He does not reduce the agent of destruction to merely secondary causes: it is still 'strange and unparalleled', intimating its divine nature. However, the result of this heavenly action does not involve the eternal damnation of the inhabitants of Capernaum. Clarke the Latitudinarian therefore re-interprets the passage to accommodate his difficulty in believing that his benevolent God would find it righteous to subject the entire populace to never-ending misery.

Clarke's interest in the etymological analysis of the word 'Hell' therefore suggests another reading of Swift's line 'And pawn'd his word Hell is not local' (l. 272). There is perhaps a pun on the meaning of 'word' here, in that it not only refers to Clarke's pledge but also to 'word' in the lexical sense. It would be appropriate in this case to see 'Hell' in quotation marks ('his word "Hell" is not local'), in the sense that Clarke's readings of 'Hell' in the Apostles' Creed and Luke's Gospel transpose the nature of Hell as the 'localized' physical place of the damned to the state of the dead in general or to a metaphorical state of 'Hell' respectively.

Swift's accusations that mortalism, materialism and atheism have captured the imagination of the Hanoverian court, and are directly related to Caroline's interest in the Newtonian philosophy, are of course satiric exaggerations, but evidence to support them was not difficult for Swift to find. Clarke claimed that his metaphysical theories were in the service of natural religion, but the theological sentiments which Swift could have discovered in Clarke's writings or in gossip might have made him suspect that the new natural philosophy was unwittingly creating a secular society.[67] Swift's writings on science sometimes suggest a rejection of its aims and methods on theological grounds, but 'Directions' never comes clean as to its exact motives, although it is doubtful that Swift truly believed that natural philosophy *per se* inherently and unavoidably results in atheism. The royal patronage of heterodox thinkers like Clarke would, at the very least, not have endeared Swift to a ruling house whose legitimacy he considered with at least some suspicion, and whose authority was further undermined by the very ideas its hirelings proliferated. Swift's references to Caroline, Clarke, Newtonianism, and the use of scientific tropes in 'Directions' function to counter Clarke's dedicatory preface in the published Leibniz–Clarke correspondence. 'Directions' undermines the connections Clarke makes between natural philosophy, the Protestant church and the house of Hanover by constructing an alternative vision which instead associates the current monarchy with metaphysical speculation which inevitably leads to materialism, atheism and hence anarchy, where the threat of divine punishment is no longer sufficient to sustain order.

These themes also coalesce in a work published in the Pope–Swift *Miscellanies* (1732) and sometimes attributed to Swift (but which is possibly by Gay), *A True and Faithful Narrative of What Passed in London*. Satirizing Whiston's millenarian prophecies, this prose satire begins with the natural philosopher announcing at one of his lectures near the Royal Exchange that an orbiting comet will in three days' time bring about the universal conflagration of the Earth. This premise is used as an occasion for social satire, ridiculing the hysterical response as news of the prediction spreads, particularly the scenes of 'Devotions both Publick and Private' as the day arrives, which give the impression that 'the whole Town had been really and seriously religious'. However, when the comet does not materialize at its appointed time, the citizens lose their recently discovered faith and 'the World went on in the old Channel'. In the narrator's long catalogue of reactions to the prediction, the very first involves a woman of high status:

> Mr. *Whiston* was sent for to a great Lady, who is very curious in the Learned Sciences, and addicted to all the Speculative Doubts of the most able Philosophers; but he was not now to be found: and since at other times, he has been known not to decline that Honour, I make no doubt he conceal'd himself to attend to the great Business of his Soul: But whether it was the Lady's Faith, or Inquisitiveness, that occasion'd her to send, is a Point I shall not presume to determine.[68]

Whiston was favoured by both Clayton and Caroline, receiving what he described as 'the queen's bounty' (an annuity of 40*l*).[69] The portrait of a lady 'addicted to all the Speculative Doubts' probably alludes to one of these women, but even if this isn't the specific case, the passage shows that the Scriblerians were concerned that a version of Newtonian natural philosophy associated with heterodox thinking was infiltrating English society from the top down. Whiston's Socinianist tendency may have been the Scriblerians' principal source of grievance with him, but his millenarian ideas of celestial catastrophe were an easier target and had comic potential.

Swift may well have suspected Newton of the anti-Trinitarianism he found in Whiston and Clarke, but he could not have made such accusations in his published works: to be a secret alchemist or astrologer is one thing, to deny the divinity of Christ is another. If this is the case, then Swift's inclusion of the fantastical millenarian theories of Whiston, or of a royal court obsessed with mathematics in the 'Voyage to Laputa' perhaps sought to attack the heterodox opinions of the Newtonians by implication. In 'Directions for a Birthday Song', unpublished during his lifetime, Swift could target the unorthodox implications of Newtonian metaphysics with much more licence. Despite his confession in 'The Dean's Reasons for Not Building at Drapier's Hill' of knowing not even a 'smatter' of metaphysics, Swift seemed to be prepared to sink himself 'over head and ears' in it if sufficiently provoked.

Afterword

> Her Knowledge, with such Pains acquir'd,
> By this new Passion grew inspir'd.
> Thro' this she made all Objects pass,
> Which gave a Tincture o'er the Mass:
> As Rivers, tho' they bend and twine,
> Still to the Sea their Course incline;
> Or, as Philosophers, who find
> Some fav'rite System to their Mind,
> In ev'ry Point to make it fit,
> Will force all Nature to submit. (*Cadenus and Vanessa*,
> ll. 716–25, in *Poems*, II, 709)

In many ways, these lines encapsulate the types of creative energy released when Swift draws upon the new natural philosophy in his writing. Here, Vanessa's love for Cadenus is figured as a prism which refracts the incident light of the things she studies. However, while Newton had shown that the colours produced by the prism are not '*Qualifications*' but '*Original* and *connate properties*' of the natural white light, Vanessa's lens of 'Passion' is 'bend[ing]' the world, producing a distorted vision of a particular 'Tincture', not revealing its true nature.[1] Through Swift's poetic dexterity, the limitations of this analogy then diffuse into a simile that seeks to satirically expose the shortcomings of any 'System' of natural knowledge (although it is not made explicit whether this makes a poke at Newtonian optics specifically). However, the elisions reveal Swift's own (poetic) surrender to the exigencies of octosyllabic metre, somewhat undercutting the severity of this repudiatory glance at reductive structures.

Again and again, Swift's satires charge the scientific impulse with failing to account for the complexity of life, simplifying all to mechanism and the material realm, though even 'The Growth of an Animal, of a Plant, or of the smallest Seed, is a Mystery to the wisest among Men' (*PW*, IX, 164).[2] While many natural philosophers were committed to a voluntarist conception of God's place in the cosmos, Swift's work suggests that their fundamentally limited explanations privileged natural causation over divine agency. Of course, many champions of natural philosophy themselves acknowledged the imperfection of human reason. Glanvill, for instance, admits that '*Mechanical* solutions' shall 'never give an account' of organic creation. However, Swift would find it unlikely that '*Philosophy* doth [...] enlarge and ennoble the spirit', allowing man to ascend his pitiful nature, as Glanvill proudly claims.[3]

Closer to home, for Swift the faults in men's minds cannot simply be attributed to bad vapours or faulty hydraulics: although if they could, then at least there would be simple ways of mending the world. His parodies of 'meletetics' present Boyle's system of reflection as mechanizing thought itself, characteristic of the dull organization of knowledge associated with the 'new Philosophy', which 'endeavour[s] to solve by some easier and shorter way'. And these weak, programmed minds are often concerned with the systematization of ostensibly trivial things, exemplified by the 'general histories' of the elements celebrated by Wotton and countered in the *Tale*'s 'Advertisement' for '*A General History of Ears*'.[4]

Despite Swift's suspicion and laughter at the attractive tendency to the general and universal within narratives of nature, this appeal is also apparent within his own satiric discourse, presenting his criticism as originating from a common-sense point of view, and pretending to a historical perspective in order to pass "final judgment" upon his targets. Moreover, some of Swift's principal satiric weapons are his allegories, which evince a sophisticated ability to exploit the multivalent nature of such writing. The fabulist mode of the Spider and Bee episode, for example, cannot help but to implore the reader to construct an allegorical system of some form or another. Nevertheless, there is a significant irony at work, in that one of the central purposes of the fable is to highlight the madness of the Modern urge to build perfect systems of interpretation, whether of nature or of texts.

Whilst Temple thought natural philosophy to have no end but 'either busying a man's brains to no purpose, or satisfying the vanity so natural to most men of distinguishing themselves', Swift's satires involving science suggest an authorial position far more moderate in attitude.[5]

Most obviously, we have the evidence of the King of Brobdingnag, who proclaims 'that whoever could make two Ears of Corn, or two Blades of Grass to grow upon a Spot of Ground where only one grew before; would deserve better of Mankind, and do more essential Service to his Country, than the whole Race of Politicians put together' (*PW*, XI, 135–36). Although this functions primarily as a swipe at the political breed, we should also take it as an endorsement of human control over nature with real practical use, as Swift would have found advocated by Francis Bacon.[6] Therefore, while we might not share all of his answers, Swift's satires prompt us to ask: what forms of enquiry are useful, and which constitute the collection of trivia? Lamenting Lord Orrery's absence from Ireland, Swift once stated that 'a Star of the first magnitude, wholly out of sight, or at too great a distance, is a very useless part of Gods works to those who grovel upon the Earth', recalling the *Broom-Stick*'s image of man's physical and mental boundaries.[7] For Swift, the accumulation of data without real methodology, the calculation of infinitesimal or colossal things, and the interest in the exotic for its own sake can be guilty of pedantry and prurience. The *moral* utility of science is therefore another concern. Natural philosophers may claim that they are making technological advancements, but this might not be in combination with ethical progress. The *Tale*-narrator's scientific and medical speculations, in a voice at times refined but uninhibited by ethical standards, form a caricature of the view of human anatomy encountered in Boyle and others, whilst the 'Voyage to Laputa' suggests that science can be a threat to life itself. Indeed, there is something powerfully prescient about the politico-military use of scientific knowledge represented by the flying island's actions against its colonies.

Swift's writing highlights numerous, sometimes legitimate, concerns with scientific enquiry, but it is evident that Swift knows he is being overly disingenuous, that his satiric distortions are often adopting extreme positions and indulging in comic possibilities, rather than always passing definite judgement.[8] This interpretation is endorsed by the personal nature of many of the attacks he makes, where it seems less libellous to laugh at someone for 'erecting certain *Edifices in the Air*' (*Tale*, p. 34), than to make accusations of political corruption or religious heterodoxy. Although some of Swift's onslaughts on individuals are "easy shots", more often they are intricate displays of his rhetorical skills, calling upon various modes of representation, and utilizing whatever ammunition (conceits and metaphors, written evidence or even gossip) seemed relevant. Swift's enemies are subject to bestial and social diminution through concrete images. They are characterized as mongrels, spiders, or lowly 'mechanicks', implying that they use knowledge as a means of self-promotion and self-aggrandizement, rather than to increase collective human achievement. Sometimes new philosophies are associated with ideas already subject to ridicule or condemnation: judicial astrology, or ancient atomism. Much of the *Tale's* unique character originates in the aggregation and accumulation of various systems of knowledge, burlesquing a number of concepts and discourses, and exploiting the inevitable tensions between different narratives of nature. Frequently, Swift deploys the natural philosophers' (and their apologists') own ideas against them: Descartes, Burnet and Bentley are literally punished by the concepts which are whirling, webbing and wheeling within their heads. Boyle's own method of similitude is employed in an inversion which caricatures him and his philosophies, pulling out the paradox that in order to justify and celebrate the divine, 'physico-theological' works linger too long on material things. The ultimate irony of this, needless to say, is that whilst Swift sometimes charges natural philosophy with incubating a materializing tendency within Modern culture, his own satires often depend upon physicalization for much of their force.

Swift's satires also categorize much writing on natural philosophy as mere oratory, as 'romantic' and 'fanciful' as literary discourse, mistaking analogy for real knowledge, and not adhering to standards of 'truth' and (what Gulliver calls) the relation of 'plain Matter of fact in the simplest Manner and Style' (*PW*, XI, 291). For Swift, this might have seemed especially striking and duplicitous given that Sprat and other supporters for natural philosophy had pompously sought to purge language of its complex relationship with things, reducing all to a rational system of signs which had no place for metaphor.

In numerous works, Swift satirically pulls the culture of Enlightenment curiosity away from the centre of eighteenth-century British society into its margins, creating a caricature of the aloof scientist that was borne out in the specialization and professionalization of disciplines in the nineteenth century, and still endures in public perception in the twenty-first. Indeed, Swift's image was one that natural philosophers and their advocates themselves kept in focus, functioning as a satiric arbiter of the 'vain pretensions of [...] the idly speculative tribes, who waste their precious time in visionary studies', as one of Swift's earliest biographers puts it.[9] John Conduitt, for instance, name-checked and paraphrased the *Tale* in his notes towards a biography of Newton, claiming that 'Fancy never got astride Sir I. N's reason' (those with knowledge of the great man's alchemy might have taken a different view). Meanwhile, in Francesco Algarotti's dialogues, which did much to popularize Newtonian ideas across Enlightenment Europe, the Marchioness of *E*—'s superstitious fears of solar catastrophe are compared to 'those of the *Laputian* school' by her enlightened tutor.[10] For all of the charges of philosophical conservatism placed at Swift's door, appropriations of his provocative satires lived long within the culture of natural knowledge, and their legacy is seen in the *Annals of Improbable Research* magazine and its associated *Ig Nobel* Prize, which keep in check, or at least laugh at, the excesses of experimental enquiry, scientific writing, and academic studies of all kinds.[11]

Despite the many criticisms of science we find in Swift's works, it is also apparent that the discoveries, methodologies and types of writing generated by the new natural philosophy served as important vehicles of satire. For example, developments in physiology which viewed the human form as analogous to mechanism put forward to Swift a distinctive way of exploring man's physical and mental vulnerabilities. However, Swift's ironies also fall upon his own satiric writing, which he self-consciously figures as a form of imaginative violation comparable to the activities on the anatomist's slab. While he may critique the sciences for excluding different modes of experience and thereby reducing all things to simple laws and relationships, his own satires often distort reality into distinct and alternative visions of what science has done or will do to man's image of the universe and of himself. Nonetheless, Swift's detailed and substantial engagements also serve to demonstrate the multifarious appropriations of the developing new sciences within their intellectual, social, economic, political, and theological communities in the early eighteenth century. Swift's responses to science reveal that satire can be an active and unique participant in contemporary debates about the methods and purposes of enquiries into nature.

Notes

Introduction

1. Abraham Cowley, 'To the Royal Society', ll. 41–46, quoted in Francis Bacon, *The Essays, or Counsels, Civil and Moral* (London: Knapton, 1691), sig. A3^v. Swift owned this edition (see *LRJS*, I, 125–26). On the Miltonic parallels, see Robert B. Hinman, *Abraham Cowley's World of Order* (Cambridge, MA: Harvard University Press, 1960), pp. 189–90.
2. See, for instance, Richard G. Olson, 'Tory-High Church Opposition to Science and Scientism in the Eighteenth Century: The Works of John Arbuthnot, Jonathan Swift, and Samuel Johnson', in *The Uses of Science in the Age of Newton*, ed. John G. Burke (Berkeley: University of California Press, 1983), pp. 171–204.
3. Cowley, 'To the Royal Society', l. 59. See Francis Bacon, *Novum Organum* (1620), 'Plan of the Work', sig. B4^v, in *The Instauratio magna Part II: Novum organum and Associated Texts*, ed. and trans. Graham Rees with Maria Wakely (Oxford: Clarendon Press, 2004), p. 33.
4. See Charles Webster, *The Great Instauration: Science, Medicine, and Reform, 1626–1660* (London: Duckworth, 1975), esp. p. 96.
5. See John R. R. Christie, 'Laputa Revisited', in *Nature Transfigured: Science and Literature, 1700–1900*, eds Christie and Sally Shuttleworth (Manchester: Manchester University Press, 1989), pp. 45–60, and Brian Vickers, 'Swift and the Baconian Idol', in *The World of Jonathan Swift: Essays for the Tercentenary*, ed. B. Vickers (Oxford: Basil Blackwell, 1968), pp. 87–128. There has been general disagreement, however, with Vickers's argument that 'Bacon stood for many things that Swift detested', and that Swift's allusions were intended to mock Bacon. See especially Irvin Ehrenpreis, 'The Doctrine of *A Tale of a Tub*', in *Proceedings of the First Münster Symposium on Jonathan Swift*, eds Hermann J. Real and Heinz J. Vienken (München: Fink, 1985), pp. 59–71 (p. 62n12).
6. Hermann J. Real, 'The "Keen Appetite for Perpetuity of Life" Abated: The Struldbruggs, Again', in *Fiktion und Geschichte in der anglo-amerikanischen Literatur: Festschrift für Heinz-Joachim Mullenbrock zum 60. Geburtstag*, eds Rudiger Ahrens and Fritz Wilhelm Neumann (Heidelberg: Carl Winter Universitatsverlag, 1998), pp. 117–35 (pp. 121–23), and the same author's 'The Dean and the Lord Chancellor: Or, Swift Saving his Bacon', in *Britannien und Europa: Studien zur Literatur-, Geistes- und Kulturgeschichte. Festschrift für Jürgen Klein*, ed. Michael Szczekalla (Frankfurt: Lang, 2010), pp. 95–111. See also Irvin Ehrenpreis, 'Jonathan Swift: Lecture on a Master Mind', *Proceedings of the British Academy*, 54 (1968), 149–64 (p. 153), and John Shanahan, '"In the Mean Time": Jonathan Swift, Francis Bacon, and Georgic Struggle', in *Swift as Priest and Satirist*, ed. Todd C. Parker (Newark: University of Delaware Press, 2009), pp. 193–214.
7. Donald Greene, 'Swift: Some Caveats', in *Studies in the Eighteenth Century II: Papers Presented at the Second David Nichol Smith Memorial Seminar Canberra 1970*, ed. R. F. Brissenden (Canberra: Australian National University Press, 1973), pp. 341–58 (esp. p. 355).

8. 'Ode to the Honble Sir William Temple', l. 38, and 'Ode to the Athenian Society', ll. 211, 213 (*Poems*, I, 27, 22). See Cowley, 'To Mr. Hobs', ll. 1–3, in *Poems* (London, 1656), p. 26. Swift owned this edition of Cowley: see *LRJS*, I, 475.

9. John Boyle, Fifth Earl of Cork and Orrery, *Remarks on the Life and Writings of Dr. Jonathan Swift*, ed. João Fróes (Newark: University of Delaware Press, 2000), p. 184 (Letter XII).

10. Bacon, *Novum Organum*, 'Plan of the Work', sig. B6^v, in *The Instauratio magna Part II*, p. 37, and *Tale*, p. 151.

11. See esp. Joseph M. Levine, *Dr. Woodward's Shield: History, Science, and Satire in Augustan England* (Berkeley: University of California Press, 1977), and Steven Shapin, *Never Pure: Historical Studies of Science as if It Was Produced by People with Bodies, Situated in Time, Space, Culture, and Society, and Struggling for Credibility and Authority* (Baltimore, MD: The Johns Hopkins University Press, 2010), pp. 142–81.

12. See *Tale*, pp. 83–84, 403–404.

13. See Karina Williamson, '"Science" and "knowledge" in Eighteenth-century Britain', *Studies in Voltaire and the Eighteenth Century*, 303 (1992), 455–58 (p. 456).

14. *An Essay on Man*, Epistle I, ll. 99–104, in *TE*, III i,27.

15. See C. P. Snow, *The Two Cultures and the Scientific Revolution* (The Rede Lecture) (Cambridge: Cambridge University Press, 1959), Judith Hawley, 'General Introduction', in *Literature and Science, 1660–1834*, gen. ed. J. Hawley, 8 vols (London: Pickering & Chatto, 2003–2004), I, xi–xvii (p. xii), and G. S. Rousseau, 'The Discourses of Literature and Science (2)', in *Enlightenment Borders: Pre- and Post-modern Discourses: Medical, Scientific* (Manchester: Manchester University Press, 1991), pp. 213–35 (pp. 217–18).

16. L. J. Jordanova, 'Introduction', in *Languages of Nature: Critical Essays on Science and Literature*, ed. Jordanova (London: Free Association Books, 1986), pp. 15–47 (p. 16), and John Christie and Sally Shuttleworth, 'Introduction: Between Literature and Science', in *Nature Transfigured*, pp. 1–12 (esp. p. 2).

17. See A. C. Elias, Jr, *Swift at Moor Park: Problems in Biography and Criticism* (Philadelphia: University of Pennsylvania Press, 1982).

18. 'An Essay upon the Ancient and Modern Learning', in *Five Miscellaneous Essays by Sir William Temple*, ed. Samuel Holt Monk (Ann Arbor: University of Michigan Press, 1963), pp. 56–57.

19. John Locke, *An Essay Concerning Human Understanding*, ed. Peter H. Nidditch (Oxford: Clarendon Press, 1979), p. 645 (Book IV, Chap. XII, 10).

20. See Douglas Lane Patey, 'Swift's Satire on "Science" and the Structure of *Gulliver's Travels*', *ELH*, 58 (1991), 809–39 (pp. 823–24), Kathleen Williams, *Jonathan Swift and the Age of Compromise* (Lawrence: University of Kansas Press, 1958), esp. pp. 49–59, J. T. Parnell, 'Swift, Sterne, and the Skeptical Tradition', *Studies in Eighteenth-Century Culture*, 23 (1994), 221–42, and Marcus Walsh, 'Swift and Religion', in *The Cambridge Companion to Jonathan Swift*, ed. Christopher Fox (Cambridge: Cambridge University Press, 2003), pp. 161–76.

21. See I Corinthians 2.5.

22. Temple, 'Some Thoughts upon Reviewing the Essay of Ancient and Modern Learning', in *Five Miscellaneous Essays*, p. 96.

23. See Hermann J. Real and Heinz J. Vienken, '"I Knew and Could Distinguish Those Two Heroes at First Sight": Homer and Aristotle in Glubbdubdrib', *Notes & Queries*, 231 (n.s. 33) (1986), 51–53.

24. John Conduitt, 'Rough Draft Preface for the Life of Newton', in King's College Library, Cambridge, Keynes MS. 130.17, f. 4, in *NP*; Thomas Sprat, *The History of the Royal-Society of London, For the Improving of Natural Knowledge* (London, 1667), p. 112.

25. See Gregory Lynall, '"An Author *bonæ notæ*, and an *Adeptus*": Swift's Alchemical Satire and Satiric Alchemy in *A Tale of a Tub*', *Swift Studies*, 24 (2009), 29–45 (pp. 42–43).

26. Roger D. Lund, 'The Eel of Science: Index Learning, Scriblerian Satire, and the Rise of Information Culture', *Eighteenth-Century Life*, 22 (1998), 18–42 (p. 39).

27. Brean Hammond, 'Scriblerian Self-Fashioning', *Yearbook of English Studies*, 18 (1988), 108–22 (p. 118).

28. George Levine, 'One Culture: Science and Literature', in *One Culture: Essays in Science and Literature*, ed. G. Levine (Chicago, IL: Chicago University Press, 1987), pp. 3–32 (p. 8).

29. Steven Shapin, 'Of Gods and Kings: Natural Philosophy and Politics in the Leibniz-Clarke Disputes', *Isis*, 72 (1981), 187–215, Larry Stewart, *The Rise of Public Science: Rhetoric, Technology, and Natural Philosophy in Newtonian Britain, 1660–1750* (Cambridge: Cambridge University Press, 1992), p. xvi, and Simon Schaffer, 'Augustan Realities: Nature's Representatives and their Cultural Resources in the Early Eighteenth Century', in *Realism and Representation: Essays on the Problem of Realism in Relation to Science, Literature and Culture*, ed. George Levine (Madison: University of Wisconsin Press, 1993), pp. 279–318.

30. See *Memoirs*, ed. Kerby-Miller, pp. 60–65.

31. See G. S. Rousseau, 'Science Books and their Readership in the High Enlightenment', in *Enlightenment Borders*, pp. 264–324 (p. 282).

32. See Anita Guerrini, 'The Tory Newtonians: Gregory, Pitcairne, and their Circle', *Journal of British Studies*, 25 (1986), 288–311, and Peter Anstey, 'Literary Responses to Robert Boyle's Natural Philosophy', in *Science, Literature and Rhetoric in Early Modern England*, eds Juliet Cummins and David Burchell (Aldershot: Ashgate, 2007), pp. 145–62 (pp. 161–62).

33. *The Spectator*, Nos. 393 and 77, in *The Spectator*, ed. Donald F. Bond, 5 vols (Oxford: Clarendon Press, 1965), III, 475, and I, 330. See also Nos. 420 and 565 (III, 574–75, and IV, 529–33), and Gregory Lynall, 'John Gay, Magnetism, and the Spectacle of Natural Philosophy: Scriblerian Pins and Needles', *British Journal for Eighteenth-Century Studies*, 30 (2007), 389–403.

34. *The Examiner*, 14 (9 November 1710), in *PW*, III, 10–11. See Pope to Arbuthnot, 17 July 1734, 26 July 1734, 2 August 1734, 25 August 1734, in *The Correspondence of Alexander Pope*, ed. George Sherburn, 5 vols (Oxford: Clarendon Press, 1956), III, 417, 419, 423, 428.

35. Steven Shapin, *A Social History of Truth: Civility and Science in Seventeenth-Century England* (Chicago, IL: University of Chicago Press, 1994), pp. 42, 93–94.

36. Phillip Harth, *Swift and Anglican Rationalism: The Religious Background of 'A Tale of a Tub'* (Chicago, IL: University of Chicago Press, 1961), pp. 59–68,

Christie, 'Laputa Revisited', pp. 49–50, and Lynall, '"An Author *bonæ notæ*, and an *Adeptus*"', p. 32.

37. Thomas Sheridan (the younger), *The Life of the Rev. Dr. Jonathan Swift* (London, 1784), pp. 9–10.

38. Marjorie Nicolson and Nora M. Mohler, 'The Scientific Background of Swift's *Voyage to Laputa*' and 'Swift's "Flying Island" in the *Voyage to Laputa*', *Annals of Science*, 2 (1937), 299–334, 405–30, and Frederick N. Smith, 'Scientific Discourse: *Gulliver's Travels* and *The Philosophical Transactions*', in *The Genres of 'Gulliver's Travels'*, ed. F. N. Smith (Newark: University of Delaware Press, 1990), pp. 139–62 (p. 141).

39. Patrick Delany, *Observations upon Lord Orrery's Remarks on the Life and Writings of Dr. Jonathan Swift* (London, 1754), p. 101.

40. See *Journal to Stella*, Letter XI (13 December 1710), in *PW*, XV, 122, and Nicolson and Mohler, 'Swift's "Flying Island" in the *Voyage to Laputa*', p. 416.

41. Beat Affentranger takes issue with critics such as Ehrenpreis ('Jonathan Swift: Lecture on a Master Mind'), who claim that Swift could distinguish between 'genuine' and so-called 'pseudo-' science. See 'The Spectacle of the Growth of Knowledge and Swift's Satires on Science' (doctoral dissertation, University of Zurich, 1997–98, accessed via www.dissertation.com [Parkland, FL, 2000]), p. 4. However, it cannot be denied that studies which are methodologically and practically absurd are often subject to Swift's scathing wit.

42. Nicolson and Mohler, 'Swift's "Flying Island" in the *Voyage to Laputa*', and Nicolson, 'The Microscope and the English Imagination', in *Science and Imagination* (Ithaca, NY: Cornell University Press, 1956), pp. 155–234 (pp. 193–99).

Chapter 1

1. John Boyle, Fifth Earl of Cork and Orrery, *Remarks on the Life and Writings of Dr. Jonathan Swift*, ed. João Fróes (Newark: University of Delaware Press, 2000), p. 145 (Letter VIII).

2. *RAML*, p. 80, and see also pp. 179–81, 186–88, 242–44, 307.

3. See Miriam Starkman, *Swift's Satire on Learning in 'A Tale of a Tub'* (Princeton, NJ: Princeton University Press, 1950; repr. New York: Octagon Books, 1968), p. 119, Jon Rowland, 'Another Turn of the Screw: Prefaces in Swift, Marvell, and Genette', *Studies in Eighteenth-Century Culture*, 21 (1991), 129–48 (p. 138), and Marjorie Nicolson and Nora M. Mohler, 'The Scientific Background of Swift's *Voyage to Laputa*', *Annals of Science*, 2 (1937), 299–334 (pp. 324–25, 328, 332).

4. Gilbert Burnet, *Bishop Burnet's History of His Own Time*, 2 vols (London, 1724–34), I, 193, quoted in *PW*, V, 271.

5. See Steven Shapin, *Never Pure: Historical Studies of Science as if It Was Produced by People with Bodies, Situated in Time, Space, Culture, and Society, and Struggling for Credibility and Authority* (Baltimore, MD: The Johns Hopkins University Press, 2010), pp. 125–27.

6. See *Occasional Reflections upon Several Subjects* (London, 1665), sig. A2^r, in *WRB*, V, 10, and H. Fisch, 'Bishop Hall's Meditations', *The Review of English Studies*, 25 (1949), 210–21.

7. See Jane E. Jenkins, 'Arguing about Nothing: Henry More and Robert Boyle on the Theological Implications of the Void', in *Rethinking the Scientific Revolution*, ed. Margaret J. Osler (Cambridge: Cambridge University Press, 2000), pp. 153–79 (pp. 155, 168). On the date of composition, see *WRB*, V, xi.

8. See Shapin, *Never Pure*, p. 100, as well as Shapin and Simon Schaffer, *Leviathan and the Air Pump: Hobbes, Boyle, and the Experimental Life* (Princeton: Princeton University Press, 1985; repr. 1989), pp. 60–69.

9. See Marie-Louise Coolahan, 'Redeeming Parcels of Time: Aesthetics and Practice of Occasional Meditation', *The Seventeenth Century*, 22 (2007), 124–43 (pp. 134–35).

10. See *A Letter to a Young Gentleman, Lately Entered into Holy Orders* (1707?), in *PW*, IX, 68, Ann Cline Kelly, 'After Eden: Gulliver's (Linguistic) Travels', *ELH*, 45 (1978), 33–54 (p. 51), and Ian Higgins, 'Language and Style', in *The Cambridge Companion to Jonathan Swift*, ed. Christopher Fox (Cambridge: Cambridge University Press, 2003), pp. 146–60 (pp. 147–49).

11. J. Paul Hunter, 'Robert Boyle and the Epistemology of the Novel', *Eighteenth-Century Fiction*, 2 (1990), 275–91 (p. 280).

12. Hunter, 'Robert Boyle and the Epistemology of the Novel', p. 278, and the same author's *Before Novels: The Cultural Contexts of Eighteenth Century English Fiction* (New York: Norton, 1990), pp. 201–208. See Lawrence M. Principe, 'Virtuous Romance and Romantic Virtuoso: The Shaping of Robert Boyle's Literary Style', *Journal of the History of Ideas*, 56 (1995), 377–97 (esp. p. 395).

13. Thomas Sprat, *The History of the Royal-Society of London, For the Improving of Natural Knowledge* (London, 1667), p. 113, and *PW*, XI, 185–86. See Ann Cline Kelly, *Swift and the English Language* (Philadelphia, PN: University of Pennsylvania Press, 1988), pp. 77–79.

14. Joseph Glanvill, *Scepsis Scientifica* (London, 1665), sig. C4^r, facs. reprt in *The Vanity of Dogmatizing: The Three 'Versions'*, ed. Stephen Medcalf (Hove: Harvester Press, 1970), and see Medcalf's introduction, pp. xli–xliv.

15. See esp. Juliet Cummins and David Burchell, 'Introduction: Ways of Knowing: Conversations between Science, Literature, and Rhetoric', in *Science, Literature and Rhetoric in Early Modern England*, eds Cummins and Burchell (Aldershot: Ashgate, 2007), pp. 1–12 (p. 9).

16. Samuel Butler, 'Miscellaneous Observations', in *Hudibras Parts I and II and Selected Other Writings*, eds John Wilders and Hugh de Quehen (Oxford: Clarendon Press, 1973), p. 285; John Wilkins, *An Essay Towards a Real Character, and a Philosophical Language* (London, 1668). On Boyle's natural philosophical writings themselves featuring a 'heavily figurative and syntactically convoluted prose style', see Robert Markley, *Fallen Languages: Crises of Representation in Newtonian England, 1660–1740* (Ithaca, NY: Cornell University Press, 1993), p. 114.

17. Thomas Shadwell, *The Virtuoso*, eds Marjorie Hope Nicolson and David Stuart Rodes (London: Arnold, 1966), pp. 18–19 (I i 267–75).

18. See esp. Peter Anstey, 'Literary Responses to Robert Boyle's Natural Philosophy', in *Science, Literature and Rhetoric in Early Modern England*, eds Cummins and Burchell, pp. 145–62, and Claude Lloyd, 'Shadwell and the Virtuosi', *PMLA*, 44 (1929), 472–94.

19. This classification is also mocked in Rochester's *A Satyre against Reason and Mankind* (ll. 6–7, in *The Works of John Wilmot, Earl of Rochester*, ed. Harold

Love [Oxford: Oxford University Press, 1999], p. 57). See also Uwe Pauschert, '"It Should Be Only *Rationis Capax*"', *Swift Studies*, 1 (1986), 67. On designs to bring 'universal improvement' through natural philosophy, see Charles Webster, *The Great Instauration: Science, Medicine, and Reform, 1626–1660* (London: Duckworth, 1975), pp. 67–77 and *passim*.

20. Barbara M. Benedict, *Curiosity: A Cultural History of Early Modern Inquiry* (Chicago, IL: University of Chicago Press, 2001), pp. 49–51.
21. Butler, *Hudibras Parts I and II and Selected Other Writings*, pp. 238, 240. Coolahan highlights that Butler parodies two genuine experiments held at Gresham College ('Redeeming Parcels of Time', p. 136).
22. Ehrenpreis, II, 91n2.
23. See George Faulkner, 'Life of Swift', in *The Works of the Reverend Dr. Jonathan Swift, Dean of St. Patrick's, Dublin*, 11 vols (Dublin, 1762), XI, 314–15, and Thomas Sheridan, *The Life of the Rev. Dr. Jonathan Swift* (London, 1784), pp. 42–44.
24. On 'personation', see *Tale*, p. 7, and Richard Terry, 'Swift's Use of "Personate" to Indicate Parody', *Notes and Queries*, 239 (1994), 196–98. *Occasional Reflections* has been suggested as an object of inspiration as well as parody for Swift. The *Biographia Britannica: Or, The Lives of the Most Eminent Persons who Have Flourished in Great Britain and Ireland, from the Earliest Ages* (ed. Andrew Kippis, 2nd edn, 5 vols [London, 1778–93], II, 501n.) and Clive T. Probyn ('Gulliver and the Relativity of Things: A Commentary on Method and Mode, with a Note on Smollett', *Renaissance and Modern Studies*, 18: 1 [1974], 63–76 [pp. 70–72]) each note the similarity between the *Travels* and Boyle's proposal for a 'Romantick story' in which an 'Observing Native' of the 'Southern Ocean' visits Europe and gives an account of customs and manners 'to condemn, or perhaps laugh at them' (*WRB*, V, 171–72). The satiric value of travel writing was not unique to Boyle or Swift, and such parallels could be accidental.
25. See Boyle, Fifth Earl of Cork and Orrery, *Remarks*, p. 145 (Letter VIII), Deane Swift, *An Essay upon the Life, Writings, and Character of Dr. Jonathan Swift* (London, 1755), facs. reprt in *Swiftiana XIV* (New York: Garland, 1974), p. 126, and W. H. Dilworth, *The Life of Dr. Jonathan Swift* (London, 1758), facs. reprt in *Swiftiana XIII: Three Biographical Pamphlets 1745–1758* (New York: Garland, 1975), p. 34. For a more sympathetic view, see Sheridan, *Life*, p. 45.
26. See Anthony Henley to Swift, 2 November 1708, in *CJS*, I, 211.
27. See also *WRB*, V, 74: 'he, that by thriftily Husbanding his time [...] has early dispatch'd the business for which he was sent into the World, needs not Gray-hairs to be reputed to have Liv'd long enough'.
28. See also *WRB*, V, 117: 'For Pious, but melancholy Persons, are oftentimes too Partial against themselves, to be competent Judges of their own Estate'.
29. See also *WRB*, V, 43, 44, 50, 147, and Leslie Moore, '"Instructive Trees": Swift's *Broom-Stick*, Boyle's *Reflections*, and Satiric Figuration', *Eighteenth-Century Studies*, 19 (1986), 313–32 (p. 328).
30. See 'A Defence of *An Essay of Dramatic Poesy*', where Dryden argues that 'a man cannot but be a rational creature' (*Of Dramatic Poesy and Other Critical Essays*, ed. George Watson, 2 vols [London: Dent and Dutton, 1962], I, 120).

31. *WRB*, V, 9, 50; Moore, '"Instructive Trees"', p. 314, 329. See also *WRB*, V, 46.
32. See *RAML*, sig. A5^{r-v}.
33. Ovid, *Metamorphoses*, trans. A. D. Melville (Oxford: Oxford University Press, 1986), p. 3 (Book I, ll. 84–85); *Cratylus*, 399c, in *Works of Plato*, trans. H. N. Fowler and others, 12 vols (London: Heinemann, 1926), VI, 59. For *Metamorphoses* in Swift's library, see *LRJS*, II, 1355–56. Swift owned two editions of Plato (see *LRJS*, II, 1437–40), and in a letter to Pope (1 May 1733) mentions 'reading Plato many years ago' (*CJS*, III, 637). See also Irene Samuel, 'Swift's Reading of Plato', *Studies in Philology*, 73 (1976), 440–62.
34. See C. A. Patrides, 'Renaissance Ideas on Man's Upright Form', *Journal of the History of Ideas*, 19 (1958), 256–58; revised in *Premises and Motifs in Renaissance Thought and Literature* (Princeton, NJ: Princeton University Press, 1982), pp. 83–89.
35. Aristotle, *Nicomachean Ethics*, Book I, Chap. 7, 1098a, in *The Complete Works of Aristotle: The Revised Oxford Translation*, ed. Jonathan Barnes, 2 vols (Princeton, NJ: Princeton University Press, 1984), II, 1735. Swift was very familiar with Aristotle's writings, and the *Nichomachean Ethics*, which was required reading for undergraduates at Trinity College Dublin (Ehrenpreis, I, 59), and *Parts of Animals* (see note 37 below) feature in an anthology he owned: see *LRJS*, I, 85–86.
36. See Walter Charleton, *The Darknes of Atheism Dispelled by the Light of Nature: A Physico-Theologicall Treatise* (London, 1652), p. 86, and Patrides, 'Renaissance Ideas on Man's Upright Form', p. 258.
37. Plato, *Timaeus*, 90a, in *Works*, IX, 245, and Aristotle, *Parts of Animals*, Book IV, Chap. 10, 686b–687a, in *Complete Works*, I, 1071.
38. *Sylva Sylvarum*, VI, 607, in *The Works of Francis Bacon*, eds James Spedding, Robert Leslie Ellis and Douglas Denon Heath, 14 vols (London, 1857–74), II, 530. See A. B. Chambers, '"I Was But an Inverted Tree": Notes toward the History of an Idea', *Studies in the Renaissance*, 8 (1961), 291–99. While Chambers' account includes the *Broom-Stick* (pp. 297–98), he does not comment upon the significance of this tradition to Swift's satiric purpose. Apparently unaware of the image's long history, Clarence M. Webster suggests that Swift draws upon George Gascoigne, who in *The Viewe of Worldly Vanities* (1576) asks 'what is man [...] but a tree turned topsie turvey?' ('A Source for Swift's *A Meditation upon a Broomstick*', *Modern Language Notes*, 51 [1936], 160). On Gascoigne and the connection of the inverted tree to human degradation in the ascetic tradition, see Valerie Rumbold, 'Headnote to the *Broom-Stick*', in *Hoaxes, Parodies, Treatises and Mock-Treatises* (Cambridge: Cambridge University Press, forthcoming).
39. Butler, *Hudibras Parts I and II and Selected Other Writings*, p. 235.
40. On this ancient trope, see A. D. Nuttall, 'Fishes in the Trees', *Essays in Criticism*, 24 (1974), 20–38. Verbally echoing the *Broom-Stick*, the Scriblerians' *Peri Bathous: or, Martinus Scriblerus, His Treatise of the Art of Sinking in Poetry* (1727) argues that poetics has been corrupted by artificial thought: 'When an audience behold [...] a man's head where his heels should be; how are they struck with transport and delight? [An author] ought therefore to render himself master of this happy and *anti-natural* way of thinking' (Chap. V, in *The Prose Works of Alexander Pope*, eds Norman Ault and Rosemary Cowler, 2 vols [Oxford: Blackwell, 1936–86], II, 192).

41. Thomas Creech, *T. Lucretius Carus The Epicurean Philosopher, His Six Books De Natura Rerum Done into English Verse* (London, 1682), p. 4; John Reynolds, *Death's Vision Represented in a Philosophical, Sacred Poem* (London, 1709).

42. Swift to Pope, 29 September 1725; Pope and Bolingbroke to Swift, 14 December 1725; in *CJS*, II, 607, 627. See also *PW*, XI, 259.

43. See Charles Peake, 'Swift and the Passions', *Modern Language Review*, 55 (1960), 169–80.

44. Douglas H. White, 'Swift and the Definition of Man', *Modern Philology*, 73: 4, Part 2 (May 1976), S48–55 (S52, 50). See also R. S. Crane, 'The Houyhnhnms, the Yahoos, and the History of Ideas', in *Reason and the Imagination: Studies in the History of Ideas, 1600–1800*, ed. J. A. Mazzeo (New York: Columbia University Press, 1962), pp. 231–53, Clive T. Probyn, 'Swift and the Human Predicament', in *The Art of Jonathan Swift*, ed. Probyn (London: Vision Press, 1978), pp. 57–80 (esp. pp. 65–66), and J. A. Downie, 'Gulliver's Fourth Voyage and Locke's *Essay concerning Human Understanding*', in *Reading Swift: Papers from the Fifth Münster Symposium on Jonathan Swift*, ed. Hermann J. Real (München: Fink, 2008), pp. 453–64.

45. See Gardner D. Stout, Jr, 'Speaker and Satiric Vision in Swift's *Tale of a Tub*', *Eighteenth-Century Studies*, 3 (1969), 175–99 (p. 189).

46. Swift to the Revd John Winder, 13 January 1698[-9], in *CJS*, I, 137.

47. Peter Harrison, 'Original Sin and the Problem of Knowledge in Early Modern Europe', *Journal of the History of Ideas*, 63 (2002), 239–59.

48. See Arthur Pollard, *Satire* (London: Methuen, 1970), p. 21.

49. Douglas Lane Patey, 'Swift's Satire on "Science" and the Structure of *Gulliver's Travels*', *ELH*, 58 (1991), 809–39 (pp. 828–33).

50. See Joseph M. Levine, *Dr. Woodward's Shield: History, Science, and Satire in Augustan England* (Berkeley: University of California Press, 1977), pp. 284–87, Ehrenpreis, II, 179–80, 189, 191, and *Oxford DNB*, s.v. 'Herbert, Thomas'. Swift discussed antiquarian topics (half-jokingly, at least) with Fountaine and Pembroke: see Swift to Pembroke, 13 June 1709, in *CJS*, I, 253.

51. On the usual charges made against the virtuoso, see esp. Walter E. Houghton, 'The English Virtuoso in the Seventeenth Century', *Journal of the History of Ideas*, 3 (1942), 51–73, and 190–219, and Shapin, *Never Pure*, p. 171.

52. As a common Scriblerian target, see Roger D. Lund, 'The Eel of Science: Index Learning, Scriblerian Satire, and the Rise of Information Culture', *Eighteenth-Century Life*, 22: 2 (May 1998), 18–42.

53. Hunter, 'Robert Boyle and the Epistemology of the Novel', p. 280.

54. See *Memoirs*, p. 92, and 'On Cutting down the Old Thorn at Market Hill' (1728), l. 25, in *Poems*, III, 849.

55. See, for instance, Mary Astell, *An Essay in Defence of the Female Sex* (London, 1696), pp. 96–108, William King, *Dialogues of the Dead: Relating to the Present Controversy Concerning the Epistles of Phalaris* (London, 1699), pp. 53–54, 66, and Richard Steele, *The Tatler*, 119, 216, 221, and esp. 236 (whose narrator at times sounds remarkably like Boyle: 'There is no study more becoming a rational Creature, than that of Natural Philosophy'), in Donald F. Bond (ed.), *The Tatler*, 3 vols (Oxford: Clarendon Press, 1987), II, 205–209; III, 132–35, 153–57, 217–20 (219).

56. Maurice Johnson identifies parallels between the *Broom-stick* and the *Tale* (particularly Sections I and IX), but does not consider whether the *Occasional*

Reflections is a source for the *Tale*. See 'A Note on Swift's *Meditation upon a Broom-stick* and *A Tale of a Tub*', *Library Chronicle* (University of Pennsylvania), 37 (1971), 136–42.

57. See also *The Christian Virtuoso, The First Part* (London, 1690–91), p. 40, in *WRB*, XI, 303.

58. *Observations upon Anthroposophia Theomagica, and Anima Magica Abscondita* (London, 1655), facs. reprt in *Henry More: Major Philosophical Works*, ed. G. A. J. Rogers, 9 vols (Bristol: Thoemmes Press, 1997), III, 73; Phillip Harth, *Swift and Anglican Rationalism: The Religious Background of 'A Tale of a Tub'* (Chicago, IL: University of Chicago Press, 1961), p. 85; Thomas Stanley, *The History of Philosophy*, 3rd edn (London, 1701), Part XI, Chap. ix, Section IV, p. 464. Harth has demonstrated Swift's use of Stanley's *History* elsewhere in the *Tale* (*Swift and Anglican Rationalism*, pp. 66–67).

59. *Some Considerations Touching the Usefulness of Experimental Natural Philosophy. The First Part* (London, 1663), p. 71, in *WRB*, III, 248, and *The Christian Virtuoso, The First Part*, in *WRB*, XI, 299. It is unlikely the sartorial system is based in a trope built on the pun 'fabric': according to the *Oxford English Dictionary*, the word was not used in the sense of a manufactured textile material until the mid-eighteenth century.

60. See Margaret G. Cook, 'Divine Artifice and Natural Mechanism: Robert Boyle's Mechanical Philosophy of Nature', *Osiris*, 2nd series, 16 (2001), 133–50 (pp. 140–41).

61. *The Christian Virtuoso*, in *WRB*, XI, 299, 300. See Marie Boas, 'The Establishment of the Mechanical Philosophy', *Osiris*, 10 (1952), 412–541 (p. 487).

62. See *Usefulness of Experimental Natural Philosophy*, Part I, in *WRB*, III, 268, and John Hedley Brooke, *Science and Religion: Some Historical Perspectives* (Cambridge: Cambridge University Press, 1991), p. 132.

63. *A Free Enquiry into the Vulgarly Receiv'd Notion of Nature* (London, 1686), Section I, pp. 7–8, in *WRB*, X, 447.

64. See Ralph Cudworth, *The True Intellectual System of the Universe* (London, 1678), Book I, Chap. V, Section V, p. 888. On '*Plastick Nature*', see esp. Book I, Chap. III, pp. 178-81. This work featured in Swift's library: see *LRJS*, I, 482–84.

65. See Roy Porter, *Flesh in the Age of Reason*, foreword by Simon Schama (London: Allen Lane, 2003), pp. 87, 89–90.

66. The continuing action of '*Journey-man* Nature' might refer generally to moderate displacements of the Prime Mover from his Creation, through the current vogue for natural theology, as Richard G. Olson suggests, but could also allude specifically to Cudworth's '*Plastick Nature*'. See 'Tory-High Church Opposition to Science and Scientism in the Eighteenth Century: The Works of John Arbuthnot, Jonathan Swift, and Samuel Johnson', in *The Uses of Science in the Age of Newton*, ed. John G. Burke (Berkeley: University of California Press, 1983), pp. 171–204 (p. 188).

67. See Porter, *Flesh in the Age of Reason*, esp. pp. 65–69.

68. See *RAML*, esp. pp. 197–98, 224, 226–27.

69. See Theodore M. Brown, 'Physiology and the Mechanical Philosophy in Mid-seventeenth-century England', *Bulletin of the History of Medicine*, 51 (1977), 25–54 (p. 54).

70. *Experiments and Considerations about the Porosity of Bodies, in Two Essays* (London, 1684), Essay I, Chap. I, p. 4, in *WRB*, X, 108. See Brown, 'Physiology and the Mechanical Philosophy', p. 50.

71. See esp. Carol Houlihan Flynn, *The Body in Swift and Defoe* (Cambridge: Cambridge University Press, 1990), and William Freedman, 'The Grotesque Body in the Hollow Tub: Swift's *Tale*', *Texas Studies in Literature and Language*, 51 (2009), 294–316.

72. *The Passions of the Soul* (1649), Part I, Section 6, in *The Philosophical Writings of Descartes*, trans. John Cottingham, Robert Stoothoff and Dugald Murdoch, 3 vols (Cambridge: Cambridge University Press, 1984–91), I, 329–30.

73. John Locke, for instance, suggested that God might 'superadd to Matter a Faculty of Thinking' (*An Essay Concerning Human Understanding*, ed. Peter H. Nidditch [Oxford: Clarendon Press, 1979], p. 541 [Book IV, Chap. III]). See John W. Yolton, *Thinking Matter: Materialism in Eighteenth-Century Britain* (Minneapolis, MN: University of Minnesota, 1983; repr. Oxford: Blackwell, 1984), esp. pp. 14–48.

74. Martin Price, *Swift's Rhetorical Art: A Study in Structure and Meaning* (New Haven, CT: Yale University Press, 1953), p. 89.

75. *The Rehearsal Transpros'd: The Second Part*, in Andrew Marvell, *The Prose Works of Andrew Marvell*, eds Annabel Patterson and others, 2 vols (New Haven, CT: Yale University Press, 2003), I, 266.

76. A. C. Guthkelch suggests Wotton's *RAML* (p. 193) as the target of this allusion, but Boyle's *Occasional Reflections* offered Swift further confirmation of the Moderns' delight in anatomy. See *A Tale of a Tub &c.*, eds Guthkelch and D. Nichol Smith, 2nd edn, corrected (Oxford: Clarendon Press, 1973), p. 123n.

77. See Michael V. DePorte, 'Digressions and Madness in *A Tale of a Tub* and *Tristram Shandy*', *Huntington Library Quarterly*, 34 (1970), 43–57 (p. 44), and the same author's *Nightmares and Hobbyhorses: Swift, Sterne, and Augustan Ideas of Madness* (San Marino, CA: Huntington Library, 1974), pp. 60–65.

78. Julien Offray de La Mettrie, *Machine Man and Other Writings*, ed. and trans. Ann Thomson (Cambridge: Cambridge University Press, 1996), p. 28.

79. See Harth, *Swift and Anglican Rationalism*, pp. 119–20. Unlike Boyle's account, Glanvill's does not proffer 'the bare change of Air' or 'an infectious Vapour' as possible causes of disruption to the system's harmony.

80. C. J. Rawson, *Gulliver and the Gentle Reader: Studies in Swift and our Time* (London: Routledge & Kegan Paul, 1973), pp. 33–36, 143. Ronald Paulson compares the passage with dissection accounts in the *Philosophical Transactions*, whilst Frederick N. Smith notes its resemblance to Thomas Willis's description of 'dissecting the Carcase of a Maid'. See Paulson, *Theme and Structure in Swift's 'Tale of a Tub'* (New Haven, CT: Yale University Press, 1960; repr. Hamden, CT: Archon Books (Shoe String Press), 1972), pp. 62–63, and Smith, *Language and Reality in Swift's 'A Tale of a Tub'* (Columbus: Ohio State University Press, 1979), pp. 63–64, 69n40.

81. Compare the metaphor of political surgery in 'A Vindication of His Excellency John, Lord Carteret' (1730), in *PW*, XII, 157–58. Swift probably approved of the anatomical models presented to Trinity College Dublin's Medical School by Dr John Scott, because 'a person may gain more perfect knowledge in anatomy [from them than] by attending many dissections' (although the

French surgeon Guillaume Desnouës dissected 'some hundreds of bodies' in order to produce them). See Scott to Swift, 7 September 1739, in *CJS*, IV, 590 and 591n.

82. See Christopher Fox, 'How to Prepare a Noble Savage: The Spectacle of Human Science', in *Inventing Human Science: Eighteenth-Century Domains*, eds Christopher Fox, Roy Porter and Robert Wokler (Berkeley: University of California Press, 1995), pp. 1–30 (p. 6), and the same author's 'Swift and the Spectacle of Human Science', in *Reading Swift: Papers from the Third Münster Symposium on Jonathan Swift*, eds Hermann J. Real and Helgard Stöver-Leidig (München: Fink, 1998), pp. 199–212 (pp. 199–200).

83. *Discourse on the Method* (1637), Part V, in *The Philosophical Writings of Descartes*, I, 140.

84. See Roger D. Lund, 'Martinus Scriblerus and the Search for the Soul', *Papers on Language and Literature*, 25: 2 (Spring 1989), 135–50 (p. 142).

85. See Peter J. Schakel, 'Swift's Voices: Innovation and Complication in the Poems Written at Market Hill', in *Reading Swift: Papers from the Fourth Münster Symposium on Jonathan Swift*, eds Hermann J. Real and Helgard Stöver-Leidig (München: Fink, 2003), pp. 311–25 (pp. 313–14), and Carole Fabricant, *Swift's Landscape* (Baltimore, MD: The Johns Hopkins University Press, 1982; repr. Notre Dame, IN: University of Notre Dame Press, 1995), pp. 207–208.

86. Arno Löffler, 'The Dean and Lady Anne: Humour in Swift's Market Hill Poems', in *Reading Swift: Papers from the Second Münster Symposium on Jonathan Swift*, eds Richard H. Rodino and Hermann J. Real (München: Fink, 1993), pp. 113–24 (pp. 118–19).

87. See 'An excellent new Panegyric on Skinnibonia', ll. 7–10, 13–14, published in James Woolley, 'Swift's "Skinnibonia": A New Poem from Lady Acheson's Manuscript', in *Reading Swift: Papers from the Fifth Münster Symposium*, pp. 309–42 (pp. 320, 328). On Swift's attitude to Epicurus and Lucretius, see Hermann J. Real, 'A Taste of Composition Rare: The *Tale*'s Matter and Void', in *Reading Swift: Papers from the Third Münster Symposium*, pp. 73–90 (esp. pp. 75–77).

Chapter 2

1. A. C. Elias, Jr, *Swift at Moor Park: Problems in Biography and Criticism* (Philadelphia: University of Pennsylvania Press, 1982), p. 48. In contrast, see Philip Pinkus, 'Swift and the Ancients-Moderns Controversy', *University of Toronto Quarterly*, 29 (1959), 46–58 (p. 51).

2. The episode has been extensively discussed. See esp. *The Battle of the Books: Eine Historisch-kritische Ausgabe*, ed. Hermann J. Real (Berlin: Walter de Gruyter, 1978), pp. xlv–liv.

3. See Ehrenpreis, I, 232–34, Hermann J. Real, 'Die Biene und die Spinne in Swift's "Battle of the Books"', *Germanisch-Romanische Monatsschrift*, n.s.23 (1973), 169–77, and Roberta F. Borkat, 'The Spider and the Bee: Jonathan Swift's Reversal of Tradition in *The Battle of the Books*', *Eighteenth-Century Life*, 3 (December 1976), 44–46.

4. Bacon, *Novum organum*, Book I, Aphorism XCV, in *The Instauratio magna Part II: Novum organum and Associated Texts*, ed. and trans. Graham Rees with

Maria Wakely (Oxford: Clarendon Press, 2004), p. 153, and *The Advancement of Learning*, ed. Michael Kiernan (Oxford: Clarendon Press, 2000), p. 24. See David K. Weiser, 'Bacon's Borrowed Imagery', *Review of English Studies*, n.s.38 (1987), 315–24 (pp. 316–18), James W. Johnson, 'That Neo-Classical Bee', *Journal of the History of Ideas*, 22 (1961), 262–66, R. H. Bowers, 'Bacon's Spider Simile', *Journal for the History of Ideas*, 17 (1956), 133–35, and Jonathan Woolfson, 'The Renaissance of Bees', *Renaissance Studies*, 24 (2009), 281–300 (p. 283). The bee's liberty to roam and to produce honey also served as a metaphor for the occasional meditator's freedom to expatiate upon any given topic: see Marie-Louise Coolahan, 'Redeeming Parcels of Time: Aesthetics and Practice of Occasional Meditation', *The Seventeenth Century*, 22 (2007), 124–43 (pp. 131–32).

5. See Ernest Tuveson, 'Swift and the World-Makers', *Journal of the History of Ideas*, 11 (1950), 54–74 (p. 69), Kathleen Williams, 'Restoration Themes in the Major Satires of Swift', *Review of English Studies*, n.s.16 (1965), 258–71 (p. 261), and Borkat, 'The Spider and the Bee', p. 45.

6. See *A Proposal for the Universal Use of Irish Manufacture* (1720), where Swift pities 'poor *Arachne*' for being cursed to '*spin* and *weave* for ever, *out of her own Bowels*, and *in a very narrow Compass*' (*PW*, IX, 18).

7. 'An Essay upon the Ancient and Modern Learning', in *Five Miscellaneous Essays by Sir William Temple*, ed. Samuel Holt Monk (Ann Arbor: The University of Michigan Press, 1963), p. 37. See Joseph M. Levine, *The Battle of the Books: History and Literature in the Augustan Age* (Ithaca, NY: Cornell University Press, 1991), pp. 19–26.

8. Thomas Burnet, *The Theory of the Earth*, 3rd edn (London, 1697), Book III, Chap. 2, p. 7. Swift owned this edition (see *LRJS*, I, 302).

9. See esp. Roy Porter, 'Creation and Credence: The Career of Theories of the Earth in Britain, 1660–1820', in *Natural Order: Historical Studies of Scientific Culture*, ed. Barry Barnes (Beverley Hills, CA: Sage, 1979), pp. 97–123, Joseph M. Levine, *Dr. Woodward's Shield: History, Science, and Satire in Augustan England* (Berkeley: University of California Press, 1977), pp. 25–27, Marjorie Hope Nicolson, *Mountain Gloom and Mountain Glory: The Development of the Aesthetics of the Infinite* (Ithaca, NY: Cornell University Press, 1959), pp. 225–70, and H. V. S. Ogden, 'Thomas Burnet's *Telluris Theoria Sacra* and Mountain Scenery', *ELH*, 14 (1947), 139–50 (esp. pp. 139, 148). On the Scriblerian attack on Woodward, see esp. Levine, *Dr. Woodward's Shield*, *passim*, Lester M. Beattie, *John Arbuthnot: Mathematician and Satirist* (Cambridge, MA: Harvard University Press, 1935), pp. 190–262, and *Memoirs*, pp. 203–206, 330.

10. Burnet, *Theory*, Book III, Chap. 12, p. 73, and Book IV, Chap. 1, p. 91.

11. Burnet, *Theory*, Book III, Chap. 10, p. 56, and Book III, Chap. 12, pp. 73, 74. See Margaret C. Jacob and W. A. Lockwood, 'Political Millenarianism and Burnet's *Sacred Theory*', *Science Studies*, 2 (1972), 265–79 (p. 273), Ernest Lee Tuveson, *Millennium and Utopia: A Study in the Background of the Idea of Progress* (Berkeley: University of California Press, 1949; repr. New York: Harper & Row, 1964), pp. 117–20, and Reiner Smolinski, 'The Logic of Millenial Thought: Sir Isaac Newton among his Contemporaries', in *Newton and Religion: Context, Nature, and Influence*, eds James E. Force and Richard H. Popkin (Dordrecht: Kluwer Academic, 1999), pp. 259–89 (pp. 267–68).

12. Richard Steele, *The Spectator*, 146 (17 August 1711), in *The Spectator*, ed. Donald F. Bond, 5 vols (Oxford: Clarendon Press, 1965), II, 76–77. See Nicolson, *Mountain Gloom and Mountain Glory, passim*.

13. See Scott Mandelbrote, 'Isaac Newton and Thomas Burnet: Biblical Criticism and the Crisis of Late Seventeenth-Century England', in *The Books of Nature and Scripture: Recent Essays on Natural Philosophy, Theology, and Biblical Criticism in the Netherlands of Spinoza's Time and the British Isles of Newton's Time*, eds James E. Force and Richard H. Popkin (Dordrecht: Kluwer Academic, 1994), pp. 149–78 (pp. 151, 157), and James E. Force, 'Providence and Newton's Pantokrator: Natural Law, Miracles, and Newtonian Science', in *Newton and Newtonianism: New Studies*, eds Force and Sarah Hutton (Dordrecht: Kluwer Academic, 2004), pp. 65–92 (p. 65).

14. See Mandelbrote, 'Isaac Newton and Thomas Burnet', p. 164. Swift was certainly aware of *Archaeologiae Philosophicae*: Temple refers to the 'great knowledge and esteem of the ancient learning' Burnet shows in this work, in contrast to the *Sacred Theory* ('Some Thoughts upon Reviewing the Essay of Ancient and Modern Learning', in *Five Miscellaneous Essays*, p. 75).

15. See Richard W. F. Kroll, *The Material Word: Literate Culture in the Restoration and Early Eighteenth Century* (Baltimore, MD: The Johns Hopkins University Press, 1991), pp. 122–23.

16. Appendix to *Archaeologiae Philosophicae*, trans. and published in Charles Blount, *The Oracles of Reason* (London, 1693), p. 80. See Tuveson, 'Swift and the World-makers', p. 65, and Kathleen Williams, *Jonathan Swift and the Age of Compromise* (Lawrence: University of Kansas Press, 1958), p. 128.

17. Tuveson, 'Swift and the World-Makers', p. 70. I have already shared some of my findings here with the Cambridge Edition of the *Tale* (see pp. 475–81).

18. Burnet, *Theory*, Book III, Chap. 7, p. 38, and Book III, Chap. 1, p. 2. See also Book III, sig. A3^r, and Book III, Chap. IV, p. 21.

19. Burnet, *Theory*, Book I, The Epistle Dedicatory, sig. A2^r, Book I, Chap. 8, p. 66, and Book III, Chap. 12, p. 74. See Louis Moréri, *The Great Historical, Geographical, and Poetical Dictionary; Being a Curious Miscellany of Sacred and Prophane History*, collected and enlarged by Jean Le Clerc, 2 vols in 1 (London, 1694), s. v. 'Beelzebub'.

20. *A Representation of the Present State of Religion, with regard to the late Excessive Growth of Infidelity, Heresy, and Profaneness* (London, 1711), pp. 16–17. See *LRJS*, I, 102–105. On Atterbury's authorship, see Larry Stewart, *The Rise of Public Science: Rhetoric, Technology, and Natural Philosophy in Newtonian Britain, 1660–1750* (Cambridge: Cambridge University Press, 1992), p. 92.

21. See Hermann J. Real, '"An Horrid Vision": Jonathan Swift's "(On) the Day of Judgment"', in *Swift and his Contexts*, eds John Irwin Fischer, Hermann J. Real and James Woolley (New York: AMS Press, 1989), pp. 65–96.

22. Everett Zimmerman argues that the dismissal of the possibility of divine providence by the *Mechanical Operation*'s narrator (p. 178) is a 'covert parody' of Burnet. However, it is just as likely that Swift is parodying Hobbes. See *Swift's Narrative Satires: Author and Authority* (Ithaca, NY: Cornell University Press, 1983), pp. 98–99.

23. John Theophilus Desaguliers, *A Course of Experimental Philosophy*, 2 vols (London, 1734–44), I, Preface, sig. C1^r.

24. Anita Guerrini, 'The Tory Newtonians: Gregory, Pitcairne, and their Circle', *Journal of British Studies*, 25 (1986), 288–311 (pp. 305–10).

25. Ehrenpreis, I, 25; Swift to William Swift, 29 November 1692, in *CJS*, I, 116.

26. Atterbury to Bishop Jonathan Trelawny, 15 June 1704, in *Memoirs and Correspondence of Francis Atterbury, D. D., Bishop of Rochester*, ed. Robert Folkestone Williams, 2 vols (London: W. H. Allen, 1869), I, 99, 100. See Ian Higgins, *Swift's Politics: A Study in Disaffection* (Cambridge: Cambridge University Press, 1994), esp. p. 141.

27. See Swift to Robert Hunter (12 January 1708/9), and Swift to John Wheldon (27 September 1727), in *CJS*, I, 230, and III, 129. Swift also knew William King, and helped him obtain the post of Gazetteer: see *Journal to Stella*, Letter XXXVIII (December 1711), in *PW*, XVI, 452, and Swift to Archbishop King, 8 [January] 1711–12, in *CJS*, I, 411.

28. See Margaret C. Jacob, *The Newtonians and the English Revolution, 1689–1720* (Ithaca, NY: Cornell University Press, 1976), esp. pp. 78–79, Howard D. Weinbrot, '"He Will Kill Me Over and Over Again": Intellectual Contexts of the Battle of the Books', in *Reading Swift: Papers from the Fourth Münster Symposium on Jonathan Swift*, eds Hermann J. Real and Helgard Stöver-Leidig (München: Fink, 2003), pp. 225–48 (esp. p. 236), and Guerrini, 'The Tory Newtonians', pp. 289, 307. Charles Boyle and Freind would find themselves in the Tower at the time of the Atterbury affair in 1723, but Freind later served as physician to Caroline (J. S. Rowlinson, 'John Freind: Physician, Chemist, Jacobite, and Friend of Voltaire's', *Notes and Records of the Royal Society of London*, 61 [2007], 109–27 [p. 116]).

29. On Freind as Swift's 'brother', see *Journal to Stella*, Letter XLIII (14 March 1711–12), in *PW*, XVI, 513. See also Letter XXII (9 May 1711), in *PW*, XV, 264–65.

30. J. E. McGuire and P. M. Rattansi, 'Newton and the "Pipes of Pan"', *Notes and Records of the Royal Society of London*, 21 (1966), 108–43 (pp. 115, 121). See also James E. Force, 'Newton, the "Ancients," and the "Moderns"', in *Newton and Religion*, pp. 237–57 (pp. 243–44).

31. Keill, *An Introduction to the True Astronomy: Or, Astronomical Lectures, Read in the Astronomical School of the University of Oxford* (London, 1721), p. ix.

32. Swift to Robert Hunter, 12 January 1708/9, in *CJS*, I, 230, and see *Oxford DNB*, s. v. 'Keill, John'.

33. 'Memoirs, Relating to That Change Which Happened in the Queen's Ministry in the Year 1710' (c.1714, pub.1765), in *PW*, VIII, 120. See Ian Higgins, 'Jonathan Swift's Political Confession', in *Politics and Literature in the Age of Swift: English and Irish Perspectives*, ed. Claude Rawson (Cambridge: Cambridge University Press, 2010), pp. 3–30.

34. See Robert M. Adams, 'The Mood of the Church and *A Tale of a Tub*', in *England in the Restoration and Early Eighteenth Century: Essays on Culture and Society*, ed. H. T. Swedenberg, Jr (Berkeley: University of California Press, 1972), pp. 71–99 (p. 84), the same author's 'In Search of Baron Somers', in *Culture and Politics from Puritanism to the Enlightenment*, ed. Perez Zagorin (Berkeley: University of California Press, 1980), pp. 165–202 (p. 186), and Higgins, *Swift's Politics*, esp. pp. 8, 34, 101, 114, 122-24, 129. For J. A. Downie, Swift always maintained his 'Old Whig' principles: see *Jonathan Swift: Political Writer* (London: Routledge & Kegan Paul, 1984; repr. 1985), esp. pp. 83–84.

35. See Margaret C. Jacob, 'Millenarianism and Science in the Late Seventeenth Century', *Journal of the History of Ideas*, 37 (1976), 335–41 (p. 335), Simon Schaffer, 'Halley's Atheism and the End of World', *Notes and Records of the Royal Society of London*, 32 (1977), 17–40 (p. 19), and Robert Markley, *Fallen Languages: Crises of Representation in Newtonian England, 1660–1740* (Ithaca, NY: Cornell University Press, 1993), p. 206. Unlike Keill, Swift's future friend Arbuthnot was more willing to entertain theorists who surveyed the 'Works of Nature with the same Geometry (tho' in a more imperfect Degree) by which the Divine Architect put them together', although he wouldn't have included Burnet and Woodward among them. See *An Examination of Dr. Woodward's Account of the Deluge* (1697), repr. in *The Miscellaneous Works of the Late Dr. Arbuthnot*, 2 vols (Glasgow, 1751), II, 235.

36. John Keill, *An Examination of Dr Burnet's Theory of the Earth. Together with Some Remarks on Mr Whiston's New Theory of the Earth* (London, 1698), p. 37. For less prominent responses, see Mandelbrote, 'Isaac Newton and Thomas Burnet', p. 171n32. Descartes' eschatology had also influenced Burnet's one-time acquaintance, Henry More, whose *An Explanation of the Grand Mystery of Godliness* (1660) explained that the conflagration would be brought about through physical means, in the form of volcanoes and comets. See Philip C. Almond, *Heaven and Hell in Enlightenment England* (Cambridge: Cambridge University Press, 1994), p. 114.

37. *The Principia: Mathematical Principles of Natural Philosophy*, 3rd edn (London, 1726), trans. I. Bernard Cohen and Anne Whitman (Berkeley: University of California Press, 1999), p. 939 (Book III, General Scholium).

38. Burnet, *Reflections upon The Theory of the Earth, Occasion'd by a Late Examination of it. In a Letter to a Friend* (London, 1699), pp. 53, 30, and see John Henry, '"Pray Do Not Ascribe that Notion to Me": God and Newton's Gravity', in *The Books of Nature and Scripture*, pp. 123–47.

39. Keill, *Examination*, p. 15, and see Wotton, *A Defense of the Reflections upon Ancient and Modern Learning, […] With Observations upon The Tale of a Tub* (London, 1705), pp. 3–6.

40. *Tale*, p. 108. On Descartes in the *Tale*, see Michael R. G. Spiller, 'The Idol of the Stove: The Background to Swift's Criticism of Descartes', *Review of English Studies*, 25 (1974), 15–24, Miriam Kosh Starkman, *Swift's Satire on Learning in 'A Tale of a Tub'* (Princeton, NJ: Princeton University Press, 1950; repr. New York: Octagon Books, 1968), pp. 32–34, Phillip Harth, *Swift and Anglican Rationalism: The Religious Background of 'A Tale of a Tub'* (Chicago, IL: University of Chicago Press, 1961), pp. 94–97, and Roger D. Lund, 'Strange Complicities: Atheism and Conspiracy in *A Tale of a Tub*', *Eighteenth-Century Life*, 13: 3 (November 1989), 34–58; repr. in *British Literature 1640–1789: A Critical Reader*, ed. Robert DeMaria, Jr (Oxford: Blackwell, 1999), pp. 142–68 (p. 152).

41. Thomas Sprat, *The History of the Royal-Society of London, for the Improving of Natural Knowledge* (London, 1667), p. 96.

42. See José Luis Bermúdez, 'Scepticism and Science in Descartes', *Philosophy and Phenomenological Research*, 57 (1997), 743–72 (p. 744).

43. See, for instance, *Discourse on the Method* (1637), Part I, in *The Philosophical Writings of Descartes*, trans. John Cottingham, Robert Stoothoff and Dugald Murdoch, 3 vols (Cambridge: Cambridge University Press, 1984–91), I, 112.

44. Tuveson notes that Boyle uses the image of a spider living in one room of a palace and ignorant of the rest of the building to illustrate the temptation to accept the 'superficial account given us of things' and neglect to use our higher faculties. See *Some Considerations Touching the Usefulness of Experimental Natural Philosophy: The First Part* (London, 1663), Essay I, p. 10, in *WRB*, III, 204–205, and Tuveson, 'Swift and the World-Makers', p. 69n50. Despite Swift's knowledge of some works of Boyle (such as the *Occasional Reflections*), it seems unlikely that he would be aware of this specific passage. Boyle's simile is at least indicative of the prevalence of the association of the spider with reductive thinking.

45. Temple, 'Some Thoughts upon Reviewing the Essay', p. 73, and John Boyle, Fifth Earl of Cork and Orrery, *Remarks on the Life and Writings of Dr. Jonathan Swift*, ed. João Fróes (Newark: University of Delaware Press, 2000), p. 207 (Letter XIV).

46. See Steven Shapin, *Never Pure* (Baltimore, MD: The Johns Hopkins University Press, 2010), pp. 142–81.

47. Brean S. Hammond, *Pope* (Brighton: Harvester New Readings, 1986), p. 107.

48. John Traugott, '*A Tale of a Tub*', in *The Character of Swift's Satire: A Revised Focus*, ed. C. J. Rawson (Newark: University of Delaware Press, 1983), pp. 83–126 (pp. 94–95). For Elias, however, the Spider highlights the 'traits which Temple unwittingly shared with the Moderns he despised' (*Swift at Moor Park*, p. 192).

49. Burnet, *Reflections upon The Theory*, pp. 40, 44, 62. For Burnet's other attacks on Keill's 'rudeness', see pp. 17, 45, 59.

50. On the interpretation of Swift's allegories, see esp. Brean S. Hammond, 'Applying Swift', in *Reading Swift: Papers from the Second Münster Symposium on Jonathan Swift*, eds Richard H. Rodino and Hermann J. Real (München: Fink, 1993), pp. 185–97.

51. See Keill, *Examination*, p. 19.

52. Keill, *Examination*, p. 36. See Burnet, *Reflections upon The Theory*, pp. 4–6, 9.

53. Brean S. Hammond, 'Scriblerian Self-Fashioning', *Yearbook of English Studies*, 18 (1988), 108–24 (p. 109).

54. See Pope's extended allusion to Swift's fable, which draws upon its imagery to characterize the professional writer as a spinning 'Scribler': 'An Epistle from Mr. *Pope*, to Dr. *Arbuthnot*', ll. 85–94, in *TE*, IV, 101–102.

55. Swift to Gay and the Duchess of Queensberry, 10 July 1732, in *CJS*, III, 499.

56. *The Spectator*, 512 (17 October 1712), in *The Spectator*, IV, 318.

57. See, for instance, Moréri, *The Great Historical [...] Dictionary*, s. v. 'Aesop', 'Socrates'.

58. See Roger D. Lund, '*A Tale of a Tub*, Swift's Apology, and the Trammels of Christian Wit', in *Augustan Subjects: Essays in Honor of Martin C. Battestin*, ed. Albert J. Rivero (Newark: University of Delaware Press, 1997), pp. 87–109 (esp. pp. 88–90).

59. Jayne Elizabeth Lewis, *The English Fable: Aesop and Literary Culture, 1651–1740* (Cambridge: Cambridge University Press, 1996), p. 59.

60. See Donald Greene, 'Augustinianism and Empiricism: A Note on Eighteenth-Century English Intellectual History', *Eighteenth-Century Studies*, 1 (1967), 33–68 (pp. 54–55), and Greene, 'Swift: Some Caveats', in *Studies in the Eighteenth Century II: Papers presented at the Second David Nichol Smith*

Memorial Seminar Canberra 1970, ed. R. F. Brissenden (Canberra: Australian National University Press, 1973), pp. 341–58 (p. 355).

61. Bacon, *Novum organum*, Book I, Aphorism XCV, p. 153.

62. Samuel Butler, *Hudibras*, Part I, Canto III, ll. 1337–40, in *Hudibras Parts I and II and Selected Other Writings*, eds John Wilders and Hugh de Quehen (Oxford: Clarendon Press, 1973), p. 101.

63. See, for instance, Colin Kiernan, 'Swift and Science', *Historical Journal*, 14 (1971), 709–22, and Richard G. Olson, 'Tory-High Church Opposition to Science and Scientism in the Eighteenth Century: The Works of John Arbuthnot, Jonathan Swift, and Samuel Johnson', in *The Uses of Science in the Age of Newton*, ed. John G. Burke (Berkeley: University of California Press, 1983), pp. 171–204.

Chapter 3

1. Eustace Budgell, *Memoirs of the Lives and Characters of the Illustrious Family of the Boyles*, 3rd edn (London, 1737): 'Appendix, relating to the Honourable Robert Boyle, Esq', p. 25.

2. Henry Guerlac and M. C. Jacob, 'Bentley, Newton, and Providence: The Boyle Lectures Once More', *Journal of the History of Ideas*, 30 (1969), 307–18 (pp. 312, 317–18). The classic account of the Boyle lectures is Jacob's *The Newtonians and the English Revolution, 1689–1720* (Ithaca, NY: Cornell University Press, 1976).

3. 'Letter IV: To Mr. Bentley, at the Palace at Worcester, from Isaac Newton, Cambridge, February 11, 1693', in *The Works of Richard Bentley*, ed. Alexander Dyce, 3 vols (London: MacPherson, 1836–38; repr. Hildesheim: Olms, 1971), III, 215. See John Henry, '"Pray Do Not Ascribe that Notion to Me": God and Newton's Gravity', in *The Books of Nature and Scripture: Recent Essays on Natural Philosophy, Theology, and Biblical Criticism in the Netherlands of Spinoza's Time and the British Isles of Newton's Time*, eds James E. Force and Richard H. Popkin (Dordrecht: Kluwer Academic, 1994), pp. 123–47, and Rome Harré, 'Knowledge', in *The Ferment of Knowledge: Studies in the Historiography of Eighteenth-Century Science*, eds G. S. Rousseau and Roy Porter (Cambridge: Cambridge University Press, 1980), pp. 11–54 (esp. pp. 25–27).

4. Bentley, *Works*, III, 178, 165, 180.

5. See John Gascoigne, 'From Bentley to the Victorians: The Rise and Fall of British Newtonian Natural Theology', *Science in Context*, 2 (1988), 219–56 (p. 223).

6. See esp. Ehrenpreis, I, 117, and Roger D. Lund, 'Strange Complicities: Atheism and Conspiracy in *A Tale of a Tub*', *Eighteenth-Century Life*, 13: 3 (November 1989), 34–58; repr. in *British Literature 1640–1789: A Critical Reader*, ed. Robert DeMaria, Jr (Oxford: Blackwell, 1999), pp. 142–68.

7. Phillip Harth, *Swift and Anglican Rationalism: The Religious Background of 'A Tale of a Tub'* (Chicago, IL: University of Chicago Press, 1961), pp. 23 and n., 145–46.

8. See John F. Tinkler, 'The Splitting of Humanism: Bentley, Swift, and the English Battle of the Books', *Journal of the History of Ideas*, 49 (1988), 453–72, and Howard D. Weinbrot, '"He Will Kill Me Over and Over Again": Intellectual

Contexts of the Battle of the Books', in *Reading Swift: Papers from the Fourth Münster Symposium on Jonathan Swift*, eds Hermann J. Real and Helgard Stöver-Leidig (München: Fink, 2003), pp. 225–48 (pp. 245–46).

9. See *Tale*, p. xxxvi.

10. All eight sermons were published separately several times in 1692 and 1693, and collectively as *The Folly and Unreasonableness of Atheism* (London, 1693 and 1699).

11. For A. H. De-Quehen, the '*Micro-Coat*' of the sartorists parodies Bentley's suggestion that men should look for the existence of God 'within themselves' ('Lucretius and Swift's *Tale of a Tub*', *University of Toronto Quarterly*, 63 [1993/1994], 287–307 [pp. 307n44, 299]; Bentley, *Works*, III, 121). The Neoplatonic idea of 'Man as a *Microcosm* or a *Little World*', perhaps encountered via Henry More, seems a more obvious echo. See *Conjectura Cabbalistica* (London, 1653), facs. reprt in *Henry More: Major Philosophical Works*, ed. G. A. J. Rogers, 9 vols (Bristol: Thoemmes Press, 1997), II, 53, and also 195. Irvin Ehrenpreis at one time claimed that 'Bentley's lectures made a tremendous stir, and they must have been known to Swift', but his masterful three-volume biography does not acknowledge this prospect: see 'Four of Swift's Sources', *Modern Language Notes*, 70 (1955), 95–100 (p. 99).

12. David Bywaters, 'Anticlericism in Swift's *Tale of a Tub*', *Studies in English Literature, 1500–1900*, 36 (1996), 579–602 (p. 588); Frank T. Boyle, *Swift as Nemesis: Modernity and Its Satirist* (Stanford, CA: Stanford University Press, 2000), esp. pp. 118–48. See also Boyle, 'New Science in the Composition of *A Tale of a Tub*', in *Reading Swift: Papers from the Fifth Münster Symposium on Jonathan Swift*, ed. Hermann J. Real (München: Fink, 2008), pp. 175–84. Boyle's case for connecting the *Principia* to the *Tale* has been criticized by Robert Phiddian (Review of *Swift as Nemesis*, in *Modern Philology*, 99 [2002], 437–39 [p. 438]). We know that Swift owned the second edition of the *Principia* (1713) (*LRJS*, II, 1314–15), and it is uncertain as to whether he possessed detailed knowledge of the work before then.

13. *RAML*, sig. A13ᵛ–A14ʳ, *Dr. Bentley's Dissertations on the Epistles of Phalaris, and the Fables of Æsop, Examin'd* (London, 1698), p. 199, Francis Atterbury, *A Short Review of the Controversy Between Mr. Boyle, and Dr. Bentley* (London, 1701), p. 8, and William King, *Dialogues of the Dead: Relating to the Present Controversy Concerning the Epistles of Phalaris* (London, 1699), pp. 23–24.

14. See, for instance, James Thomson, *A Poem Sacred to the Memory of Sir Isaac Newton* (London, 1727).

15. See esp. Mark McDayter, 'The Haunting of St. James's Library: Librarians, Literature, and *The Battle of the Books*', *Huntington Library Quarterly*, 66 (2003), 1–26 (pp. 5–9).

16. R. J. Dingley, 'Dr Bentley's Centripetal Tendency', *Notes & Queries*, 229 (n.s.31) (1984), 378–79, and Boyle, *Swift as Nemesis*, pp. 124–25. Richard N. Ramsey hints that Swift would have been aware of the impact of the *Principia* at the time of the *Battel*, but does not explore this possibility ('Swift's Strategy in *The Battle of the Books*', *Papers on Language and Literature*, 20 [1984], 382–89 [p. 387]).

17. See, for instance, [Edmond Halley], 'An Accompt of Some Books, II: Newton, *Philosophiæ Naturalis Principia Mathematica*', *Philosophical Transactions*, 16 (1687), 291–97, which uses the phrase four times. For Newton's description

of centripetal forces, see *The Principia: Mathematical Principles of Natural Philosophy*, 3rd edn (London, 1726), trans. I. Bernard Cohen and Anne Whitman (Berkeley: University of California Press, 1999), pp. 444–61 (Book I, Section II).

18. See also *RAML*, pp. 264–65.
19. See Lund, 'Strange Complicities', p. 161, citing Bentley, *Works*, III, 27. The 'Professors' among the Taylor-worshippers in Section II of the *Tale* apply this Pauline aphorism absurdly and blasphemously to their contention that 'Man was an Animal compounded of two *Dresses*, the *Natural* and the *Celestial Suit*, which were the Body and the Soul' (p. 50), perhaps suggesting an additional poke at the the physico-theological pretensions of Bentley and Wotton.
20. E. W. Gudger, 'The Five Great Naturalists of the Sixteenth Century: Belon, Rondelet, Salviani, Gesner and Aldrovandi: A Chapter in the History of Ichthyology', *Isis*, 22 (1934), 21–40 (pp. 36–37).
21. See John M. Bullitt, *Jonathan Swift and the Anatomy of Satire: A Study of Satiric Technique* (Cambridge, MA: Harvard University Press, 1953), p. 47.
22. *The Principia*, p. 820 (Book III, Proposition 17, Theorem 15). See Mercator, *Institutionum Astronomicarum Libri Duo* (London, 1676), pp. 286–87, cited in Derek T. Whiteside, 'Newton's Early Thoughts on Planetary Motion: A Fresh Look', *The British Journal for the History of Science*, 2 (1964), pp. 117–137 (p. 131n48).
23. See Grant McColley, 'The Theory of the Diurnal Rotation of the Earth', *Isis*, 26 (1937), 392–402.
24. See James E. Force, 'Providence and Newton's *Pantokrator*: Natural Law, Miracles, and Newtonian Science', in *Newton and Newtonianism: New Studies*, eds Force and Sarah Hutton (Dordrecht: Kluwer Academic, 2004), pp. 65–92 (pp. 69–70).
25. See David Kubrin, 'Newton and the Cyclical Cosmos: Providence and the Mechanical Philosophy', *Journal of the History of Ideas*, 28 (1967), 325–46 (p. 326n4).
26. On key types of argument in the Boyle lectures, see John J. Dahm, 'Science and Apologetics in the Early Boyle Lectures', *Church History*, 39 (1970), 172–86 (pp. 176–77, 180–81).
27. Newton to Bentley, 10 December 1692, and Newton to Burnet, January 1680/81, in *The Correspondence of Isaac Newton*, III, 236, and II, 333–34.
28. Dingley, 'Dr Bentley's Centripetal Tendency', 378–79.
29. See *Cadenus and Vanessa*, l. 827, in *Poems*, II, 712.
30. See, for instance, Thomas Salusbury, *Mathematical Collections and Translations*, 2 vols (London, 1661), I, 65.
31. William Whiston, *A New Theory of the Earth* (London, 1696), pp. 126, 369–70, 447.
32. On the political character of this conflict, see Robert Markley, *Fallen Languages: Crises of Representation in Newtonian England, 1660–1740* (Ithaca, NY: Cornell University Press, 1993), pp. 204–207.
33. See John Keill, *An Examination of Dr Burnet's Theory of the Earth. Together with Some Remarks on Mr Whiston's New Theory of the Earth* (London, 1698), pp. 62–83, and Thomas Burnet, *The Theory of the Earth*, 3rd edn (London, 1697), pp. 133–34.

34. Wotton, *A Defense of the Reflections upon Ancient and Modern Learning,* [...]
With Observations upon The Tale of a Tub (London, 1705), pp. 8, 9. Swift certainly read Wotton's *Defense*: the *Observations* appended to it informed many
of the footnotes added to the 1710 *Tale*.
35. Keill, *Examination*, p. 71. See also Keill, *An Introduction to the True Astronomy*,
p. ii.
36. *A Short Account of Dr. Bentley's Humanity and Justice ... In a Letter to the
Honourable Charles Boyle, Esq.* (London, 1699), p. 80.
37. Bernard le Bovier de Fontenelle, *Entretiens sur la Pluralité des Mondes* (Paris,
1686), and John Wilkins, *The Discovery of a World in the Moone* (London,
1638).
38. On the inadvertent dissemination of their opponents' ideas being a problem for the Boyle lecturers, see Andrew Pyle, 'Introduction', in *A Defence of
Natural and Revealed Religion: Being an Abridgement of the Sermons preached at
the Lecture founded by Robert Boyle*, ed. Gilbert Burnet, 4 vols (London, 1737;
facs. reprt Bristol: Thoemmes Press, 2000), I, xlviii–xlix.
39. See Thomas Hobbes, *Leviathan*, ed. Richard Tuck (Cambridge: Cambridge
University Press, 1991; repr. 1994), Chap. XLV, pp. 443–44, and *Tractatus
theologico-politicus*, in *The Chief Works of Benedict de Spinoza*, trans. R. H.
M. Elwes, rev. edn, 2 vols (London: George Bell & Sons, 1903–1905), I, 120.
40. See Gerard Reedy, SJ, 'A Preface to Anglican Rationalism', in *Eighteenth-
Century Contexts: Historical Inquiries in Honor of Phillip Harth*, eds Howard
D. Weinbrot, Peter J. Schakel and Stephen E. Karian (Wisconsin: University
of Wisconsin Press, 2001), pp. 44–59 (p. 56), and Thomas Franklin Mayo,
'Epicurus in England (1650–1725)' (unpublished doctoral dissertation,
Columbia University, Texas, 1933), p. 200.
41. Michael V. DePorte, 'Swift, God, and Power', in *Walking Naboth's Vineyard:
New Studies of Swift*, eds Christopher Fox and Brenda Tooley (Notre Dame,
IN: University of Notre Dame Press, 1995), pp. 73–97 (p. 81). See also
DePorte, 'Contemplating Collins: Freethinking in Swift', in *Reading Swift:
Papers from the Third Münster Symposium on Jonathan Swift*, eds Hermann
J. Real and Helgard Stöver-Leidig (München: Fink, 1998), pp. 103–15.
42. See W. R. Albury, 'Halley's Ode on the *Principia* of Newton and the Epicurean
Revival in England', *Journal of the History of Ideas*, 39 (1978), 24–43 (p. 38).
43. See Hermann J. Real and Heinz J. Vienken, '"I Knew and Could Distinguish
those Two Heroes at First Sight": Homer and Aristotle in Glubbdubdrib',
Notes & Queries, 231 (n.s.33) (1986), 51–53.
44. James Burnet, Lord Monboddo, *Antient Metaphysics: or, the Science of
Universals*, 2nd edn (London, 1782), p. 451.
45. Jean Le Clerc, *Bibliothèque Ancienne et Moderne*, 15 (Paris, 1721), 441-45, repr.
in *Swift: The Critical Heritage*, ed. Kathleen Williams (London: Routledge,
1970), p. 59, Atterbury to Bishop Jonathan Trelawney, 15 June 1704, in
Memoirs and Correspondence of Francis Atterbury, D. D., Bishop of Rochester, ed.
Robert Folkestone Williams, 2 vols (London: W. H. Allen, 1869), I, 99, and
King, *Some Remarks upon the Tale of a Tub. In a Letter* (London, 1704), repr. in
The Original Works of William King, 3 vols (London, 1776), I, 215–16.
46. See esp. *RAML*, p. 80.
47. On the possible use of a persona in the 'Apology', see Frank H. Ellis, 'No
Apologies, Dr. Swift!', *Eighteenth-Century Life*, 21: 3 (November 1997), 71–76,

and Judith C. Mueller, 'Writing under Constraint: Swift's "Apology" for *A Tale of a Tub'*, *ELH*, 60 (1993), 101–15.

48. Samuel Clarke, *A Discourse Concerning the Unchangeable Obligations of Natural Religion, and the Truth and Certainty of the Christian Revelation*, 2nd edn (London, 1708), pp. 28–29, 31. See Frank T. Boyle, 'Profane and Debauched Deist: Swift in the Contemporary Response to *A Tale of a Tub'*, *Eighteenth-Century Ireland*, 3 (1988), 25–38, and *Swift as Nemesis*, pp. 151–55. Clarke produced a Latin translation of the *Opticks* (*Optice*, 1706).
49. *OED*, s. v. 'banter'.
50. For Edmund Curll, one of Wotton's key remarks is his disregard of the *Tale* as 'banter'. See *A Complete Key to The Tale of a Tub* (London, 1710), p. 30.
51. 'Upon the Gardens of Epicurus; or, Of Gardening, in the Year 1685', in *Five Miscellaneous Essays by Sir William Temple*, ed. Samuel Holt Monk (Ann Arbor: The University of Michigan Press, 1963), p. 4.

Chapter 4

1. Barbara M. Benedict, *Curiosity: A Cultural History of Early Modern Inquiry* (Chicago, IL: University of Chicago Press, 2001), p. 110.
2. See John Mullan, 'Swift, Defoe, and Narrative Forms', in *The Cambridge Companion to English Literature, 1650–1740*, ed. Steven N. Zwicker (Cambridge: Cambridge University Press, 1998), pp. 250–75 (pp. 251–53).
3. See esp. Marjorie Nicolson, 'The Microscope and English Imagination', in *Science and Imagination* (Ithaca, NY: Cornell University Press, 1956), pp. 155–234 (pp. 194–99), and Frederick N. Smith, 'Scientific Discourse: *Gulliver's Travels* and *The Philosophical Transactions'*, in *The Genres of 'Gulliver's Travels'*, ed. Smith (Newark: University of Delaware Press, 1990), pp. 139–62 (pp. 140–43).
4. Swift to Gay and the Duchess of Queensberry, 10 July 1732, in *CJS*, III, 501.
5. Swift to Arbuthnot, 25 July 1714 and 3 July 1714, in *CJS*, II, 26, and I, 630.
6. *The Humble Petition of the Colliers* (1716), and *God's Revenge Against Punning* (1716), both republished in *Miscellanies in Prose and Verse by Pope, Swift and Gay* (1727–32), ed. Alexander Pettit, 4 vols (London: Pickering & Chatto, 2002), IV, 72–78, 53–56. See esp. Marjorie Hope Nicolson and G. S. Rousseau, *'This Long Disease, My Life': Alexander Pope and the Sciences* (Princeton, NJ: Princeton University Press, 1968), pp. 156–66, 178–87, and G. S. Rousseau, 'Wicked Whiston and the English Wits', in *Enlightenment Borders: Pre- and Post-modern Discourses: Medical, Scientific* (Manchester: Manchester University Press, 1991), pp. 325–41. On Derham's theories of solar destruction, see Marjorie Nicolson and Nora M. Mohler, 'The Scientific Background of Swift's *Voyage to Laputa'*, *Annals of Science*, 2 (1937), 299–334 (pp. 310–12).
7. On Whiston as a target of the 'Voyage to Laputa', see esp. Nicolson and Mohler, 'The Scientific Background of Swift's *Voyage to Laputa'*, pp. 312–16, Dennis Todd, 'Laputa, the Whore of Babylon, and the Idols of Science', *Studies in Philology*, 75 (1978), 93–120 (pp. 107–109), and David Charles Leonard, 'Swift, Whiston, and the Comet', *English Language Notes*, 16 (1979), 284–87.
8. See *The Correspondence of Dr. John Arbuthnot*, ed. Angus Ross (München: Fink, 2006), pp. 67–68.

9. Ehrenpreis, III, 620; Swift to Ford, 9 October 1733, in *CJS*, III, 692, and see Swift to Mrs Whiteway, 16 and 22 April 1737, in *CJS*, IV, 425.

10. 'Character of Doctor Sheridan' (c. 1738), in *PW*, V, 216; Swift to Sheridan, 11 and 25 September 1725, in *CJS*, II, 595, 605. See Irvin Ehrenpreis, *The Personality of Jonathan Swift* (London: Methuen, 1958), pp. 109–14, and also Swift (with Thomas Sheridan), *The Intelligencer*, ed. James Woolley (Oxford: Clarendon Press, 1992), pp. 6–19. On Sheridan's reputation as a high Tory and possible Jacobite, see Swift's satirical 'The History of the Second Solomon' (c. 1729), in *PW*, V, 223, 226, and Swift to Thomas Tickell, 18 September 1725, in *CJS*, II, 599.

11. Swift to Ford, 16 August 1725, and Swift to Pope, 29 September 1725, in *CJS*, II, 588, 606.

12. See *LRJS*, IV, 238, 286, 227; Boyle, *Experiments and Considerations Touching Colours* (London, 1670), pp. 42–49. Boyle's story was suggested as a target by Nicolson and Mohler ('The Scientific Background of Swift's *Voyage to Laputa*', pp. 323–24), but they were unaware of its most likely textual source.

13. See Ehrenpreis, II, 95, 151, 365, and *The Account Books of Jonathan Swift*, transcribed and with an introduction by Paul V. Thompson and Dorothy Jay Thompson (Newark: University of Delaware Press, 1984), p. lv.

14. See Joseph Beaumont, *A Proposal for the More Effectual Improvement of the Channel and Harbour of Dublin* (Dublin?, 1710?), *Mathematical Sleaing-Tables: Or, The Great and only Mistery of Weaving Linnen-Cloth Explain'd* (Dublin, 1712), and Swift to John Wheldon, 27 September 1727, in *CJS*, III, 129. On Beaumont's government award for the tables, see *Journal to Stella*, Letters III (11 September 1710), IV (22 September 1710), V (3 October 1710), in *PW*, XV, 14, 27, 40.

15. 'On the Little House by the Churchyard of Castleknock' (c. 1710), ll. 1–8, 11–12, in *Poems*, I, 126–27. For an example of the friendly banter between the three men, see Swift to Archdeacon Thomas Walls, 7 August 1713, in *CJS*, I, 526–27.

16. See *CJS*, III, 195, 220, 221, 222, 418, and *Letters, Written by the Late Jonathan Swift, D.D.*, ed. Deane Swift, 6 vols (London, 1768), IV, 1–2n.

17. John Conduitt, 'Miscellanea', in King's College, Cambridge, Keynes MS. 130.5, ff. 4ᵛ–5ʳ, in *NP*.

18. Richard S. Westfall, *Never at Rest: A Biography of Isaac Newton* (Cambridge: Cambridge University Press, 1980), p. 595.

19. '*Mrs. B—n*', in Anon., *The Toasters Compleat, with the last Additions* (London, 1704), p. 5.

20. *Journal to Stella*, Letter XIX (24 March 1710/11) and Letter X (25 November 1710), in *PW*, XV, 229 and 109. For other references to Barton see *PW*, XV, 17, 31, 107, 131, 172, 210, 230, 238, 309, 316; XVI, 380, 383, 395, 417, and *CJS*, III, 304 and III, 711–12. Seven unrecovered letters between Swift and Barton were exchanged during April to August 1709 (see *CJS*, III, 712n).

21. Conduitt, 'Notes on Newton's Character', in King's College Library, Cambridge, Keynes MS 130.7, f. 2ʳ, in *NP*, and Swift to Robert Hunter, 22 March 1708–1709, in *CJS*, I, 244.

22. See Conduitt, 'Miscellanea', f. 1ʳ.

23. *The Works of Jonathan Swift, D. D.*, ed. Sir Walter Scott, 19 vols (Edinburgh, 1814), I, 332.

24. See Ricardo Quintana, *The Mind and Art of Jonathan Swift* (London: Oxford University Press, 1936), p. 316, and Herbert Davis, 'Swift and the Pedants', in *Jonathan Swift: Essays on His Satire and Other Studies* (New York: Oxford University Press, 1964), pp. 199–215 (p. 206).
25. On satiric 'miscegenation', see John R. R. Christie, 'Laputa Revisited', in *Nature Transfigured: Science and Literature, 1700–1900*, eds Christie and Sally Shuttleworth (Manchester: Manchester University Press, 1989), pp. 45–60.
26. See Patrick Kelly, 'Swift on Money and Economics', in *The Cambridge Companion to Jonathan Swift*, ed. Christopher Fox (Cambridge: Cambridge University Press, 2003), pp. 128–45 (pp. 135, 131), and Sabine Baltes, *The Pamphlet Controversy about Wood's Halfpence (1722-25) and the Tradition of Irish Constitutional Nationalism* (Frankfurt am Main: Lang, 2003), pp. 107–108.
27. See Swift to Ford, 11 March 1724-5, in *CJS*, II, 547.
28. Ehrenpreis, III, 206.
29. Swift to Francis Grant, 23 March 1733–34, in *CJS*, III, 730–31. On Swift's strategies in *The Drapier's Letters*, see Irvin Ehrenpreis, *Acts of Implication: Suggestion and Covert Meaning in the Works of Dryden, Swift, Pope, and Austen* (Berkeley: University of California Press, 1981), pp. 65–82.
30. Newton, Southwell and Scrope to the Treasury, 27 April 1724, in *The Correspondence of Isaac Newton*, eds A. Rupert Hall and Laura Tilling, 7 vols (Cambridge: Cambridge University Press for the Royal Society, 1959–77), VII, 276–77.
31. See Kelly, 'Swift on Money and Economics', p. 144n25.
32. Newton, Southwell and Scrope to the Treasury, in *Correspondence*, VII, 276. See Oliver W. Ferguson, *Jonathan Swift and Ireland* (Urbana, IL: University of Illinois Press, 1962), p. 104.
33. David Bindon, *Some Reasons Shewing the Necessity the People of Ireland are under, for continuing to refuse Mr. Wood's Coinage* (Dublin, 1724), p. 21, and Sir Michael Creagh, *Remarks upon Mr. Wood's Coyn and Proceedings* (Dublin, 1724), facs. reprt in *Swiftiana IV: On the Drapier's Letters, etc. 1724* (New York: Garland, 1975), p. 4.
34. See Swift to George Faulkner, 6 January 1737–38, in *CJS*, IV, 488.
35. Albert Goodwin, 'Wood's Halfpence', *The English Historical Review*, 51 (1936), 647–74 (p. 649).
36. See *The Drapier's Letters*, ed. Herbert Davis (Oxford: Clarendon Press, 1935), p. 229, J. M. Treadwell, 'Swift, William Wood and the Factual Basis of Satire', *Journal of British Studies* 15 (1976), 76–91, and Johann N. Schmidt, 'Swift's Uses of Fact and Fiction: *The Drapier's Letters*', in *Proceedings of the First Münster Symposium on Jonathan Swift*, ed. Hermann J. Real and Heinz J. Vienken (München: Fink, 1985), pp. 247–56. Newton told his friend, the Boyle lecturer William Derham, that an agent of a person 'of Quality' had sought to speed up the introduction of the coinage through offering a bribe, but he refused (Derham, 'Remarks on Sr Is. Newton', with a covering letter to John Conduitt [18 July 1733], in King's College Library, Cambridge, Keynes MS. 133, ff. 12–13, in *NP*).
37. Anon., *A Letter from a Young Lady, to the Revd. D–n S—t* ([Dublin], 1724), facs. reprt in *Swiftiana IV*, p. 7.
38. See E. G. R. Taylor, *The Mathematical Practitioners of Tudor and Stuart England* (Cambridge: Cambridge University Press, for the Institute of Navigation, 1954), p. 426, and Westfall, *Never at Rest*, pp. 834–36.

39. In early 1712, a 'Projector' with an 'Invention for finding out the Longitude' applied for Swift's recommendation to the ministry, but Swift had been told such a thing would be 'as improbable as the Philosopher's Stone, or perpetual Motion' (Swift to Archbishop King, 29 March 1712, in *CJS*, I, 421). This 'Projector' is believed to be none other than Whiston, whose 'bomb-vessels' proposal would invite the Scriblerians' ridicule, but whose petitions for a reward resulted in the passing of the Act. In September 1727, another of the 'Projectors of the Longitude', John Wheldon, who had been mis-informed Swift was a 'Lover of the Mathematicks' (possibly a joke by Sheridan), approached the Dean, but received the reply that 'Newton, Halley, and Keil have all told me they doubted the Thing was impossible' (see *CJS*, III, 128, 129). See also 'Holyhead Journal, 1727', in *PW*, V, 206. On the Scriblerian satires on Whiston's project, see esp. *Memoirs*, pp. 334–35, Nicolson and Rousseau, *'This Long Disease, My Life'*, pp. 174–78, and Chris Worth, 'Swift's "Flying Island": Buttons and Bomb-Vessels', *Review of English Studies*, n.s.42 (1991), 343–60.

40. See *Artephius, His Secret Booke*, appended to *Nicolas Flamel, His Exposition of the Hieroglyphicall Figures* (London, 1624), facs. reprt ed. Laurinda Dixon (New York: Garland, 1994), p. 60, and Louis Moréri, *The Great Historical, Geographical, and Poetical Dictionary; Being a Curious Miscellany of Sacred and Prophane History*, collected and enlarged by Jean Le Clerc, 2 vols in 1 (London, 1694), s. v. 'Philosopher's Stone'.

41. See *Poems*, III, 841–42, and also James Kelly, 'Jonathan Swift and the Irish Economy in the 1720s', *Eighteenth-Century Ireland*, 6 (1991), 7–36 (p. 13).

42. 'The Virtues of *Sid Hamet* the Magician's Rod' (1710), in *Poems*, I, 133 (ll. 40–42). See Christine Gerrard, *The Patriot Opposition to Walpole: Politics, Poetry, and National Myth, 1725–1742* (Oxford: Clarendon Press, 1994), pp. 174–77.

43. See also St George Ashe's speech to Lord Clarendon, 25 January 1685/6, published in Ehrenpreis, I, 276. On the dating of *Polite Conversation*, see *PW*, IV, xxviii.

44. Steven Shapin, *A Social History of Truth: Civility and Science in Seventeenth-Century England* (Chicago, IL: University of Chicago Press, 1994), pp. 42, 93–94, and Larry Stewart, *The Rise of Public Science: Rhetoric, Technology, and Natural Philosophy in Newtonian Britain, 1660–1750* (Cambridge: Cambridge University Press, 1992), esp. pp. 175, 202.

45. Arthur E. Case, 'Personal and Political satire in *Gulliver's Travels*', in *Four Essays on 'Gulliver's Travels'* (Princeton, NJ: Princeton University Press, 1945; repr. Gloucester, MA: Peter Smith, 1958), pp. 69–96, J. M. Treadwell, 'Jonathan Swift: The Satirist as Projector', *Texas Studies in Literature and Language*, 17 (1975), 439–60, and Pat Rogers, 'Gulliver and the Engineers', *Modern Language Review*, 70 (1975), 260–70.

46. Simon Schaffer, 'Augustan Realities: Nature's Representatives and their Cultural Resources in the Early Eighteenth Century', in *Realism and Representation: Essays on the Problem of Realism in Relation to Science, Literature and Culture*, ed. George Levine (Madison: University of Wisconsin Press, 1993), pp. 279–318.

47. See *Tale*, pp. 38, 180.

48. Conduitt, 'Three drafts of a passage praising Newton's manual dexterity', in King's College Library, Cambridge, Keynes MS. 130.9, f. 4^v, in *NP*.

49. On the conflict between the philosophical and the technical in Newtonianism, see Larry Stewart, 'The Trouble with Newton in the Eighteenth Century', in *Newton and Newtonianism: New Studies*, eds James E. Force and Sarah Hutton (Dordrecht: Kluwer Academic, 2004), pp. 221–237 (pp. 228–30).

50. Thomas Sprat, *The History of the Royal-Society of London, For the Improving of Natural Knowledge* (London, 1667), p. 67.

51. See *PW*, XI, xxi.

52. See esp. Ian Higgins, *Swift's Politics: A Study in Disaffection* (Cambridge: Cambridge University Press, 1994), p. 177. David Renaker suggests unconvincingly that Laputa represents the French Cartesians ('Swift's Laputians as a Caricature of the Cartesians', *PMLA*, 94 [1979], 936–44). Meanwhile, Dolores J. Palomo argues that Lagado resembles the University of Leiden ('The Dutch Connection: The University of Leiden and Swift's Academy of Lagado', *The Huntington Library Quarterly*, 41 [1977], 27–35), but many of the experiments are reminiscent of those conducted by the Royal Society at Gresham College and Crane Court, and published in the *Philosophical Transactions*.

53. *Works*, ed. Scott, I, 331–32; Nicolson and Mohler, 'The Scientific Background of Swift's *Voyage to Laputa*', p. 307. Swift owned the *Principia*'s second edition (1713): see *LRJS*, II, 1314–15.

54. A. Rupert Hall, 'Newton versus Leibniz: From Geometry to Metaphysics', in *The Cambridge Companion to Newton*, eds I. Bernard Cohen and George E. Smith (Cambridge: Cambridge University Press, 2002), pp. 431–54 (p. 444).

55. See, for instance, 'A Letter from the Rev. Dr. Samuel Clarke to Mr. Benjamin Hoadly, F. R. S. Occasion'd by the Present Controversy among Mathematicians, concerning the Proportion of Velocity and Force in Bodies in Motion', *Philosophical Transactions*, 35: 401 (1727–28), 381–88 (p. 382).

56. Steven Shapin, 'Of Gods and Kings: Natural Philosophy and Politics in the Leibniz-Clarke Disputes', *Isis*, 72 (1981), 187–215 (p. 190).

57. See Valerie Rumbold, 'Burying the Fanatic Partridge: Swift's Holy Week Hoax', in *Politics and Literature in the Age of Swift: English and Irish Perspectives*, ed. Claude Rawson (Cambridge: Cambridge University Press, 2010), pp. 81–115 (pp. 97–99).

58. N. F. Lowe, 'Why Swift Killed Partridge', *Swift Studies*, 6 (1991), 70–82.

59. Flamsteed had links with astrologers in his early career, but it is doubtful Swift would have known of these. See Michael Hunter, 'Science and Astrology in Seventeenth-Century England: An Unpublished Polemic by John Flamsteed', in *Astrology, Science and Society: Historical Essays*, ed. Patrick Curry (Woodbridge: Boydell and Brewer, 1987), pp. 261–86 (p. 264). On Partridge and Gadbury, see Patrick Curry, 'Saving Astrology in Restoration England: "Whig" and "Tory" Reforms', in *Astrology, Science and Society*, pp. 245–59 (pp. 249–52).

60. See Simon Schaffer, 'Newton's Comets and the Transformation of Astrology', in *Astrology, Science and Society*, pp. 219–43.

61. Conduitt, 'Account of Newton's Life at Cambridge', in King's College Library, Cambridge, Keynes MS. 130.4, f. 2^r. See also Conduitt's notes towards his 'Life of Newton' (several of which contain additions in Barton's hand), in Keynes MS. 130.10, ff. 2^{r-v}, Keynes MS. 129 (A), f. 2^v, Keynes MS. 129 (B), f. 2^r, and 'Memorandums relating to Sir Isaac Newton given me by Mr Abraham

Demoivre in November 1727', in University of Chicago Library, Joseph Halle Schaffner Collection, MS. 1075.7, f. 1^r. All are transcribed in *NP*.

62. See *PW*, II, x–xi, Lowe, 'Why Swift Killed Partridge', *passim*, and Rumbold, 'Burying the Fanatic Partridge', p. 82.

63. William Petty, *Several Essays in Political Arithmetick* (London, 1699), sig. M7^r. Swift owned this edition: see *LRJS*, II, 1413–16.

64. See Mary Poovey, *A History of the Modern Fact: Problems of Knowledge in the Sciences of Wealth and Society* (Chicago, IL: University of Chicago Press, 1998), pp. 120–38, and Toby Barnard, *Improving Ireland? Projectors, Prophets and Profiteers, 1641–1786* (Dublin: Four Courts Press, 2008), esp. pp. 41–50.

65. See esp. George Wittowsky, 'Swift's *Modest Proposal*: The Biography of an Early Georgian Pamphlet', *Journal of the History of Ideas*, 4 (1943), 75–104, and Peter M. Briggs, 'John Graunt, Sir William Petty, and Swift's *Modest Proposal*', *Eighteenth-Century Life*, 29: 2 (Spring 2005), 3–24.

66. Robert P. Fitzgerald, however, argues 'Newton did not really have a significant role in politics or political theory. It is more meaningful to read [the passage] as referring in specific to Bodin and Hobbes and in general to theoreticians of the abstract' ('Science and Politics in Swift's Voyage to Laputa', *Journal of English and Germanic Philology*, 87 [1988], 213–29 [p. 224]). Despite the connection between politics, astrology and the music of the spheres in Jean Bodin's *Les Six Livres De La République* (1579), which Swift read and annotated (see *PW*, V, 244), the Irish context of the voyage suggests Newton or Petty are more likely targets.

67. *An Essay on the Usefulness of Mathematical Learning* (1701), in *The Life and Works of John Arbuthnot*, ed. George A. Aitken (Oxford: Clarendon Press, 1892), pp. 409–35 (p. 429). Swift owned two editions of Plato: see *LRJS*, II, 1437–40.

68. On Pythagoras's claim that he alone could hear the music of the spheres, see Iamblichus, *On the Pythagorean Way of Life*, eds John Dillon and Jackson Hershbell (Atlanta, GA: Scholars Press, 1991), Chap. 15, p. 91. See also 'His Grace's Answer to Jonathan', l. 36, in *Poems*, II, 362. In 'The Dean and the Lord Chancellor: Or, Swift Saving his Bacon' in *Britannien und Europa: Studien zur Literatur-, Geistes- und Kulturgeschichte. Festschrift für Jürgen Klein*, ed. Michael Szczekalla (Frankfurt: Lang, 2010), pp. 95–111, Hermann J. Real emphasizes the importance of the inaudibility of the music of the spheres to mortal men, indicating another example of the Laputians' futile endeavours.

69. See Brean Hammond, *Pope* (Brighton: Harvester New Readings, 1986), p. 117.

70. Deane Swift was perhaps the first to suggest this: see *An Essay upon the Life, Writings, and Character of Dr. Jonathan Swift* (London, 1755), facs. reprt in *Swiftiana XIV* (New York: Garland, 1974), p. 214.

71. See Marjorie Nicolson and Nora M. Mohler, 'Swift's "Flying Island" in the *Voyage to Laputa*', *Annals of Science*, 2 (1937), 405–30, Sidney Gottlieb, 'The Emblematic Background of Swift's Flying Island', *Swift Studies*, 1 (1986), 24–31, Paul J. Korshin, 'The Intellectual Context of Swift's Flying Island', *Philological Quarterly*, 50 (1971), 630–46, and Robert C. Merton, 'The "Motionless" Motion of Swift's Flying Island', *Journal of the History of Ideas*, 27 (1966), 275–77.

72. See, for instance, William Derham, 'Some Magnetical Experiments and Observations', and Nehemiah Grew, 'Of the Number of Acres contained

in England', in *The Philosophical Transactions from the Year MDCC (where Mr. Lowthorp ends) to the year MDCCXX. Abridg'd, and Dispos'd under General Heads*, ed. Benjamin Motte, 2 vols (London, 1721), II, 241–43, 278–82.

73. Charles Harding Firth, 'The Political Significance of *Gulliver's Travels*', *Proceedings of the British Academy* (1919–20), 237–59 (p. 253).

74. Nicolson and Mohler, 'Swift's "Flying Island"', pp. 416–17.

75. On the extensive use of analogy in the *Transactions*, see Smith, 'Scientific Discourse', pp. 146–48.

76. C. D. M. (Corolini di Marco), *The Flying Island, &c. Being a Key to Gulliver's Voyage to Laputa, Balnibarbi, Glubbdubdrib, Luggnag, and Japan. In a Third Letter to Dean Swift* (London, 1726), p. 15, and see *Gulliver's Travels*, eds Claude Rawson and Ian Higgins (Oxford: Oxford University Press, 2005), p. 324.

77. See *PW*, XII, 8, 66, 132, and Ferguson, *Jonathan Swift and Ireland*, pp. 9–10.

78. *Gulliver's Travels*, ed. Paul Turner (Oxford: Oxford University Press, 1971; repr. 1994), p. 331, and C. D. M., *The Flying Island*, p. 15.

79. Derham, 'Some Magnetical Experiments and Observations', and Richard Helsham, *A Course of Lectures in Natural Philosophy* (Dublin, [1739]), pp. 19–20. The experiment also resembles Newton's investigation of the effect of gravity on pendulum clocks. See *The Principia: Mathematical Principles of Natural Philosophy*, 3rd edn (London, 1726), trans. I. Bernard Cohen and Anne Whitman (Berkeley: University of California Press, 1999), pp. 826–32 (Book III, Proposition 20, Problem 4).

80. Case, 'Personal and Political Satire in *Gulliver's Travels*', pp. 81–89.

81. Swift to Ford, 9 October 1733, in *CJS*, III, 693. See Michael Treadwell, 'The Text of *Gulliver's Travels*, Again', *Swift Studies*, 10 (1995), 62–79 (pp. 72–78), and 'Benjamin Motte, Andrew Tooke and *Gulliver's Travels*', in *Proceedings of the First Münster Symposium*, pp. 287–304.

82. F. P. Lock, *The Politics of 'Gulliver's Travels'* (Oxford: Clarendon Press, 1980), pp. 85, 102, 101; Case, 'Personal and Political Satire in *Gulliver's Travels*', pp. 81–89. See also Firth, 'The Political Significance of *Gulliver's Travels*', pp. 256–58.

83. See *TE*, VI, 317.

84. See, for instance, Phillip Harth, 'The Problem of Political Allegory in *Gulliver's Travels*', *Modern Philology*, 73: 4 (May 1976), S40–S47, and J. A. Downie, 'Political Characterization in *Gulliver's Travels*', *Yearbook of English Studies*, 7 (1977), 108–20.

85. Irvin Ehrenpreis, 'The Allegory of *Gulliver's Travels*', *Swift Studies*, 4 (1989), 13–28 (p. 23), and Brean S. Hammond, 'Applying Swift', in *Reading Swift: Papers from the Second Münster Symposium on Jonathan Swift*, eds Richard H. Rodino and Hermann J. Real (München: Fink, 1993), pp. 185–97 (p. 187). See also Hammond, 'Allegory in Swift's "Voyage to Laputa"', in *KM 80: A Birthday Album for Kenneth Muir* (Liverpool: Liverpool University Press, 1987), pp. 65–67.

86. Pope to Swift, 16 November 1726, in *CJS*, III, 52. See also Gay and Pope to Swift, [7] November 1726, in *CJS*, III, 47.

87. See *PW*, X, xix–xx, and Herbert Davis, 'Moral Satire', in *Swift, 'Gulliver's Travels': A Casebook*, ed. Richard Gravil (Basingstoke: Macmillan, 1974), pp. 120–35 (p. 128).

88. Edward Said, 'Swift the Intellectual', in *The World, the Text, and the Critic* (Cambridge, MA: Harvard University Press, 1983), pp. 72–89 (pp. 77, 83).

89. See Treadwell, 'Benjamin Motte, Andrew Tooke and *Gulliver's Travels*', pp. 287–304.

90. See Lester M. Beattie, *John Arbuthnot: Mathematician and Satirist* (Cambridge, MA: Harvard University Press, 1935), pp. 7–20, and John Arbuthnot, *Tables of Ancient Coins, Weights and Measures, explain'd and exemplified in several dissertations* (London, 1727), p. 109.

91. Gay and Pope to Swift, [7] November 1726, and Arbuthnot to Swift, 17 October 1725, in *CJS*, III, 47; II, 615.

92. See *Gulliver's Travels*, eds Rawson and Higgins, p. 353.

93. Pope, 'Part of the Ninth Ode of the Fourth Book', ll. 9–12, in *TE*, IV, 159.

94. See G. S. Rousseau, 'The Discourses of Literature and Science (1)', in *Enlightenment Borders*, pp. 202–12 (p. 207).

Chapter 5

1. Swift to Gay, 20 November 1729, in *CJS*, III, 268.

2. Swift to Thomas Swift, 3 May 1692, in *CJS*, I, 111. See Ehrenpreis, *Swift*, I, 61 and 279, and also *Tale*, p. 110.

3. See Peter J. Schakel, 'Swift's Voices: Innovation and Complication in the Poems Written at Market Hill', in *Reading Swift: Papers from the Fourth Münster Symposium on Jonathan Swift*, eds Hermann J. Real and Helgard Stöver-Leidig (München: Fink, 2003), pp. 311–25.

4. Swift to Pope, 31 October 1729, in *CJS*, III, 262.

5. See *LRJS*, II, 1167–71, and IV, 273–74.

6. Swift to Pope, 13 February 1728[-9], in *CJS*, III, 209.

7. See esp. Benjamin Hoadly's biographical preface to *Sermons by Samuel Clarke*, ed. John Clarke, 7th edn, 11 vols (London, 1749), I, ix–xlxix.

8. See Larry Stewart, *The Rise of Public Science: Rhetoric, Technology, and Natural Philosophy in Newtonian Britain, 1660–1750* (Cambridge: Cambridge University Press, 1992), p. 87.

9. See J. P. Ferguson, *Dr. Samuel Clarke: An Eighteenth-Century Heretic* (Kineton: Roundwood Press, 1976), pp. 24–25.

10. For instance, see Clarke, *A Demonstration of the Being and Attributes of God*, 2nd edn (London, 1706), p. 204. Sheridan owned the first and second editions: see *LRJS*, IV, 233.

11. Clarke, *A Discourse Concerning the Unchangeable Obligations of Natural Religion, and the Truth and Certainty of the Christian Revelation*, 2nd edn (London, 1708), p. 30. See Frank T. Boyle, 'Profane and Debauched Deist: Swift in the Contemporary Response to *A Tale of a Tub*', *Eighteenth-Century Ireland*, 3 (1988), 25–38, and *Swift as Nemesis: Modernity and its Satirist* (Stanford, CA: Stanford University Press, 2000), pp. 151–55.

12. Clarke, *The Scripture-Doctrine of the Trinity* (London, 1712), p. 352. On Arius, see Swift's sermon *On the Trinity*, in *PW*, IX, 160.

13. See Steven Shapin, 'Of Gods and Kings: Natural Philosophy and Politics in the Leibniz-Clarke Disputes', *Isis*, 72 (1981), 187–215 (p. 207), and Stewart, *The Rise of Public Science*, pp. 89–90.

14. Gay to Parnell, April–May 1714, in *The Letters of John Gay*, ed. C. F. Burgess (Oxford: Clarendon Press, 1966), p. 7.

15. Whiston, *A New Theory of the Earth* (London, 1696), pp. 126, 369–70.

16. See Marjorie Hope Nicolson and G. S. Rousseau, *'This Long Disease, My Life': Alexander Pope and the Sciences* (Princeton, NJ: Princeton University Press, 1968), esp. pp. 141–49.

17. Whiston, *Primitive Christianity Reviv'd*, 5 vols (London, 1711–12), I, ix, and see Scott Mandelbrote, 'Newton and Eighteenth-century Christianity', in *The Cambridge Companion to Newton*, eds I. Bernard Cohen and George E. Smith (Cambridge: Cambridge University Press, 2002), pp. 409–30 (pp. 409, 412).

18. *The Principia: Mathematical Principles of Natural Philosophy*, 3rd edn (London, 1726), trans. I. Bernard Cohen and Anne Whitman (Berkeley: University of California Press, 1999), p. 940. See Stephen D. Snobelen, '"God of Gods, and Lord of Lords": The Theology of Isaac Newton's General Scholium to the *Principia*', *Osiris*, 2nd series, 16 (2001), 169–208 (esp. pp. 176–77, 180–86).

19. Larry Stewart, 'The Trouble with Newton in the Eighteenth Century', in *Newton and Newtonianism: New Studies*, eds James E. Force and Sarah Hutton (Dordrecht: Kluwer Academic, 2004), pp. 221–37 (p. 224). See also Stewart, 'Seeing through the Scholium: Religion and Reading Newton in the Eighteenth Century', *History of Science*, 34 (1996), 123–65, and Scott Mandelbrote, 'Eighteenth-Century Reactions to Newton's Anti-Trinitarianism', in *Newton and Newtonianism*, pp. 93–111 (p. 97).

20. Rob Iliffe, 'Prosecuting Athanasius: Protestant Forensics and the Mirrors of Persecution', in *Newton and Newtonianism*, pp. 113–54 (pp. 117, 119).

21. *PW*, IV, 37, 63. See Roger D. Lund, 'Introduction', in *The Margins of Orthodoxy: Heterodox Writing and Cultural Response, 1660–1750*, ed. Lund (Cambridge: Cambridge University Press, 1995), pp. 1–29 (pp. 6–9), and Michael V. DePorte, 'Contemplating Collins: Freethinking in Swift', in *Reading Swift: Papers from the Third Münster Symposium on Jonathan Swift*, eds Hermann J. Real and Helgard Stöver-Leidig (München: Fink, 1998), pp. 103–15 (p. 103).

22. See Marcus Walsh, 'Swift and Religion', in *The Cambridge Companion to Jonathan Swift*, ed. Christopher Fox (Cambridge: Cambridge University Press, 2003), pp. 161–76.

23. Joseph Spence, *Observations, Anecdotes, and Characters of Books and Men*, ed. James M. Osborn, 2 vols (Oxford: Clarendon Press, 1966), I, 135 (No. 304, December 1743), and Pope, *The Dunciad in Four Books*, ed. Valerie Rumbold (Harlow: Longman, 1999), p. 331 (Book 4, ll. 459, 465–68). See *TE*, V, 385–86n., B. W. Young, '"See Mystery to Mathematics Fly!": Pope's *Dunciad* and the Critique of Religious Rationalism', *Eighteenth-Century Studies*, 26 (1993), 435–48, and Arthur Friedman, 'Pope and Deism', in *Pope and his Contemporaries: Essays Presented to George Sherburn*, eds James L. Clifford and Louis A. Landa (Oxford: Oxford University Press, 1949), pp. 89–95 (p. 92). In the *Memoirs*, Clarke is probably one of several philosophers ridiculed by the numerically inclined biblical speculations of Martinus and Crambe (Chap. VII, pp. 123–24).

24. *An Essay on Man*, Epistle I, ll. 17–18, 21–22, in *TE*, III i, 14–15, and Spence, *Observations*, I, 134 (No. 303, December 1743).

25. Clarke, 'The Answer to *A Seventh* Letter, Concerning the Argument *a priori*', in *Several Letters to the Reverend Dr Clarke, from a Gentleman in Gloucestershire,*

Relating to the First Volume of the Foregoing Sermons; with the Drs Answers Thereunto, 3rd edn (London, 1725), pp. 40–46 (p. 42).

26. James Noggle, 'Skepticism and the Sublime Advent of Modernity in the 1742 *Dunciad*', *Eighteenth Century: Theory and Interpretation*, 37 (1996), 22–41 (p. 23).

27. See Christopher Fox, *Locke and the Scriblerians: Identity and Consciousness in Early Eighteenth-Century Britain* (Berkeley: University of California Press, 1988), esp. pp. 101, 107–108, and also *Memoirs*, pp. 280–93.

28. William Coxe, *Memoirs of the Life and Administration of Sir Robert Walpole*, 3 vols (London, 1798), I, 274; Caroline to Leibniz, 26 November 1715, in *LCC*, p. 190.

29. Coxe, *Memoirs of the Life and Administration of Sir Robert Walpole*, I, 275, and *The Diary of Mary, Countess Cowper, Lady of the Bedchamber to the Princess of Wales, 1714–1720*, ed. Spencer Cowper, 2nd edn (London: for John Murray, 1865), p. 17 (see also pp. 14, 74).

30. See A. Rupert Hall and Marie Boas Hall, 'Clarke and Newton', *Isis*, 52 (1961), 583–85, and Domenico Bertoloni Meli, 'Newton and the Leibniz-Clarke Correspondence', in *The Cambridge Companion to Newton*, pp. 455–64 (pp. 459–60).

31. See *Alma: or, The Progress of the Mind*, Canto III, ll. 334–41, in *The Literary Works of Matthew Prior*, eds H. Bunker Wright and Monroe K. Spears, 2 vols (Oxford: Clarendon Press, 1959), I, 509.

32. See *Principia*, p. 932, and James E. Force, 'Providence and Newton's *Pantokrator*: Natural Law, Miracles, and Newtonian Science', in *Newton and Newtonianism*, pp. 65–92 (esp. pp. 69–70).

33. Carolyn Iltis, 'The Leibnizian-Newtonian Debates: Natural Philosophy and Social Psychology', *British Journal for the History of Science*, 6 (1973), 343–77 (pp. 347–48).

34. Shapin, 'Of Gods and Kings', p. 202. See also Larry Stewart, 'Samuel Clarke, Newtonianism, and the Factions of Post-Revolutionary England', *Journal of the History of Ideas*, 42 (1981), 52–72.

35. See Ian Higgins, *Swift's Politics: A Study in Disaffection* (Cambridge: Cambridge University Press, 1994), esp. pp. 11, 151, 171, 186.

36. Arbuthnot to Swift, [*c.* 20 September 1726], in *CJS*, III, 28 (see also [5 April 1726], in *CJS*, II, 636); Swift to Mrs. Henrietta Howard, [October 1726], in *CJS*, III, 41 (and see Swift to Lady Elisabeth Germain, [8] January 1732–3, in *CJS*, III, 574–77); 'The History of the Second Solomon' (c. 1729), in *PW*, V, 226.

37. See Judith Colton, 'Merlin's Cave and Queen Caroline: Garden Art as Political Propaganda', *Eighteenth-Century Studies*, 10 (1976), 1–20 (pp. 1–2), Joanna Marschner, 'Queen Caroline of Anspach and the European Princely Museum Tradition', in *Queenship in Britain, 1660–1837: Royal Patronage, Court Culture and Dynastic Politics*, ed. Clarissa Campbell Orr (Manchester: Manchester University Press, 2002), pp. 130–42 (p. 133), and Pope to Gay, 2 October 1732, in *The Correspondence of Alexander Pope*, ed. George Sherburn, 5 vols (Oxford: Clarendon Press, 1956), III, 318.

38. 'A Conclusion Drawn from an Epigram on the Queen, To the Drapier', in *Poems*, II, 664.

39. *An Epistle to Burlington*, l. 78, in *TE*, III ii, 144; Pope to William Oliver, 27 May 1740, in *The Correspondence of Alexander Pope*, IV, 244.

40. Swift had composed a far more explicit condemnation of the Hanoverians in about 1718, in a manuscript poem (acquired by Walter Scott) which dealt with the possible promiscuity of George I. See James Woolley, 'Writing Libels on the Germans: Swift's "Wicked Treasonable Libel"', in *Swift: The Enigmatic Dean – Festschrift for Hermann Josef Real*, eds Rudolf Freiburg, Arno Loffler and Wolfgang Zach (Tubingen: Stauffenburg, 1998), pp. 303–16.

41. The 'Letter from Dr. Swift to Mr. Pope' (1721), for instance, treats the Act of Settlement with some ambivalence: see *PW*, IX, 31, and Higgins, *Swift's Politics*, p. 89.

42. John Theophilus Desaguliers, *The Newtonian System of the World, The Best Model of Government: An Allegorical Poem* (London, 1728), p. 33 (ll. 181–82), and Thomas Sheridan, *An Ode, To be Perform'd at the Castle of Dublin, On the 1st of March 1729–30. Being the Birth-day of her most Serene Majesty Queen Caroline: By the Special Command of His Excellency John Lord Carteret* (Dublin, 1730), p. 3 (ll. 1, 4). See also *The Dunciad*, IV, 411–12 (p. 326), where Pope continues, in satiric fashion, the association of Caroline with Newtonian optics: 'Did Nature's pencil ever blend such rays, / Such vary'd light in one promiscuous blaze?'.

43. See Mandelbrote, 'Newton and Eighteenth-century Christianity', pp. 411–12.

44. See *LCC*, p. 43n.

45. See Ezio Vailati, *Leibniz & Clarke: A Study of their Correspondence* (New York: Oxford University Press, 1997), pp. 170–72, and Margula R. Perl, 'Physics and Metaphysics in Newton, Leibniz, and Clarke', *Journal of the History of Ideas*, 30 (1969), 507–26 (pp. 510–11). Clarke and Leibniz's argument is, of course, a rehashing of an older and predominantly Epicurean dispute about the nature of matter; one which Swift utilized as an appropriate conceit in his assault on professional writing in the *Tale* (pp. 96–97). See also Joseph Addison, *The Spectator*, 420 (2 July 1712), in Bond (ed.), *The Spectator*, III, 576.

46. Newton, Extract from *Optice* (1706), Query 31, in *LCC*, Appendix A, p. 178. See Vailati, *Leibniz & Clarke*, p. 168.

47. 'Dr. Clarke's Fifth Reply', in *LCC*, p. 112. See Iltis, 'The Leibnizian-Newtonian Debates', p. 353.

48. See B. J. T. Dobbs, 'Stoic and Epicurean doctrines in Newton's system of the world', in *Atoms, Pneuma and Tranquillity: Epicurean and Stoic Themes in European Thought*, ed. Margaret J. Osler (Cambridge: Cambridge University Press, 1991), pp. 221–38 (pp. 222–23).

49. Diogenes Laertius, *Lives of the Eminent Philosophers*, trans. R. D. Hicks, 2 vols (Cambridge, MA: Harvard University Press, 1925), II, 569.

50. See Margaret J. Osler, 'The Intellectual Sources of Robert Boyle's Philosophy of Nature: Gassendi's Voluntarism and Boyle's Physico-Theological Project', in *Philosophy, Science, and Religion in England 1640–1700*, eds Richard Kroll, Richard Ashcraft and Perez Zagorin (Cambridge: Cambridge University Press, 1992), pp. 178–98 (pp. 179–80), and Thomas Stanley, *The History of Philosophy: Containing the Lives, Opinions, Actions and Discourses of the Philosophers of Every Sect*, 2nd edn (London, 1687), Part XIII, Chap. VIII, p. 863.

51. *The Works of Richard Bentley*, ed. Alexander Dyce, 3 vols (London: MacPherson, 1836–38; repr. Hildesheim: Olms, 1971), III, 74, and see *WRB*, X, 522.

52. *T. Lucretius Carus The Epicurean Philosopher, His Six Books De Natura Rerum Done into English Verse*, trans. Thomas Creech (London, 1682), pp. 91–92.

See Swift, 'Pethox the Great', ll. 27–28: 'as *Epicurus* shows / The World from justling Seeds arose' (*Poems*, I, 324).

53. See Nora Crow Jaffe, *The Poet Swift* (Hanover, NH: University Press of New England, 1977), p. 53.

54. See Ferguson, *Dr. Samuel Clarke*, pp. 222–23.

55. Calvin, *Institutes of the Christian Religion*, trans. Henry Beveridge, 3 vols (Edinburgh: Calvin Translation Society, 1845), II, 629 (III. xxv. 12). See C. A. Patrides, 'Renaissance and Modern Views on Hell', *The Harvard Theological Review*, 57 (1964), 217–36 (p. 223).

56. On the difficulty of using the term 'latitudinarianism', see Richard Kroll, 'Introduction', in *Philosophy, Science, and Religion in England 1640–1700*, pp. 1–28.

57. See Paul C. Davies, 'The Debate on Eternal Punishment in Late Seventeenth- and Eighteenth-Century English Literature', *Eighteenth-Century Studies*, 4 (1971), 257–76.

58. *Dr. Faustus*, v 124–26, in *The Complete Works of Christopher Marlowe*, eds Roma Gill and others, 5 vols (Oxford: Clarendon Press, 1987–1998), II, 19.

59. Compare *Mr. C—ns's Discourse*: 'if you happen to think there is no Hell, there certainly is none, and consequently you cannot be damned; I answer further, that wherever there is no *Lawyer*, *Physician*, or *Priest*, that Country is *Paradise*' (*PW*, IV, 39).

60. Whiston, *Historical Memoirs of the Life and Writings of Dr. Samuel Clarke* (London, 1730), p. 98. Whiston's ideas were eventually published in *The Eternity of Hell Torments Considered* (London, 1740).

61. Clarke, *A Fourth Defense of an Argument made use of in a Letter to Mr Dodwel, to prove the Immateriality and Natural Immortality of the Soul* (London, 1708), p. 61. See Fox, *Locke and the Scriblerians*, p. 108.

62. See Ferguson, *Dr. Samuel Clarke*, pp. 36–37. Sheridan owned Dodwell's *Epistolary Discourse*: see *LRJS*, IV, 239.

63. Clarke, *A Letter to Mr Dodwell; Wherein all the Arguments in his Epistolary Discourse against the Immortality of the Soul are particularly answered, and the Judgment of the Fathers concerning that Matter truly represented* (London, 1706), p. 101. Sheridan owned the 6th edn (London, 1731): see *LRJS*, IV, 233.

64. Philip C. Almond, *Heaven and Hell in Enlightenment England* (Cambridge: Cambridge University Press, 1994), pp. 65, 176–77n124. In contrast, D. P. Walker argues that 'What Newton and Samuel Clarke thought about the eternity of hell we know only through Whiston': see *The Decline of Hell: Seventeenth-Century Discussions of Eternal Torment* (London: Routledge & Kegan Paul, 1964), p. 95.

65. Clarke, *The Exposition of the Church-Catechism* (Dublin, 1730), p. 49, and see *LRJS*, IV, 233.

66. Clarke, *A Paraphrase on the Four Evangelists*, 2 vols (London, 1722), II, 109.

67. Compare Louis A. Landa, who finds 'no overt answer' to whether Swift believed that 'science enforced religious faith and truth or constituted in some way a challenge to them'. See Landa, Review of 'Swift and Natural Science', by George Reuben Potter, *Philological Quarterly*, 21 (1942), 219–21 (p. 221).

68. *A True and Faithful Narrative of What Passed in London*, in *John Gay: Poetry and Prose*, eds Vinton A. Dearing and Charles E. Beckwith, 2 vols (Oxford: Clarendon

Press, 1974), II, 473, 466. Regarding its authorship and dating, see esp. Nicolson and Rousseau, *'This Long Disease'*, pp. 178–82, G. S. Rousseau, 'Wicked Whiston and the English Wits', in *Enlightenment Borders: Pre- and Post-modern Discourses: Medical, Scientific* (Manchester: Manchester University Press, 1991), pp. 325–41 (pp. 330–33), and Leland D. Peterson, 'Jonathan Swift and a Prose "Day of Judgment"', *Modern Philology*, 81 (May 1984), 401–406.

69. *Memoirs of the Life and Writings of Mr. William Whiston*, 2nd edn (London, 1753), p. 290. See also *Memoirs and Correspondence of Francis Atterbury, D. D., Bishop of Rochester*, ed. Robert Folkestone Williams, 2 vols (London: W. H. Allen, 1869), II, 239.

Afterword

1. 'A Letter of Mr. Isaac Newton, Professor of the Mathematicks in the University of Cambridge; containing his New Theory about Light and Colors', *Philosophical Transactions*, 6: 80 (19 February 1671/2), 3075–87 (p. 3081).

2. See Louis A. Landa, 'Swift, the Mysteries, and Deism', in *Essays in Eighteenth-Century English Literature* (Princeton, NJ: Princeton University Press, 1980), pp. 89–106 (p. 99).

3. Joseph Glanvill, *Scepsis Scientifica* (London, 1665), pp. 33, 176; facs. reprt in *The Vanity of Dogmatizing: The Three 'Versions'*, ed. Stephen Medcalf (Hove: Harvester Press, 1970).

4. *The Importance of the Guardian Considered* (1713), in Swift, *English Political Writings 1711–1714: The Conduct of the Allies and Other Works*, eds Bertrand A. Goldgar and Ian Gadd (Cambridge: Cambridge University Press, 2008), p. 236; *RAML*, pp. 240–44; *Tale*, p. 4.

5. 'Upon the Gardens of Epicurus; or, Of Gardening, in the Year 1685', in *Five Miscellaneous Essays by Sir William Temple*, ed. Samuel Holt Monk (Ann Arbor: The University of Michigan Press, 1963), p. 4.

6. See Francis Bacon, *The Advancement of Learning*, ed. Michael Kiernan (Oxford: Clarendon Press, 2000), pp. 31–32.

7. Swift to Lord Orrery, [16 April 1733], in *CJS*, III, 627.

8. I would not go as far as George Reuben Potter, though, who claims Swift 'really did not take the natural sciences seriously as objects for condemnation'. See 'Swift and Natural Science', *Philological Quarterly*, 20 (1941), 97–118 (p. 117), together with Louis A. Landa's important review (*Philological Quarterly*, 21 [1942], 219–21).

9. W. H. Dilworth, *The Life of Dr. Jonathan Swift* (London, 1758), facs. reprt in *Swiftiana XIII: Three Biographical Pamphlets 1745–1758* (New York: Garland, 1975), p. 68. See also John Boyle, Fifth Earl of Cork and Orrery, *Remarks on the Life and Writings of Dr. Jonathan Swift*, ed. João Fróes (Newark: University of Delaware Press, 2000), p. 185 (Letter XII).

10. John Conduitt, 'Notes on Newton's Character', in King's College Library, Cambridge, Keynes MS 130.7, f. 7^r, in *NP*; Francesco Algarotti, *Sir Isaac Newton's Philosophy Explain'd For the Use of the Ladies*, trans., 2 vols (London, 1739), I, 41.

11. See <http://www.improbable.com>.

Bibliography

Primary Works

1 Works written by Swift

The Account Books of Jonathan Swift, transcribed and with an introduction by Paul V. Thompson and Dorothy Jay Thompson (Newark: University of Delaware Press, 1984).

The Battle of the Books: Eine Historisch-kritische Ausgabe, ed. Hermann J. Real (Berlin: Walter de Gruyter, 1978).

The Correspondence of Jonathan Swift, D. D., ed. David Woolley, 4 vols (Frankfurt am Main: Lang, 1999–2007).

The Drapier's Letters, ed. Herbert Davis (Oxford: Clarendon Press, 1935).

English Political Writings 1711–1714: The Conduct of the Allies and Other Works, eds Bertrand A. Goldgar and Ian Gadd (Cambridge: Cambridge University Press, 2008) [*The Cambridge Edition of the Works of Jonathan Swift*, VIII].

Gulliver's Travels, ed. Paul Turner (Oxford: Oxford University Press, 1971; repr. 1994).

Gulliver's Travels, eds Claude Rawson and Ian Higgins (Oxford: Oxford University Press, 2005).

Hoaxes, Parodies, Treatises and Mock-Treatises, ed. Valerie Rumbold (Cambridge: Cambridge University Press, forthcoming) [*The Cambridge Edition of the Works of Jonathan Swift*, II].

The Intelligencer (with Thomas Sheridan), ed. James Woolley (Oxford: Clarendon Press, 1992).

Jonathan Swift: The Complete Poems, ed. Pat Rogers (Harmondsworth: Penguin, 1983).

Letters, Written by the Late Jonathan Swift, D.D., ed. Deane Swift, 6 vols (London, 1768).

Miscellanies, written by Jonathan Swift, D.D., 5th edn (London, 1736).

The Poems of Jonathan Swift, ed. Harold Williams, 2nd edn, 3 vols (Oxford: Clarendon Press, 1958).

The Prose Writings of Jonathan Swift, eds Herbert Davis and others, 14 vols (Oxford: Blackwell, 1939–68).

A Tale of a Tub &c., eds A. C. Guthkelch and D. Nichol Smith, 2nd edn, corrected (Oxford: Clarendon Press, 1973).

A Tale of a Tub and Other Works, ed. Marcus Walsh (Cambridge: Cambridge University Press, 2010) [*The Cambridge Edition of the Works of Jonathan Swift*, I].

The Works of Jonathan Swift, D. D. Dean of St. Patrick's, Dublin, Accurately revised in Twelve Volumes, adorned with copper-plates, with some account of the author's life, and notes historical and explanatory, ed. John Hawkesworth, 12 vols (London, 1754–55).

The Works of Jonathan Swift, D. D., ed. Sir Walter Scott, 19 vols (Edinburgh, 1814).

The Works of the Reverend Dr. Jonathan Swift, Dean of St. Patrick's, Dublin, ed. George Faulkner, 11 vols (Dublin, 1762).

2   Other primary works

Alexander, H. G., ed., *The Leibniz-Clarke Correspondence* (Manchester: Manchester University Press, 1956).

Algarotti, Francesco, *Sir Isaac Newton's Philosophy Explain'd for the Use of the Ladies*, trans., 2 vols (London, 1739).

Annals of Improbable Research, accessed via <http://www.improbable.com>.

Anon., *A Letter from a Young Lady, to the Revd. D—n S—t* (Dublin, 1724), facs. reprt in *Swiftiana IV: On the Drapier's Letters, etc. 1724* (New York: Garland, 1975).

Anon., *A Short Account of Dr. Bentley's Humanity and Justice .. In a Letter to the Honourable Charles Boyle, Esq.* (London, 1699).

Anon., *The Toasters Compleat, with the last Additions* (London, 1704).

Arbuthnot, John, *The Correspondence of Dr. John Arbuthnot*, ed. Angus Ross (München: Fink, 2006).

——, *The Life and Works of John Arbuthnot*, ed. George A. Aitken (Oxford: Clarendon Press, 1892).

——, *The Miscellaneous Works of the Late Dr. Arbuthnot*, 2 vols (Glasgow, 1751).

——, *Tables of Ancient Coins, Weights and Measures, explain'd and exemplified in several dissertations* (London, 1727).

Aristotle, *The Complete Works of Aristotle: The Revised Oxford Translation*, ed. Jonathan Barnes, 2 vols (Princeton, NJ: Princeton University Press, 1984).

Astell, Mary, *An Essay in Defence of the Female Sex* (London, 1696).

Atterbury, Francis, *Memoirs and Correspondence of Francis Atterbury, D. D., Bishop of Rochester*, ed. Robert Folkestone Williams, 2 vols (London: W. H. Allen, 1869).

——, *A Short Review of the Controversy Between Mr. Boyle, and Dr. Bentley* (London, 1701).

Bacon, Francis, *The Advancement of Learning*, ed. Michael Kiernan (Oxford: Clarendon Press, 2000) [*The Oxford Bacon*, IV].

——, *The Essays, or Counsels, Civil and Moral* (London: Knapton, 1691).

——, *The Instauratio magna Part II: Novum organum and Associated Texts*, ed. and trans. Graham Rees with Maria Wakely (Oxford: Clarendon Press, 2004) [*The Oxford Bacon*, XI].

——, *The Works of Francis Bacon*, eds James Spedding, Robert Leslie Ellis and Douglas Denon Heath, 14 vols (London, 1857–74).

Beaumont, Joseph, *Mathematical Sleaing-Tables: Or, The Great and only Mistery of Weaving Linnen-Cloth Explain'd* (Dublin, 1712).

——, *A Proposal for the More Effectual Improvement of the Channel and Harbour of Dublin* (Dublin?, 1710?).

Bentley, Richard, *The Works of Richard Bentley*, ed. Alexander Dyce, 3 vols (London: MacPherson, 1836–38; repr. Hildesheim: Olms, 1971).

Bindon, David, *Some Reasons Shewing the Necessity the People of Ireland are under, for continuing to refuse Mr. Wood's Coinage* (Dublin, 1724).

Blount, Charles, *The Oracles of Reason* (London, 1693).

Bond, Donald F., ed., *The Spectator*, 5 vols (Oxford: Clarendon Press, 1965).

——, *The Tatler*, 3 vols (Oxford: Clarendon Press, 1987).

Boyle, Charles, *Dr. Bentley's Dissertations on the Epistles of Phalaris, and the Fables of Æsop, Examin'd* (London, 1698).

Boyle, John, Fifth Earl of Cork and Orrery, *Remarks on the Life and Writings of Dr. Jonathan Swift*, ed. João Fróes (Newark: University of Delaware Press, 2000).

Boyle, Robert, *Experiments and Considerations Touching Colours* (London, 1670).

——, *The Works of Robert Boyle*, eds Michael Hunter and Edward B. Davis, 14 vols (London: Pickering & Chatto, 1999–2000).

Budgell, Eustace, *Memoirs of the Lives and Characters of the Illustrious Family of the Boyles*, 3rd edn (London, 1737).

Burnet, Gilbert, ed., *A Defence of Natural and Revealed Religion: Being an Abridgement of the Sermons preached at the Lecture founded by Robert Boyle* (London, 1737), facs. reprt, intro. by Andrew Pyle, preface by Alan P. F. Sell (Bristol: Thoemmes Press, 2000).

Burnet, James, Lord Monboddo, *Antient Metaphysics: or, the Science of Universals*, 2nd edn (London, 1782).

Burnet, Thomas, *Reflections upon The Theory of the Earth, Occasion'd by a Late Examination of it. In a Letter to a Friend.* (London, 1699).

——, *The Theory of the Earth*, 3rd edn (London, 1697).

Butler, Samuel, *Hudibras Parts I and II and Selected Other Writings*, eds John Wilders and Hugh de Quehen (Oxford: Clarendon Press, 1973).

C. D. M. (Corolini di Marco), *The Flying Island, &c. Being a Key to Gulliver's Voyage to Laputa, Balnibarbi, Glubbdubdrib, Luggnag, and Japan. In a Third Letter to Dean Swift* (London, 1726).

Charleton, Walter, *The Darknes of Atheism Dispelled by the Light of Nature: A Physico-Theologicall Treatise* (London, 1652).

Cheyne, George, *Philosophical Principles of Natural Religion* (London, 1705).

Church of England, *A Representation of the Present State of Religion, with regard to the late Excessive Growth of Infidelity, Heresy, and Profaneness* (London, 1711).

Clarke, Samuel, *A Demonstration of the Being and Attributes of God*, 2nd edn (London, 1706).

——, *A Discourse Concerning the Unchangeable Obligations of Natural Religion, and the Truth and Certainty of the Christian Revelation*, 2nd edn (London, 1708).

——, *The Exposition of the Church-Catechism* (Dublin, 1730).

——, *A Fourth Defense of an Argument made use of in a Letter to Mr Dodwel, to prove the Immateriality and Natural Immortality of the Soul* (London, 1708).

——, 'A Letter from the Rev. Dr. Samuel Clarke to Mr. Benjamin Hoadly, F. R. S. Occasion'd by the Present Controversy among Mathematicians, concerning the Proportion of Velocity and Force in Bodies in Motion', *Philosophical Transactions*, 35: 401 (1727–28), 381–88.

——, *A Letter to Mr Dodwell; Wherein all the Arguments in his Epistolary Discourse against the Immortality of the Soul are particularly answered, and the Judgment of the Fathers concerning that Matter truly represented* (London, 1706).

——, *A Paraphrase on the Four Evangelists*, 2 vols (London, 1722).

——, *The Scripture-Doctrine of the Trinity* (London, 1712).

——, *Sermons by Samuel Clarke*, ed. John Clarke, 7th edn, 11 vols (London, 1749).

——, *Several Letters to the Reverend Dr Clarke, from a Gentleman in Gloucestershire, Relating to the First Volume of the Foregoing Sermons; with the Drs Answers Thereunto*, 3rd edn (London, 1725).

Conduitt, John, 'Account of Newton's life at Cambridge', in King's College Library, Cambridge, Keynes MS. 130.4, in *The Newton Project* <http://www.newtonproject.sussex.ac.uk>.

——, 'Memorandums relating to Sir Isaac Newton given me by Mr Abraham Demoivre in November 1727', in University of Chicago Library, Joseph Halle Schaffner Collection, MS. 1075.7, in *The Newton Project*.

——, 'Miscellanea', in King's College Library, Cambridge, Keynes MS. 130.5, in *The Newton Project*.

——, 'Notes on Newton's Character', in King's College Library, Cambridge, Keynes MS. 130.7, in *The Newton Project*.

——, Notes towards the 'Life of Newton', in King's College Library, Cambridge, Keynes MS. 130.10, Keynes MS. 129 (A), and Keynes MS. 129 (B), in *The Newton Project*

——, 'Rough draft preface for the Life of Newton', in King's College Library, Cambridge, Keynes MS. 130.17, in *The Newton Project*.

——, 'Three drafts of a passage praising Newton's manual dexterity', in King's College Library, Cambridge, Keynes MS. 130.9, in *The Newton Project*.

Cowper, Mary, *The Diary of Mary, Countess Cowper, Lady of the Bedchamber to the Princess of Wales, 1714–1720*, ed. Spencer Cowper, 2nd edn (London: for John Murray, 1865).

Coxe, William, *Memoirs of the Life and Administration of Sir Robert Walpole*, 3 vols (London, 1798).

Creagh, Sir Michael, *Remarks upon Mr. Wood's Coyn and Proceedings* (Dublin, 1724), facs. reprt in *Swiftiana IV: On the Drapier's Letters, etc. 1724* (New York: Garland, 1975).

Creech, Thomas, trans., *T. Lucretius Carus The Epicurean Philosopher, His Six Books De Natura Rerum Done into English Verse* (London, 1682).

Cudworth, Ralph, *The True Intellectual System of the Universe* (London, 1678).

Curll, Edmund, *A Complete Key to The Tale of a Tub; With Some Account of the Authors, the Occasion and Design if Writing it, and Mr. Wotton's Remarks examin'd* (London, 1710).

de La Mettrie, Julien Offray, *Machine Man and Other Writings*, ed. and trans. Ann Thomson (Cambridge: Cambridge University Press, 1996).

Delany, Patrick, *Observations upon Lord Orrery's Remarks on the Life and Writings of Dr. Jonathan Swift* (London, 1754).

Derham, William, 'Remarks on Sr Is. Newton', with a covering letter to John Conduitt (18 July 1733), in King's College Library, Cambridge, Keynes MS. 133, in *The Newton Project*.

Derham, William, 'Some Magnetical Experiments and Observations', in *The Philosophical Transactions from the Year MDCC (where Mr. Lowthorp ends) to the year MDCCXX. Abridg'd, and Dispos'd under General Heads*, ed. Benjamin Motte, 2 vols (London, 1721), II, 241–43.

Desaguliers, John Theophilus, *A Course of Experimental Philosophy*, 2 vols (London, 1734–44).

——, *The Newtonian System of the World, The Best Model of Government: An Allegorical Poem* (London, 1728).

Descartes, René, *The Philosophical Writings of Descartes*, trans. John Cottingham, Robert Stoothoff and Dugald Murdoch, 3 vols (Cambridge: Cambridge University Press, 1984–91).

Diogenes Laertius, *Lives of the Eminent Philosophers*, trans. R. D. Hicks, 2 vols (Cambridge, MA: Harvard University Press, 1925).

Dilworth, W. H., *The Life of Dr. Jonathan Swift* (London, 1758), facs. reprt in *Swiftiana XIII: Three Biographical Pamphlets 1745–1758* (New York: Garland, 1975).

Dixon, Laurinda, ed., *Nicolas Flamel, His Exposition of the Hieroglyphicall Figures* (London, 1624), facs. reprt (New York: Garland, 1994).

Dryden, John, *Of Dramatic Poesy and Other Critical Essays*, ed. George Watson, 2 vols (London: Dent and Dutton, 1962).

Gay, John, *John Gay: Poetry and Prose*, eds Vinton A. Dearing and Charles E. Beckwith, 2 vols (Oxford: Clarendon Press, 1974).

——, *The Letters of John Gay*, ed. C. F. Burgess (Oxford: Clarendon Press, 1966).

Glanvill, Joseph, *Scepsis Scientifica* (London, 1665), facs. reprt in *The Vanity of Dogmatizing: The Three 'Versions'*, ed. Stephen Medcalf (Hove: Harvester Press, 1970).

Grew, Nehemiah, 'Of the Number of Acres contained in England', in *The Philosophical Transactions from the Year MDCC (where Mr. Lowthorp ends) to the year MDCCXX. Abridg'd, and Dispos'd under General Heads*, ed. Benjamin Motte, 2 vols (London, 1721), II, 278–82.

[Halley, Edmond], 'An Accompt of Some Books, II: Newton, *Philosophiæ Naturalis Principia Mathematica'*, *Philosophical Transactions*, 16 (1687), 291–97.

Helsham, Richard, *A Course of Lectures in Natural Philosophy* (Dublin, [1739]).

Hobbes, Thomas, *Leviathan*, ed. Richard Tuck (Cambridge: Cambridge University Press, 1991; repr. 1994).

Hoppen, K. Theodore, ed., *Papers of the Dublin Philosophical Society 1683–1709*, 2 vols (Dublin: Irish Manuscripts Commission, 2008).

Iamblichus, *On the Pythagorean Way of Life*, eds John Dillon and Jackson Hershbell (Atlanta, GA: Scholars Press, 1991).

Keill, John, *An Examination of Dr Burnet's Theory of the Earth. Together with Some Remarks on Mr Whiston's New Theory of the Earth* (London, 1698).

——, *An Introduction to Natural Philosophy: or, Philosophical Lectures Read in the University of Oxford, Anno Dom. 1700*, 2nd edn (London, 1726).

——, *An Introduction to the True Astronomy: Or, Astronomical Lectures, Read in the Astronomical School of the University of Oxford* (London, 1721).

King, William, *Dialogues of the Dead: Relating to the Present Controversy Concerning the Epistles of Phalaris* (London, 1699).

——, *The Original Works of William King*, 3 vols (London, 1776).

Kippis, Andrew, ed., *Biographia Britannica: Or, The Lives of the Most Eminent Persons who have Flourished in Great Britain and Ireland, from the Earliest Ages*, 2nd edn, 5 vols (London, 1778–93).

Locke, John, *An Essay Concerning Human Understanding*, ed. Peter H. Nidditch (Oxford: Clarendon Press, 1979).

Marlowe, Christopher, *The Complete Works of Christopher Marlowe*, eds Roma Gill and others, 5 vols (Oxford: Clarendon Press, 1987–98).

Marvell, Andrew, *The Prose Works of Andrew Marvell*, eds Annabel Patterson and others, 2 vols (New Haven, CT: Yale University Press, 2003).

More, Henry, *Henry More: Major Philosophical Works*, ed. G. A. J. Rogers, 9 vols (Bristol: Thoemmes Press, 1997).

Moréri, Louis, *The Great Historical, Geographical, and Poetical Dictionary; Being a Curious Miscellany of Sacred and Prophane History*, collected and enlarged by Jean Le Clerc, 2 vols in 1 (London, 1694).

Motte, Benjamin, ed., *The Philosophical Transactions from the Year MDCC (where Mr. Lowthorp ends) to the year MDCCXX. Abridg'd, and Dispos'd under General Heads*, 2 vols (London, 1721).

Newton, Isaac, *The Correspondence of Isaac Newton*, eds A. Rupert Hall and Laura Tilling, 7 vols (Cambridge: Cambridge University Press for the Royal Society, 1959–77).

——, 'A Letter of Mr. Isaac Newton, Professor of the Mathematicks in the University of Cambridge; containing his New Theory about Light and Colors', *Philosophical Transactions*, 6: 80 (19 February 1671/2), 3075–87.

——, *The Principia: Mathematical Principles of Natural Philosophy*, 3rd edn (London, 1726), trans. I. Bernard Cohen and Anne Whitman (Berkeley: University of California Press, 1999).

Ovid, *Metamorphoses*, trans. A. D. Melville (Oxford: Oxford University Press, 1986).

Petty, William, *Several Essays in Political Arithmetick* (London, 1699).

Plato, *Works*, trans. H. N. Fowler and others, 12 vols (London: Heinemann, 1926).

Pope, Alexander, *The Correspondence of Alexander Pope*, ed. George Sherburn, 5 vols (Oxford: Clarendon Press, 1956).

——, *The Dunciad in Four Books*, ed. Valerie Rumbold (Harlow: Longman, 1999).

——, *The Prose Works of Alexander Pope*, eds Norman Ault and Rosemary Cowler, 2 vols (Oxford: Blackwell, 1936–86).

——, *The Twickenham Edition of the Works of Alexander Pope*, eds John Butt and others, 11 vols (London: Methuen, 1939–69).

Pope, Alexander, and others, *The Memoirs of the Extraordinary Life, Works, and Discoveries of Martinus Scriblerus*, ed. Charles Kerby-Miller (New Haven, CT: Yale University Press, 1950; repr. Oxford: Oxford University Press, 1988).

——, *Miscellanies in Prose and Verse by Pope, Swift and Gay* (1727–32), ed. Alexander Pettit, 4 vols (London: Pickering & Chatto, 2002).

Reynolds, John, *Death's Vision Represented in a Philosophical, Sacred Poem* (London, 1709).

Salusbury, Thomas, *Mathematical Collections and Translations*, 2 vols (London, 1661).

Shadwell, Thomas, *The Virtuoso*, eds Marjorie Hope Nicolson and David Stuart Rodes (London: Arnold, 1966).

Sheridan, Thomas, *An Ode, To be Perform'd at the Castle of Dublin, On the 1st of March 1729–30. Being the Birth-day of her most Serene Majesty Queen Caroline: By the Special Command of His Excellency John Lord Carteret* (Dublin, 1730).

Sheridan, Thomas (the younger), *The Life of the Rev. Dr. Jonathan Swift* (London, 1784).

Spence, Joseph, *Observations, Anecdotes, and Characters of Books and Men*, ed. James M. Osborn, 2 vols (Oxford: Clarendon Press, 1966).

Spinoza, Benedict de, *The Chief Works of Benedict de Spinoza*, trans. R. H. M. Elwes, rev. edn, 2 vols (London: George Bell & Sons, 1903–1905).

Sprat, Thomas, *The History of the Royal-Society of London, For the Improving of Natural Knowledge* (London, 1667).

Stanley, Thomas, *The History of Philosophy: Containing the Lives, Opinions, Actions and Discourses of the Philosophers of Every Sect*, 2nd edn (London, 1687), and 3rd edn (London, 1701).

Swift, Deane, *An Essay upon the Life, Writings, and Character of Dr. Jonathan Swift* (London, 1755), facs. reprt in *Swiftiana XIV* (New York: Garland, 1974).

Temple, William, *Five Miscellaneous Essays by Sir William Temple*, ed. Samuel Holt Monk (Ann Arbor: The University of Michigan Press, 1963).

——, *Miscellanea: The Third Part*, ed. Jonathan Swift (London, 1701).

Thomson, James, *A Poem Sacred to the Memory of Sir Isaac Newton* (London, 1727).

Vaughan, Thomas, *The Works of Thomas Vaughan*, ed. Alan Rudrum with Jennifer Drake-Brockman (Oxford: Clarendon Press, 1984).

Whiston, William, *The Eternity of Hell Torments Considered* (London, 1740).

——, *Historical Memoirs of the Life and Writings of Dr. Samuel Clarke* (London, 1730).

——, *The Literal Accomplishment of Scripture Prophecies* (London, 1724).

——, *Memoirs of the Life and Writings of Mr. William Whiston*, 2nd edn (London, 1753).

——, *A New Theory of the Earth* (London, 1696).

——, *Primitive Christianity Reviv'd*, 5 vols (London, 1711–12).

Wilkins, John, *An Essay Towards a Real Character, and a Philosophical Language* (London, 1668).

Wilmot, John, Earl of Rochester, *The Works of John Wilmot, Earl of Rochester*, ed. Harold Love (Oxford: Oxford University Press, 1999).

Wotton, William, *A Defense of the Reflections upon Ancient and Modern Learning, [...] With Observations upon The Tale of a Tub* (London, 1705).

——, *Reflections upon Ancient and Modern Learning* (London, 1694; repr. Hildesheim: Olms, 1968).

Secondary Works

Adams, Robert M., 'In Search of Baron Somers', in *Culture and Politics from Puritanism to the Enlightenment*, ed. Perez Zagorin (Berkeley: University of California Press, 1980), pp. 165–202.

——, 'The Mood of the Church and *A Tale of a Tub*', in *England in the Restoration and Early Eighteenth Century: Essays on Culture and Society*, ed. H. T. Swedenberg, Jr (Berkeley: University of California Press, 1972), pp. 71–99.

Affentranger, Beat, 'The Spectacle of the Growth of Knowledge and Swift's Satires on Science' (doctoral dissertation, University of Zurich, 1997–98, accessed via <http://www.dissertation.com> [Parkland, FL, 2000]).

Albury, W. R., 'Halley's Ode on the *Principia* of Newton and the Epicurean Revival in England', *Journal of the History of Ideas*, 39 (1978), 24–43.

Alexander, Peter, *Ideas, Qualities and Corpuscles: Locke and Boyle on the External World* (Cambridge: Cambridge University Press, 1985).

Almond, Philip C., *Heaven and Hell in Enlightenment England* (Cambridge: Cambridge University Press, 1994).

Anstey, Peter, 'Literary Responses to Robert Boyle's Natural Philosophy', in *Science, Literature and Rhetoric in Early Modern England*, eds Juliet Cummins and David Burchell (Aldershot: Ashgate, 2007), pp. 145–62.

Armintor, Deborah Needleman, 'The Sexual Politics of Microscopy in Brobdingnag', *Studies in English Literature, 1500–1900*, 47 (2007), 619–40.

Baltes, Sabine, *The Pamphlet Controversy about Wood's Halfpence (1722–25) and the Tradition of Irish Constitutional Nationalism* (Frankfurt am Main: Lang, 2003).

Barnard, Toby, *Improving Ireland? Projectors, Prophets and Profiteers, 1641–1786* (Dublin: Four Courts Press, 2008).

Beattie, Lester M., *John Arbuthnot: Mathematician and Satirist* (Cambridge, MA: Harvard University Press, 1935).

Benedict, Barbara M., *Curiosity: A Cultural History of Early Modern Inquiry* (Chicago, IL: University of Chicago Press, 2001).

Bermúdez, José Luis, 'Scepticism and Science in Descartes', *Philosophy and Phenomenological Research*, 57 (1997), 743–72.

Boas, Marie, 'The Establishment of the Mechanical Philosophy', *Osiris*, 10 (1952), 412–541.

Boas Hall, Marie, 'Boyle's Method of Work: Promoting his Corpuscular Philosophy', *Notes and Records of the Royal Society of London*, 41 (1987), 111–43.

Borkat, Roberta F., 'The Spider and the Bee: Jonathan Swift's Reversal of Tradition in *The Battle of the Books*', *Eighteenth-Century Life*, 3 (December 1976), 44–46.

Bowers, R. H., 'Bacon's Spider Simile', *Journal for the History of Ideas*, 17 (1956), 133–35.

Boyle, Frank T., 'New Science in the Composition of *A Tale of a Tub*', in *Reading Swift: Papers from the Fifth Münster Symposium on Jonathan Swift*, ed. Hermann J. Real (München: Fink, 2008), pp. 175–84.

——, 'Profane and Debauched Deist: Swift in the Contemporary Response to *A Tale of a Tub*', *Eighteenth-Century Ireland*, 3 (1988), 25–38.

——, *Swift as Nemesis: Modernity and Its Satirist* (Stanford, CA: Stanford University Press, 2000).

Briggs, Peter M., 'John Graunt, Sir William Petty, and Swift's *Modest Proposal*', *Eighteenth-Century Life*, 29: 2 (Spring 2005), 3–24.

Brown, Theodore M., 'The College of Physicians and the Acceptance of iatro-mechanism in England, 1665–1695', *Bulletin of the History of Medicine*, 44 (1970), 12–30.

——, 'Physiology and the Mechanical Philosophy in Mid-seventeenth-century England', *Bulletin of the History of Medicine*, 51 (1977), 25–54.

Bullitt, John M., *Jonathan Swift and the Anatomy of Satire: A Study of Satiric Technique* (Cambridge, MA: Harvard University Press, 1953).

Bywaters, David, 'Anticlericism in Swift's *Tale of a Tub*', *Studies in English Literature, 1500–1900*, 36 (1996), 579–602.

Carey, Daniel, 'Swift among the Freethinkers', *Eighteenth-Century Ireland*, 12 (1997), 89–99.

Carnochan, W. B., 'The Occasion of Swift's "Day of Judgement"', *PMLA*, 87 (1972), 518–20.

Case, Arthur E., *Four Essays on 'Gulliver's Travels'* (Princeton, NJ: Princeton University Press, 1945; repr. Gloucester, MA: Peter Smith, 1958).

Chambers, A. B., '"I Was But an Inverted Tree": Notes Toward the History of an Idea', *Studies in the Renaissance*, 8 (1961), 291–99.

Christie, John R. R., 'Laputa Revisited', in *Nature Transfigured: Science and Literature, 1700–1900*, eds Christie and Sally Shuttleworth (Manchester: Manchester University Press, 1989), pp. 45–60.

Christie, John, and Sally Shuttleworth, 'Introduction: Between Literature and Science', in *Nature Transfigured: Science and Literature, 1700–1900* (see Christie, above), pp. 1–12.

Clucas, Stephen, '"The Infinite Variety of Formes and Magnitudes": 16th- and 17th-Century English Corpuscular Philosophy and Aristotelian Theories of Matter and Form', *Early Science and Medicine*, 2 (1997), 251–71.

Colie, Rosalie L., 'Spinoza in England, 1665–1730', *Proceedings of the American Philosophical Society*, 107 (1963), 183–219.

Colton, Judith, 'Merlin's Cave and Queen Caroline: Garden Art as Political Propaganda', *Eighteenth-Century Studies*, 10 (1976), 1–20.

Cook, Margaret G., 'Divine Artifice and Natural Mechanism: Robert Boyle's Mechanical Philosophy of Nature', *Osiris*, 2nd series, 16 (2001), 133–50.

Coolahan, Marie-Louise, 'Redeeming Parcels of Time: Aesthetics and Practice of Occasional Meditation', *The Seventeenth Century*, 22 (2007), 124–43.

Craig, John, *Newton at the Mint* (Cambridge: Cambridge University Press, 1946).

——, 'The Royal Society and the Royal Mint', *Notes and Records of the Royal Society of London*, 19 (1964), 156–67.

Crane, R. S., 'The Houyhnhnms, the Yahoos, and the History of Ideas', in *Reason and the Imagination: Studies in the History of Ideas, 1600–1800*, ed. J. A. Mazzeo (New York: Columbia University Press, 1962), pp. 231–53.

Craven, Kenneth, *Jonathan Swift and the Millennium of Madness: The Information Age in Swift's 'A Tale of a Tub'* (Leiden: Brill, 1992).

Cummins, Juliet, and David Burchell, 'Introduction: Ways of Knowing: Conversations between Science, Literature, and Rhetoric', in *Science, Literature and Rhetoric in Early Modern England* (see Anstey, above), pp. 1–12.

Curry, Patrick, 'Saving Astrology in Restoration England: "Whig" and "Tory" Reforms', in *Astrology, Science and Society: Historical Essays*, ed. Curry (Woodbridge: Boydell and Brewer, 1987), pp. 245–59.

Dahm, John J., 'Science and Apologetics in the Early Boyle Lectures', *Church History*, 39 (1970), 172–86.

Dargan, H. M., 'The Nature of Allegory as Used by Swift', *Studies in Philology*, 13 (1916), 159–79.

Davies, Paul C., 'The Debate on Eternal Punishment in Late Seventeenth- and Eighteenth-Century English Literature', *Eighteenth-Century Studies*, 4 (1971), 257–76.

Davis, Herbert, 'Moral Satire', in *Swift, 'Gulliver's Travels': A Casebook*, ed. Richard Gravil (Basingstoke: Macmillan, 1974; repr. 1986), pp. 120–35; first published in Davis, *The Satire of Jonathan Swift* (New York: Macmillan, 1947), as revised in *Jonathan Swift: Essays on His Satire and Other Studies* (New York: Oxford University Press, 1964), pp. 143–58.

——, 'Swift and the Pedants', in *Jonathan Swift: Essays on His Satire and Other Studies*, pp. 199–215.

DePorte, Michael V., 'Contemplating Collins: Freethinking in Swift', in *Reading Swift: Papers from the Third Münster Symposium on Jonathan Swift*, eds Hermann J. Real and Helgard Stöver-Leidig (München: Fink, 1998), pp. 103–15.

——, 'Digressions and Madness in *A Tale of a Tub* and *Tristram Shandy*', *Huntington Library Quarterly*, 34 (1970), 43–57.

——, *Nightmares and Hobbyhorses: Swift, Sterne, and Augustan Ideas of Madness* (San Marino, CA: Huntington Library, 1974).

——, 'Swift, God, and Power', in *Walking Naboth's Vineyard: New Studies of Swift*, eds Christopher Fox and Brenda Tooley (Notre Dame, IN: University of Notre Dame Press, 1995), pp. 73–97.

De-Quehen, A. H., 'Lucretius and Swift's *Tale of a Tub*', *University of Toronto Quarterly*, 63 (1993–94), 287–307.

Dingley, R. J., 'Dr Bentley's Centripetal Tendency', *Notes & Queries*, 229 (n.s.31) (1984), 378–79.

Dobbs, B. J. T., 'Stoic and Epicurean doctrines in Newton's system of the world', in *Atoms, Pneuma and Tranquillity: Epicurean and Stoic Themes in European Thought*, ed. Margaret J. Osler (Cambridge: Cambridge University Press, 1991), pp. 221–38.

Downie, J. A., 'Gulliver's Fourth Voyage and Locke's *Essay concerning Human Understanding*', in *Reading Swift: Papers from the Fifth Münster Symposium* (see Frank T. Boyle, above), pp. 453–64.

——, *Jonathan Swift: Political Writer* (London: Routledge & Kegan Paul, 1984; repr. 1985).

——, 'Political Characterization in *Gulliver's Travels*', *Yearbook of English Studies*, 7 (1977), 108–20.

Ehrenpreis, Irvin, *Acts of Implication: Suggestion and Covert Meaning in the Works of Dryden, Swift, Pope, and Austen* (Berkeley: University of California Press, 1981).

——, 'The Allegory of *Gulliver's Travels*', *Swift Studies*, 4 (1989), 13–28.

——, 'The Doctrine of *A Tale of a Tub*', in *Proceedings of the First Münster Symposium on Jonathan Swift*, eds Hermann J. Real and Heinz J. Vienken (München: Fink, 1985), pp. 59–71.

——, 'Four of Swift's Sources', *Modern Language Notes*, 70 (1955), 95–100.

——, 'Jonathan Swift: Lecture on a Master Mind', *Proceedings of the British Academy*, 54 (1968), 149–64.

——, *The Personality of Jonathan Swift* (London: Methuen, 1958).

——, *Swift: The Man, His Works, and the Age*, 3 vols (London: Methuen, 1962–83).

Elias, A. C., Jr, *Swift at Moor Park: Problems in Biography and Criticism* (Philadelphia: University of Pennsylvania Press, 1982).

Ellis, Frank H., 'No Apologies, Dr. Swift!', *Eighteenth-Century Life*, 21: 3 (November 1997), 71–76.

England, A. B., *Energy and Order in the Poetry of Swift* (Lewisburg, PA: Bucknell University Press, 1980).

Fabricant, Carole, *Swift's Landscape* (Baltimore, MD: The Johns Hopkins University Press, 1982; repr. Notre Dame, IN: University of Notre Dame Press, 1995).

Ferguson, J. P., *Dr. Samuel Clarke: An Eighteenth-Century Heretic* (Kineton: Roundwood Press, 1976).

Ferguson, Oliver W., *Jonathan Swift and Ireland* (Urbana, IL: University of Illinois Press, 1962).

Firth, Charles Harding, 'The Political Significance of *Gulliver's Travels*', *Proceedings of the British Academy* (1919–20), 237–59.

Fisch, H., 'Bishop Hall's Meditations', *The Review of English Studies*, 25 (1949), 210–21.

Fitzgerald, Robert P., 'Science and Politics in Swift's Voyage to Laputa', *Journal of English and Germanic Philology*, 87 (1988), 213–29.

Force, James E., 'The God of Abraham and Isaac (Newton)', in *The Books of Nature and Scripture: Recent Essays on Natural Philosophy, Theology, and Biblical Criticism in the Netherlands of Spinoza's Time and the British Isles of Newton's Time*, eds Force and Richard H. Popkin (Dordrecht: Kluwer Academic, 1994), pp. 179–200.

——, 'Newton, the "Ancients," and the "Moderns"', in *Newton and Religion: Context, Nature, and Influence*, eds Force and Richard H. Popkin (Dordrecht: Kluwer Academic, 1999), pp. 237–57.

——, 'Providence and Newton's Pantokrator: Natural Law, Miracles, and Newtonian Science', in *Newton and Newtonianism: New Studies*, eds Force and Sarah Hutton (Dordrecht: Kluwer Academic, 2004), pp. 65–92.

Fox, Christopher, 'How to Prepare a Noble Savage: The Spectacle of Human Science', in *Inventing Human Science: Eighteenth-Century Domains*, eds Fox, Roy Porter and Robert Wokler (Berkeley: University of California Press, 1995), pp. 1–30.

——, *Locke and the Scriblerians: Identity and Consciousness in Early Eighteenth-Century Britain* (Berkeley: University of California Press, 1988).

——, 'Swift and the Spectacle of Human Science', in *Reading Swift: Papers from the Third Münster Symposium* (see DePorte, above), pp. 199–212.

Freedman, William, 'The Grotesque Body in the Hollow Tub: Swift's *Tale*', *Texas Studies in Literature and Language*, 51 (2009), 294–316.

Freiburg, Rudolf, '"Strip, Tear, Pull, Rent, Flay off all": The Mechanical Reduction of Satire in Swift's *Tale*', in *Reading Swift: Papers from the Third Münster Symposium* (see DePorte, above), pp. 57–72.

Friedman, Arthur, 'Pope and Deism', in *Pope and his Contemporaries: Essays Presented to George Sherburn*, eds James L. Clifford and Louis A. Landa (Oxford: Oxford University Press, 1949), pp. 89–95.

Frye, Northrop, *An Anatomy of Criticism: Four Essays* (Princeton, NJ: Princeton University Press, 1957).

Gascoigne, John, 'From Bentley to the Victorians: The Rise and Fall of British Newtonian Natural Theology', *Science in Context*, 2 (1988), 219–56.

Gerrard, Christine, *The Patriot Opposition to Walpole: Politics, Poetry, and National Myth, 1725–1742* (Oxford: Clarendon Press, 1994).

Goodwin, Albert, 'Wood's Halfpence', *The English Historical Review*, 51 (1936), 647–74.

Gottlieb, Sidney, 'The Emblematic Background of Swift's Flying Island', *Swift Studies*, 1 (1986), 24–31.

Greene, Donald, 'Augustinianism and Empiricism: A Note on Eighteenth-Century English Intellectual History', *Eighteenth-Century Studies*, 1 (1967), 33–68.

——, 'Swift: Some Caveats', in *Studies in the Eighteenth Century II: Papers presented at the Second David Nichol Smith Memorial Seminar Canberra 1970*, ed. R. F. Brissenden (Canberra: Australian National University Press, 1973), pp. 341–58.

Greene, Herbert Eveleth, 'The Allegory as Employed by Spenser, Bunyan, and Swift', *PMLA*, 4 (1889), 145–93.

Gudger, E. W., 'The Five Great Naturalists of the Sixteenth Century: Belon, Rondelet, Salviani, Gesner and Aldrovandi: A Chapter in the History of Ichthyology', *Isis*, 22 (1934), 21–40.

Guerlac, Henry, and M. C. Jacob, 'Bentley, Newton, and Providence: The Boyle Lectures Once More', *Journal of the History of Ideas*, 30 (1969), 307–18.

Guerrini, Anita, 'The Tory Newtonians: Gregory, Pitcairne, and their Circle', *Journal of British Studies*, 25 (1986), 288–311.

Hall, A. Rupert, 'Newton versus Leibniz: From Geometry to Metaphysics', in *The Cambridge Companion to Newton*, eds I. Bernard Cohen and George E. Smith (Cambridge: Cambridge University Press, 2002), pp. 431–54.

Hall, A. Rupert, and Marie Boas Hall, 'Clarke and Newton', *Isis*, 52 (1961), 583–85.

Hammond, Brean S., 'Allegory in Swift's "Voyage to Laputa"', in *KM 80: A Birthday Album for Kenneth Muir* (Liverpool: Liverpool University Press, 1987), pp. 65–67.

——, 'Applying Swift', in *Reading Swift: Papers from the Second Münster Symposium on Jonathan Swift*, eds Richard H. Rodino and Hermann J. Real (München: Fink, 1993), pp. 185–97.

——, *Pope* (Brighton: Harvester New Readings, 1986).

——, 'Scriblerian Self-Fashioning', *Yearbook of English Studies*, 18 (1988), 108–22.

Harré, Rome, 'Knowledge', in *The Ferment of Knowledge: Studies in the Historiography of Eighteenth-Century Science*, eds G. S. Rousseau and Roy Porter (Cambridge: Cambridge University Press, 1980), pp. 11–54.

Harrison, Charles T., 'The Ancient Atomists and English Literature of the Seventeenth Century', *Harvard Studies in Classical Philology*, 45 (1934), 1–79.

——, 'Bacon, Hobbes, Boyle, and the Ancient Atomists', *Harvard Studies and Notes in Philology and Literature*, 15 (1933), 191–218.

Harrison, Peter, 'Original Sin and the Problem of Knowledge in Early Modern Europe', *Journal of the History of Ideas*, 63 (2002), 239–59.

Harth, Phillip, 'The Problem of Political Allegory in *Gulliver's Travels*', *Modern Philology*, 73: 4 (May 1976), S40–S47.

——, *Swift and Anglican Rationalism: The Religious Background of 'A Tale of a Tub'* (Chicago, IL: University of Chicago Press, 1961).

Hawley, Judith, 'General Introduction', in *Literature and Science, 1660–1834*, gen. ed. J. Hawley, 8 vols (London: Pickering & Chatto, 2003–2004), I, xi–xvii.

Hedley Brooke, John, *Science and Religion: Some Historical Perspectives* (Cambridge: Cambridge University Press, 1991).

Henry, John, '"Pray Do Not Ascribe that Notion to Me": God and Newton's Gravity', in *The Books of Nature and Scripture* (see Force, above), pp. 123–47.

Higgins, Ian, 'Jonathan Swift's Political Confession', in *Politics and Literature in the Age of Swift: English and Irish Perspectives*, ed. Claude Rawson (Cambridge: Cambridge University Press, 2010), pp. 3–30.

——, 'Language and Style', in *The Cambridge Companion to Jonathan Swift*, ed. Christopher Fox (Cambridge: Cambridge University Press, 2003), pp. 146–60.

——, *Swift's Politics: A Study in Disaffection* (Cambridge: Cambridge University Press, 1994).

Hill, John M., 'Corpuscular Fundament: Swift and the Mechanical Philosophy', *Enlightenment Essays*, 6 (Spring 1975), 37–49.

Hinman, Robert B., *Abraham Cowley's World of Order* (Cambridge, MA: Harvard University Press, 1960), pp. 189–90.

Hoppen, K. Theodore, *The Common Scientist in the Seventeenth Century: A Study of Dublin Philosophical Society 1683–1708* (London: Routledge & Kegan Paul, 1970).

Houghton, Walter E., 'The English Virtuoso in the Seventeenth Century', *Journal of the History of Ideas*, 3 (1942), 51–73, and 190–219.

Houlihan Flynn, Carol, *The Body in Swift and Defoe* (Cambridge: Cambridge University Press, 1990).

Hunter, J. Paul, *Before Novels: The Cultural Contexts of Eighteenth Century English Fiction* (New York: Norton, 1990).

——, 'Robert Boyle and the Epistemology of the Novel', *Eighteenth-Century Fiction*, 2 (1990), 275–91.

Hunter, Michael, 'Latitudinarianism and the "Ideology" of the Early Royal Society: Thomas Sprat's *History of the Royal Society* (1667) Reconsidered', in *Philosophy, Science, and Religion in England 1640–1700*, eds Richard Kroll,

Richard Ashcraft and Perez Zagorin (Cambridge: Cambridge University Press, 1992), pp. 199–229.

——, 'Science and Astrology in Seventeenth-Century England: An Unpublished Polemic by John Flamsteed', in *Astrology, Science and Society: Historical Essays* (see Curry, above), pp. 261–86.

Iliffe, Rob, 'Prosecuting Athanasius: Protestant Forensics and the Mirrors of Persecution', in *Newton and Newtonianism: New Studies* (see Force, above), pp. 113–54.

Iltis, Carolyn, 'The Leibnizian-Newtonian Debates: Natural Philosophy and Social Psychology', *British Journal for the History of Science*, 6 (1973), 343–77.

Ingram, Allan, 'Madness at *Tub* Time: Swift Writing Insanity', in *Reading Swift: Papers from the Fifth Münster Symposium* (see Frank T. Boyle, above), pp. 165–73.

Jacob, Margaret C., 'Millenarianism and Science in the Late Seventeenth Century', *Journal of the History of Ideas*, 37 (1976), 335–41.

——, *The Newtonians and the English Revolution, 1689–1720* (Ithaca, NY: Cornell University Press, 1976).

Jacob, Margaret C., and W. A. Lockwood, 'Political Millenarianism and Burnet's *Sacred Theory*', *Science Studies*, 2 (1972), 265–79.

Jaffe, Nora Crow, *The Poet Swift* (Hanover, NH: University Press of New England, 1977).

Jenkins, Jane E., 'Arguing about Nothing: Henry More and Robert Boyle on the Theological Implications of the Void', in *Rethinking the Scientific Revolution*, ed. Margaret J. Osler (Cambridge: Cambridge University Press, 2000), pp. 153–79.

Johnson, Christopher D., 'The Nature of Fallen Things: Another Look at Lucretius and *A Tale of a Tub*', *Swift Studies*, 21 (2006), 39–47.

Johnson, James W., 'That Neo-Classical Bee', *Journal of the History of Ideas*, 22 (1961), 262–66.

Johnson, Maurice, 'A Note on Swift's *Meditation upon a Broom-stick* and *A Tale of a Tub*', *Library Chronicle* (University of Pennsylvania), 37 (1971), 136–42.

Johnson, Monte, and Catherine Wilson, 'Lucretius and the History of Science', in *The Cambridge Companion to Lucretius*, eds Stuart Gillespie and Philip Hardie (Cambridge: Cambridge University Press, 2007), pp. 131–48.

Jordanova, L. J., 'Introduction', in *Languages of Nature: Critical Essays on Science and Literature*, ed. Jordanova (London: Free Association Books, 1986), pp. 15–47.

Kargon, Robert Hugh, *Atomism in England from Hariot to Newton* (Oxford: Clarendon Press, 1966).

Keithley, Walter H., 'Jonathan Swift, a Grub-Street Hack, and the Problem of the Popularization of Science in *A Tale of a Tub*', *Swift Studies*, 20 (2005), 51–69.

Kelly, Ann Cline, 'After Eden: Gulliver's (Linguistic) Travels', *ELH*, 45 (1978), 33–54.

——, *Swift and the English Language* (Philadelphia: University of Pennsylvania Press, 1988).

Kelly, James, 'Jonathan Swift and the Irish Economy in the 1720s', *Eighteenth-Century Ireland*, 6 (1991), 7–36.

Kelly, Patrick, 'Swift on Money and Economics', in *The Cambridge Companion to Jonathan Swift* (see Higgins, above), pp. 128–45.

Kiernan, Colin, 'Swift and Science', *Historical Journal*, 14 (1971), 709–22.

Klein, Jürgen, and Gerhild Riemann, 'Enigmatic Folly or Foolish Enigma: Speculations on *Gulliver's Travels*, Book III', in *Swift: The Enigmatic Dean – Festschrift for Hermann Josef Real*, eds Rudolf Freiburg, Arno Loffler and Wolfgang Zach (Tubingen: Stauffenburg, 1998), pp. 91–98.

Korshin, Paul J., 'The Intellectual Context of Swift's Flying Island', *Philological Quarterly*, 50 (1971), 630–46.

Koyre, Alexandre, and I. Bernard Cohen, 'Newton & the Leibniz-Clarke Correspondence, with notes on Newton, Conti, & Des Maizeaux', *Archives Internationales d'Histoire des Sciences*, 15 (1962), 63–126.

Kroll, Richard W. F., 'Introduction', in *Philosophy, Science, and Religion in England 1640–1700* (see Hunter, above), pp. 1–28.

——, *The Material Word: Literate Culture in the Restoration and Early Eighteenth Century* (Baltimore, MD: The Johns Hopkins University Press, 1991).

Kubrin, D. C., 'Newton and the Cyclical Cosmos: Providence and the Mechanical Philosophy', *Journal of the History of Ideas*, 28 (1967), 325–46.

Landa, Louis A., 'The Dismal Science in Houyhnhnmland', *Novel: A Forum on Fiction*, 13 (1979), 38–49.

——, Review of 'Swift and Natural Science', by George Reuben Potter, *Philological Quarterly*, 21 (1942), 219–21.

——, 'Swift's Economic Views and Mercantilism', *ELH*, 10 (1943), 310–35.

——, 'Swift, the Mysteries, and Deism', in *Essays in Eighteenth-Century English Literature* (Princeton, NJ: Princeton University Press, 1980), pp. 89–106; first published in *Studies in English, Department of English, The University of Texas 1944* (Austin: University of Texas Press, 1945), pp. 239–56.

Leonard, David Charles, 'Swift, Whiston, and the Comet', *English Language Notes*, 16 (1979), 284–87.

Levine, George, 'One Culture: Science and Literature', in *One Culture: Essays in Science and Literature*, ed. G. Levine (Chicago, IL: Chicago University Press, 1987), pp. 3–32.

Levine, Joseph M., *The Battle of The Books: History and Literature in the Augustan Age* (Ithaca, NY: Cornell University Press, 1991).

——, *Dr. Woodward's Shield: History, Science, and Satire in Augustan England* (Berkeley: University of California Press, 1977).

Lewis, Jayne Elizabeth, *The English Fable: Aesop and Literary Culture, 1651–1740* (Cambridge: Cambridge University Press, 1996).

Limouze, A. S., 'A Note on Virgil and the *Battle of the Books*', *Philological Quarterly*, 27 (1948), 85–89.

Lloyd, Claude, 'Shadwell and the Virtuosi', *PMLA*, 44 (1929), 472–94.

Lock, F. P., *The Politics of 'Gulliver's Travels'* (Oxford: Clarendon Press, 1980).

Löffler, Arno, 'The Dean and Lady Anne: Humour in Swift's Market Hill Poems', in *Reading Swift: Papers from the Second Münster Symposium* (see Hammond, above), pp. 113–24.

Lowe, N. F., 'Why Swift Killed Partridge', *Swift Studies*, 6 (1991), 70–82.

Lund, Roger D., '*A Tale of a Tub*, Swift's Apology, and the Trammels of Christian wit', in *Augustan Subjects: Essays in Honor of Martin C. Battestin*, ed. Albert J. Rivero (Newark: University of Delaware Press, 1997), pp. 87–109.

——, 'The Eel of Science: Index Learning, Scriblerian Satire, and the Rise of Information Culture', *Eighteenth-Century Life*, 22 (1998), 18–42.

——, ed., *The Margins of Orthodoxy: Heterodox Writing and Cultural Response, 1660–1750* (Cambridge: Cambridge University Press, 1995).

——, 'Martinus Scriblerus and the Search for the Soul', *Papers on Language and Literature*, 25: 2 (Spring 1989), 135–50.

——, 'Strange Complicities: Atheism and Conspiracy in *A Tale of a Tub*', *Eighteenth-Century Life*, 13: 3 (November 1989), 34–58, repr. in *British Literature 1640–1789: A Critical Reader*, ed. Robert DeMaria, Jr (Oxford: Blackwell, 1999), pp. 142–68.

Lynall, Gregory, '"An Author *bonæ notæ*, and an *Adeptus*": Swift's Alchemical Satire and Satiric Alchemy in *A Tale of a Tub*', *Swift Studies*, 24 (2009), 29–45.

——, 'John Gay, Magnetism, and the Spectacle of Natural Philosophy: Scriblerian Pins and Needles', *British Journal for Eighteenth-Century Studies*, 30 (2007), 389–403.

Mandelbrote, Scott, 'Eighteenth-Century Reactions to Newton's Anti-Trinitarianism', in *Newton and Newtonianism: New Studies* (see Force, above), pp. 93–111.

——, 'Isaac Newton and Thomas Burnet: Biblical Criticism and the Crisis of Late Seventeenth-Century England', in *The Books of Nature and Scripture* (see Force, above), pp. 149–78.

——, 'Newton and Eighteenth-century Christianity', in *The Cambridge Companion to Newton* (see Hall, above), pp. 409–30.

Maresca, Thomas E., 'Personification vs. Allegory', in *Enlightening Allegory: Theory, Practice, and Contexts of Allegory in the Late Seventeenth and Eighteenth Centuries*, ed. Kevin L. Cope (New York: AMS Press, 1993), pp. 21–39.

Markley, Robert, *Fallen Languages: Crises of Representation in Newtonian England, 1660–1740* (Ithaca, NY: Cornell University Press, 1993).

Marschner, Joanna, 'Queen Caroline of Anspach and the European princely museum tradition', in *Queenship in Britain, 1660–1837: Royal Patronage, Court Culture and Dynastic Politics*, ed. Clarissa Campbell Orr (Manchester: Manchester University Press, 2002), pp. 130–42.

Matthew, Colin, and Brian Harrison, eds, *Oxford Dictionary of National Biography* (Oxford: Oxford University Press, 2004).

Mayo, Thomas Franklin, 'Epicurus in England (1650–1725)' (unpublished doctoral dissertation, Columbia University, Texas, 1933).

McColley, Grant, 'The Theory of the Diurnal Rotation of the Earth', *Isis*, 26 (1937), 392–402.

McDayter, Mark, 'The Haunting of St. James's Library: Librarians, Literature, and *The Battle of the Books*', *Huntington Library Quarterly*, 66 (2003), 1–26.

McGuire, J. E., and P. M. Rattansi, 'Newton and the "Pipes of Pan"', *Notes and Records of the Royal Society of London*, 21 (1966), 108–42.

Meli, Domenico Bertoloni, 'Caroline, Leibniz, and Clarke', *Journal of the History of Ideas*, 60 (1999), 469–86.

——, 'Newton and the Leibniz-Clarke Correspondence', in *The Cambridge Companion to Newton* (see Hall, above), pp. 455–64.

Merton, Robert C., 'The "Motionless" Motion of Swift's Flying Island', *Journal of the History of Ideas*, 27 (1966), 275–77.

Mezciems, Jenny, 'The Unity of Swift's "Voyage to Laputa": Structure as Meaning in Utopian Fiction', *Modern Language Review*, 72 (1977), 1–21.

Montag, Warren, *The Unthinkable Swift: The Spontaneous Philosophy of a Church of England Man* (London: Verso, 1994).

Moore, Leslie, '"Instructive Trees": Swift's *Broom-Stick*, Boyle's *Reflections*, and Satiric Figuration', *Eighteenth-Century Studies*, 19 (1986), 313–32.

Moore, John Robert, 'A Possible Model for the Organization of *A Tale of a Tub*', *Notes & Queries*, 199 (1954), 288–90.

Morel, Pierre-Marie, 'Epicurean atomism', in *The Cambridge Companion to Epicureanism*, ed. James Warren (Cambridge: Cambridge University Press, 2009), pp. 65–83.

Mueller, Judith C., 'Writing under Constraint: Swift's "Apology" for *A Tale of a Tub*', *ELH*, 60 (1993), 101–15.

Mullan, John, 'Swift, Defoe, and Narrative Forms', in *The Cambridge Companion to English Literature, 1650–1740*, ed. Steven N. Zwicker (Cambridge: Cambridge University Press, 1998), pp. 250–75.

Nash, Richard, 'Entrapment and Ironic Modes in *Tale of a Tub*', *Eighteenth-Century Studies*, 24 (1991), 415–31.

Nicolson, Marjorie Hope, *Mountain Gloom and Mountain Glory: The Development of the Aesthetics of the Infinite* (Ithaca, NY: Cornell University Press, 1959).

——, *Newton Demands the Muse: Newton's Opticks and the Eighteenth Century Poets* (Princeton, NJ: Princeton University Press, 1946; repr. Hamden, CT: Archon, 1963).

——, *Science and Imagination* (Ithaca, NY: Cornell University Press, 1956).

Nicolson, Marjorie, and Nora M. Mohler, 'The Scientific Background of Swift's *Voyage to Laputa*' and 'Swift's "Flying Island" in the *Voyage to Laputa*', *Annals of Science*, 2 (1937), 299–334 and 405–30.

Nicolson, Marjorie Hope, and G. S. Rousseau, *'This Long Disease, My Life': Alexander Pope and the Sciences* (Princeton, NJ: Princeton University Press, 1968).

Noggle, James, 'Skepticism and the Sublime Advent of Modernity in the 1742 *Dunciad*', *Eighteenth Century: Theory and Interpretation*, 37 (1996), 22–41.

Nuttall, A. D., 'Fishes in the Trees', *Essays in Criticism*, 24 (1974), 20–38.

Oakleaf, David, *A Political Biography of Jonathan Swift* (London: Pickering & Chatto, 2008).

Oxford English Dictionary, 2nd edn (Oxford: Oxford University Press, 1989).

Ogden, H. V. S., 'Thomas Burnet's *Telluris Theoria Sacra* and Mountain Scenery', *ELH*, 14 (1947), 139–50.

Olson, Richard G., 'Tory-High Church Opposition to Science and Scientism in the Eighteenth Century: The Works of John Arbuthnot, Jonathan Swift, and Samuel Johnson', in *The Uses of Science in the Age of Newton*, ed. John G. Burke (Berkeley: University of California Press, 1983), pp. 171–204.

Olson, Robert C., 'Swift's use of the *Philosophical Transactions* in Section V of *A Tale of a Tub*', *Studies in Philology*, 49 (1952), 459–67.

Osler, Margaret J., 'The Intellectual Sources of Robert Boyle's Philosophy of Nature: Gassendi's Voluntarism and Boyle's Physico-theological Project', in *Philosophy, Science, and Religion in England 1640–1700* (see Coudert, above), pp. 178–98.

Palomo, Dolores J., 'The Dutch Connection: The University of Leiden and Swift's Academy of Lagado', *The Huntington Library Quarterly*, 41 (1977), 27–35.

Parnell, J. T., 'Swift, Sterne, and the Skeptical Tradition', *Studies in Eighteenth-Century Culture*, 23 (1994), 221–42.

Passmann, Dirk F., and Heinz J. Vienken, *The Library and Reading of Jonathan Swift: A Bio-Bibliographical Handbook, Part I: Swift's Library in Four Volumes* (Frankfurt am Main: Lang, 2003).

Patey, Douglas Lane, 'Swift's Satire on "Science" and the Structure of *Gulliver's Travels*', *ELH*, 58 (1991), 809–39.

Patrides, C. A., *Premises and Motifs in Renaissance Thought and Literature* (Princeton, NJ: Princeton University Press, 1982).

——, 'Renaissance Ideas on Man's Upright Form', *Journal of the History of Ideas*, 19 (1958), 256–58.

——, 'Renaissance and Modern Views on Hell', *The Harvard Theological Review*, 57 (1964), 217–36.

Paulson, Ronald, *Theme and Structure in Swift's 'Tale of a Tub'* (New Haven, CT: Yale University Press, 1960; repr. Hamden, CT: Archon Books [Shoe String Press], 1972).

Pauschert, Uwe, '"It Should Be Only *Rationis Capax*"', *Swift Studies*, 1 (1986), 67.

Peake, Charles, 'Swift and the Passions', *Modern Language Review*, 55 (1960), 169–80.

Perl, Margula R., 'Physics and Metaphysics in Newton, Leibniz, and Clarke', *Journal of the History of Ideas*, 30 (1969), 507–26.

Peterson, Leland D., 'Jonathan Swift and a Prose "Day of Judgment"', *Modern Philology*, 81 (1984), 401–406.

Phiddian, Robert, Review of *Swift as Nemesis*, by Frank Boyle, *Modern Philology*, 99 (2002), 437–39.

——, *Swift's Parody* (Cambridge: Cambridge University Press, 1995).

Philmus, Robert M., 'Mechanical Operations of the Spirit and *A Tale of a Tub*', *English Studies in Canada*, 10 (1984), 391–406.

Pinkus, Philip, 'Swift and the Ancients-Moderns Controversy', *University of Toronto Quarterly*, 29 (1959), 46–58.

——, *Swift's Vision of Evil: A Comparative Study of 'A Tale of a Tub' and 'Gulliver's Travels'*, 2 vols (Victoria, BC, Canada: English Literary Studies, University of Victoria, 1975–77).

Pollard, Arthur, *Satire* (London: Methuen, 1970).

Poovey, Mary, *A History of the Modern Fact: Problems of Knowledge in the Sciences of Wealth and Society* (Chicago, IL: University of Chicago Press, 1998).

Porter, Roy, 'Creation and Credence: The Career of Theories of the Earth in Britain, 1660–1820', in *Natural Order: Historical Studies of Scientific Culture*, ed. Barry Barnes (Beverley Hills, CA: Sage, 1979), pp. 97–123.

——, *Flesh in the Age of Reason*, foreword by Simon Schama (London: Allen Lane, 2003).

Potter, George Reuben, 'Swift and Natural Science', *Philological Quarterly*, 20 (1941), 97–118.

Price, Martin, *Swift's Rhetorical Art: A Study in Structure and Meaning* (New Haven, CT: Yale University Press, 1953).

Principe, Lawrence M., 'Virtuous Romance and Romantic Virtuoso: The Shaping of Robert Boyle's Literary Style', *Journal of the History of Ideas*, 56 (1995), 377–97.

Probyn, Clive T., 'Gulliver and the Relativity of Things: A Commentary on Method and Mode, with a Note on Smollett', *Renaissance and Modern Studies*, 18: 1 (1974), 63–76.

——, 'Swift and the Human Predicament', in *The Art of Jonathan Swift*, ed. Probyn (London: Vision Press, 1978), pp. 57–80.

——, 'Swift and the Physicians: Aspects of Satire and Status', *Medical History*, 18 (1974), 249–61.

——, 'Swift's Anatomy of the Brain: The Hexagonal Bite of Poetry', *Notes & Queries*, 219 (n.s.21) (1974), 250–51.

Quilligan, Maureen, *The Language of Allegory: Defining the Genre* (Ithaca, NY: Cornell University Press, 1979).

Quinlan, Maurice J., 'Swift's Literalization of Metaphor as a Rhetorical Device', *PMLA*, 82 (1967), 516–21.

Quintana, Ricardo, *The Mind and Art of Jonathan Swift* (London: Oxford University Press, 1936).

Ramsey, Richard N., 'Swift's Strategy in *The Battle of the Books*', *Papers on Language and Literature*, 20 (1984), 382–89.

Rawson, C. J., 'The Character of Swift's Satire', in *Focus: Swift*, ed. Rawson (London: Sphere Books, 1971), pp. 17–75.

——, *Gulliver and the Gentle Reader: Studies in Swift and our Time* (London: Routledge & Kegan Paul, 1973).

Real, Hermann J., 'Die Biene und die Spinne in Swift's "Battle of the Books"', *Germanisch-Romanische Monatsschrift*, n.s.23 (1973), 169–77.

——, 'The Dean and the Lord Chancellor: Or, Swift Saving his Bacon', in *Britannien und Europa: Studien zur Literatur-, Geistes- und Kulturgeschichte. Festschrift für Jürgen Klein*, ed. Michael Szczekalla (Frankfurt: Lang, 2010), pp. 95–111.

——, '"An Horrid Vision": Jonathan Swift's "(On) the Day of Judgment"', in *Swift and His Contexts*, eds John Irwin Fischer, Hermann J. Real and James Woolley (New York: AMS Press, 1989), pp. 65–96.

——, 'The "Keen Appetite for Perpetuity of Life" Abated: The Struldbruggs, Again; Festschrift fur Heinz-Joachim Mullenbrock zum 60. Geburtstag', in *Fiktion und Geschichte in der anglo-amerikanischen Literatur*, eds Rudiger Ahrens and Fritz Wilhelm Neumann (Heidelberg: Carl Winter Universitatsverlag, 1998), pp. 117–35.

——, 'A Taste of Composition Rare: The *Tale*'s Matter and Void', in *Reading Swift: Papers from the Third Münster Symposium* (see DePorte, above), pp. 73–90.

Real, Hermann J., and Heinz J. Vienken, '"I Knew and Could Distinguish Those Two Heroes at First Sight": Homer and Aristotle in Glubbdubdrib', *Notes & Queries*, 231 (n.s.33) (1986), 51–53.

Reedy, Gerard, S. J., 'A Preface to Anglican Rationalism', in *Eighteenth-Century Contexts: Historical Inquiries in Honor of Phillip Harth*, eds Howard D. Weinbrot, Peter J. Schakel and Stephen E. Karian (Wisconsin: University of Wisconsin Press, 2001), pp. 44–59.

Renaker, David, 'Swift's Laputians as a Caricature of the Cartesians', *PMLA*, 94 (1979), 936–44.

Riley, Patrick, 'Rousseau, Fénelon, and the Quarrel between the Ancients and the Moderns', in *The Cambridge Companion to Rousseau*, ed. P. Riley (Cambridge: Cambridge University Press, 2001), pp. 78–93.

Rivers, Isabel, *Reason, Grace, and Sentiment: A Study of the Language of Religion and Ethics in England, 1660–1780*, 2 vols (Cambridge: Cambridge University Press, 1991–2000).

Roberts, Marie Mulvey, 'The Flying Island and the Invisible College in Book Three of *Gulliver's Travels*', *Notes & Queries*, 229 (n.s.31) (1984), 391–93.

——, 'Science, Magic and Masonry: Swift's Secret Texts', in *Secret Texts: The Literature of Secret Societies*, eds Roberts and Hugh Ormsby-Lennon (New York: AMS Press, 1995), pp. 97–113.

Rogers, Pat, 'Gulliver and the Engineers', *Modern Language Review*, 70 (1975), 260–70.

——, *Hack and Dunces: Pope, Swift and Grub Street* (London: Methuen, 1980).

——, 'Plunging in the Southern Waves: Swift's Poem on the Bubble', *Yearbook of English Studies*, 18 (1988), 41–50.

——, Review of *Swift at Moor Park*, by A. C. Elias, Jr, *Modern Language Review*, 79 (1984), 667–69.

Rosenheim, Edward W., Jr., *Swift and the Satirist's Art* (Chicago, IL: University of Chicago Press, 1963).

Rothstein, Eric, 'In Brobdingnag: Captain Gulliver, Dr. Derham, and Master Tom Thumb', *Études Anglaises*, 37 (1984), 129–41.

Rousseau, G. S., *Enlightenment Borders: Pre- and Post-modern Discourses: Medical, Scientific* (Manchester: Manchester University Press, 1991).

——, *Nervous Acts: Essays on Literature, Culture and Sensibility* (Basingstoke: Palgrave Macmillan, 2004).

Rowland, Jon, 'Another Turn of the Screw: Prefaces in Swift, Marvell, and Genette', *Studies in Eighteenth-Century Culture*, 21 (1991), 129–48.

Rowlinson, J. S., 'John Freind: Physician, Chemist, Jacobite, and Friend of Voltaire's', *Notes and Records of the Royal Society of London*, 61 (2007), 109–27.

Rumbold, Valerie, 'Burying the Fanatic Partridge: Swift's Holy Week Hoax', in *Politics and Literature in the Age of Swift: English and Irish Perspectives*, ed. Claude Rawson (Cambridge: Cambridge University Press, 2010), pp. 81–115.

Said, Edward W., 'Swift the Intellectual', in *The World, the Text, and the Critic* (Cambridge, MA: Harvard University Press, 1983), pp. 72–89.

Samuel, Irene, 'Swift's Reading of Plato', *Studies in Philology*, 73 (1976), 440–62.

Sawday, Jonathan, *Engines of the Imagination: Renaissance Culture and the Rise of the Machine* (Abingdon: Routledge, 2007).

Schaffer, Simon, 'Augustan Realities: Nature's Representatives and Their Cultural Resources in the Early Eighteenth Century', in *Realism and Representation: Essays on the Problem of Realism in Relation to Science, Literature and Culture*, ed. George Levine (Madison: University of Wisconsin Press, 1993), pp. 279–318.

——, 'Halley's Atheism and the End of World', *Notes and Records of the Royal Society of London*, 32 (1977), 17–40.

——, 'Newton's Comets and the Transformation of Astrology', in *Astrology, Science and Society: Historical Essays* (see Curry, above), pp. 219–43.

Schakel, Peter J., 'Swift's Voices: Innovation and Complication in the Poems Written at Market Hill', in *Reading Swift: Papers from the Fourth Münster Symposium on Jonathan Swift*, eds Hermann J. Real and Helgard Stöver-Leidig (München: Fink, 2003), pp. 311–25.

Schmidt, Johann N., 'Swift's Uses of Fact and Fiction: The Drapier's Letters', in *Proceedings of the First Münster Symposium* (see Ehrenpreis, above), pp. 247–56.

Schofield, Robert E., *Mechanism and Materialism: British Natural Philosophy in an Age of Reason* (Princeton, NJ: Princeton University Press, 1970).

Scruggs, Charles, 'Swift's Use of Lucretius in *A Tale of a Tub*', *Texas Studies in Literature and Language*, 15 (1973), 39–50.

Shanahan, John, '"In the Mean Time": Jonathan Swift, Francis Bacon, and Georgic Struggle', in *Swift as Priest and Satirist*, ed. Todd C. Parker (Newark: University of Delaware Press, 2009), pp. 193–214.

Shapin, Steven, *Never Pure: Historical Studies of Science as if It Was Produced by People with Bodies, Situated in Time, Space, Culture, and Society, and Struggling for*

Credibility and Authority (Baltimore, MD: The Johns Hopkins University Press, 2010).

——, 'Of Gods and Kings: Natural Philosophy and Politics in the Leibniz-Clarke Disputes', *Isis*, 72 (1981), 187–215.

——, *A Social History of Truth: Civility and Science in Seventeenth-Century England* (Chicago, IL: University of Chicago Press, 1994).

——, 'Social Uses of Science', in *The Ferment of Knowledge* (see Harré, above), pp. 93–139.

Shapin, Steven, and Simon Schaffer, *Leviathan and the Air Pump: Hobbes, Boyle, and the Experimental Life* (Princeton, NJ: Princeton University Press, 1985).

Shuttleton, David E., '"A Modest Examination": John Arbuthnot and the Scottish Newtonians', *British Journal for Eighteenth-Century Studies*, 18 (1995), 47–62.

Smith, Frederick N., *Language and Reality in Swift's 'A Tale of a Tub'* (Columbus: Ohio State University Press, 1979).

——, 'Science, Imagination, and Swift's Brobdingnagians', *Eighteenth-Century Life*, 14: 1 (February 1990), 100–14.

——, 'Scientific Discourse: *Gulliver's Travels* and *The Philosophical Transactions*', in *The Genres of 'Gulliver's Travels'*, ed. Smith (Newark: University of Delaware Press, 1990), pp. 139–62.

Smolinski, Reiner, 'The Logic of Millenial Thought: Sir Isaac Newton among his Contemporaries', in *Newton and Religion* (see Force, above), pp. 259–89.

Snobelen, Stephen D., '"God of Gods, and Lord of Lords": The Theology of Isaac Newton's General Scholium to the *Principia*', *Osiris*, 2nd series, 16 (2001), 169–208.

Snow, C. P., *The Two Cultures and the Scientific Revolution* (The Rede Lecture) (Cambridge: Cambridge University Press, 1959).

Spellman, W. M., *John Locke and the Problem of Depravity* (Oxford: Oxford University Press, 1988).

Spiller, Michael R. G., 'The Idol of the Stove: The Background to Swift's Criticism of Descartes', *Review of English Studies*, 25 (1974), 15–24.

Starkman, Miriam Kosh, *Swift's Satire on Learning in 'A Tale of a Tub'* (Princeton, NJ: Princeton University Press, 1950; repr. New York: Octagon Books, 1968).

Stewart, Larry, *The Rise of Public Science: Rhetoric, Technology, and Natural Philosophy in Newtonian Britain, 1660–1750* (Cambridge: Cambridge University Press, 1992).

——, 'Samuel Clarke, Newtonianism, and the Factions of Post-Revolutionary England', *Journal of the History of Ideas*, 42 (1981), 52–72.

——, 'Seeing through the Scholium: Religion and Reading Newton in the Eighteenth Century', *History of Science*, 34 (1996), 123–65.

——, 'The Trouble with Newton in the Eighteenth Century', in *Newton and Newtonianism: New Studies* (see Force, above), pp. 221–37.

Stout, Gardner D., Jr, 'Speaker and Satiric Vision in Swift's *Tale of a Tub*', *Eighteenth-Century Studies*, 3 (1969), 175–99.

Taylor, E. G. R., *The Mathematical Practitioners of Tudor and Stuart England* (Cambridge: Cambridge University Press, for the Institute of Navigation, 1954).

Terry, Richard, 'Swift's Use of "Personate" to Indicate Parody', *Notes & Queries*, n.s.41 (1994), 196–98.

Tinkler, John F., 'The Splitting of Humanism: Bentley, Swift, and the English Battle of the Books', *Journal of the History of Ideas*, 49 (1988), 453–72.

Todd, Dennis, 'Laputa, the Whore of Babylon, and the Idols of Science', *Studies in Philology*, 75 (1978), 93–120.

Traugott, John, '*A Tale of a Tub*', in *The Character of Swift's Satire: A Revised Focus*, ed. C. J. Rawson (Newark: University of Delaware Press, 1983), pp. 83–126.

Treadwell, J. M., 'Jonathan Swift: The Satirist as Projector', *Texas Studies in Literature and Language*, 17 (1975), 439–60.

——, 'Swift, William Wood and the Factual Basis of Satire', *Journal of British Studies*, 15 (1976), 76–91.

Treadwell, Michael, 'Benjamin Motte, Andrew Tooke and *Gulliver's Travels*', in *Proceedings of the First Münster Symposium* (see Ehrenpreis, above), pp. 287–304.

——, 'The Text of *Gulliver's Travels*, Again', *Swift Studies*, 10 (1995), 62–79.

Tuveson, Ernest Lee, *Millennium and Utopia: A Study in the Background of the Idea of Progress* (Berkeley: University of California Press, 1949; repr. New York: Harper & Row, 1964).

——, 'Swift and the World-Makers', *Journal of the History of Ideas*, 11 (1950), 54–74.

Vailati, Ezio, *Leibniz & Clarke: A Study of their Correspondence* (New York: Oxford University Press, 1997).

Vickers, Brian, 'Swift and the Baconian Idol', in *The World of Jonathan Swift: Essays for the Tercentenary*, ed. B. Vickers (Oxford: Blackwell, 1968), pp. 87–128.

Walker, D. P., *The Decline of Hell: Seventeenth-Century Discussions of Eternal Torment* (London: Routledge & Kegan Paul, 1964).

Walsh, Marcus, 'Swift and Religion', in *The Cambridge Companion to Jonathan Swift* (see Higgins, above), pp. 161–76.

——, 'Text, "Text", and Swift's *A Tale of a Tub*', *Modern Language Review*, 85 (1990), 290–303.

Ward, David, *Jonathan Swift: An Introductory Essay* (London: Methuen, 1973).

Webster, Charles, *The Great Instauration: Science, Medicine, and Reform, 1626–1660* (London: Duckworth, 1975).

Webster, Clarence M., 'A Source for Swift's *A Meditation upon a Broomstick*', *Modern Language Notes*, 51 (1936), 160.

Weinbrot, Howard D., '"He Will Kill Me Over and Over Again": Intellectual Contexts of the Battle of the Books', in *Reading Swift: Papers from the Fourth Münster Symposium* (see Schakel, above), pp. 225–48.

——, *Menippean Satire Reconsidered: From Antiquity to the Eighteenth Century* (Baltimore, MD: The Johns Hopkins University Press, 2005).

Weiser, David K., 'Bacon's Borrowed Imagery', *Review of English Studies*, n.s.38 (1987), 315–24.

Westfall, Richard S., *Never At Rest: A Biography of Isaac Newton* (Cambridge: Cambridge University Press, 1980).

White, Douglas H., 'Swift and the Definition of Man', *Modern Philology*, 73: 4, Part 2 (May 1976), S48–55.

White, R. J., *Dr. Bentley: A Study in Academic Scarlet* (London: Eyre & Spottiswoode, 1965).

Whiteside, Derek T., 'Newton's Early Thoughts on Planetary Motion: A Fresh Look', *The British Journal for the History of Science*, 2 (1964), 117–137.

Williams, Harold, *The Text of 'Gulliver's Travels'* (Cambridge: Cambridge University Press, 1952).

Williams, Kathleen, *Jonathan Swift and the Age of Compromise* (Lawrence: University of Kansas Press, 1958).

——, 'Restoration Themes in the Major Satires of Swift', *Review of English Studies*, n.s.16 (1965), 258–71.

——, ed., *Swift: The Critical Heritage* (London: Routledge & Kegan Paul, 1970).

Williamson, Karina, '"Science" and "Knowledge" in Eighteenth-century Britain', *Studies in Voltaire and the Eighteenth Century*, 303 (1992), 455–58.

Wilson, Catherine, *Epicureanism at the Origins of Modernity* (Oxford: Oxford University Press, 2008).

Wittowsky, George, 'Swift's *Modest Proposal*: The Biography of an Early Georgian Pamphlet', *Journal of the History of Ideas*, 4 (1943), 75–104.

Wolper, Roy S., 'Swift's Enlightened Gulls', *Studies on Voltaire and the Eighteenth Century*, 58 (1967), 1915–37.

Womersley, David, 'Swift's Shapeshifting', in *Swift's Travels: Eighteenth-Century British Satire and its Legacy*, eds Nicholas Hudson and Aaron Santesso (Cambridge: Cambridge University Press, 2008), pp. 108–23.

Wood, P. B., 'Methodology and Apologetics: Thomas Sprat's *History of the Royal Society*', *The British Journal for the History of Science*, 13 (1980), 1–26.

Woolfson, Jonathan, 'The Renaissance of Bees', *Renaissance Studies*, 24 (2009), 281–300.

Woolley, James, 'Swift's "Skinnibonia": A New Poem from Lady Acheson's Manuscript', in *Reading Swift: Papers from the Fifth Münster Symposium* (see Frank T. Boyle, above), pp. 309–42.

——, 'Writing Libels on the Germans: Swift's "Wicked Treasonable Libel"', in *Swift: The Enigmatic Dean* (see Klein and Riemann, above), pp. 303–16.

Wootton, David, 'New Histories of Atheism', in *Atheism from the Reformation to the Enlightenment*, eds Michael Hunter and David Wootton (Oxford: Clarendon Press, 1992), pp. 13–53.

Worth, Chris, 'Swift's "Flying Island": Buttons and Bomb-Vessels', *Review of English Studies*, n.s.42 (1991), 343–60.

Yolton, John W., *Thinking Matter: Materialism in Eighteenth-Century Britain* (Minneapolis, MN: University of Minnesota, 1983; repr. Oxford: Blackwell, 1984).

Young, B. W., '"See Mystery to Mathematics Fly!": Pope's *Dunciad* and the Critique of Religious Rationalism', *Eighteenth-Century Studies*, 26 (1993), 435–48.

Zimmerman, Everett, *Swift's Narrative Satires: Author and Authority* (Ithaca, NY: Cornell University Press, 1983).

Index